Inequality, Identity, and the Politics of Northern Ireland

Inequality, Identity, and the Politics of Northern Ireland

Challenges of Peacebuilding and Conflict Transformation

Curtis C. Holland

LEXINGTON BOOKS
Lanham • Boulder • New York • London

Rowman & Littlefield
Bloomsbury Publishing Inc, 1359 Broadway, New York, NY 10018, USA
Bloomsbury Publishing Plc, 50 Bedford Square, London, WC1B 3DP, UK
Bloomsbury Publishing Ireland, 29 Earlsfort Terrace, Dublin 2, D02 AY28, Ireland
www.bloomsbury.com

Published by Lexington Books
An imprint of The Rowman & Littlefield Publishing Group, Inc.
4501 Forbes Boulevard, Suite 200, Lanham, Maryland 20706
www.rowman.com
86-90 Paul Street, London EC2A 4NE
Copyright © 2022 by The Rowman & Littlefield Publishing Group, Inc.

British Library Cataloguing in Publication Information available

Library of Congress Cataloging-in-Publication Data
ISBN 978-1-7936-4882-2 (cloth : alk. Paper)
ISBN 978-1-7936-4883-9 (electronic)

For my parents, Carl and Gail Holland, and my sister, Jennifer.
And for my lovely wife and best friend, Marie Aline Sillice.

Contents

Acknowledgments

I would like to thank mentors and colleagues who provided helpful suggestions on earlier drafts of this work or posed thoughtful questions that contributed to its development, including Lee Blackstone, Neil Jarman, Jack Levin, Glenn Pierce, Gordana Rabrenovic, Liza Weinstein, and Gilda Zwerman. I would also like to thank the editorial staff at Lexington, specifically Courtney Morales, Shelby Russell, Dominique McIndoe, and Emma Ebert for their friendly support and hard work during the review and publication process.

Research discussed in the book was supported by a faculty development grant from SUNY at Old Westbury.

PERMISSIONS

Chapters 2, 3, and 4 of this manuscript are modified drafts of these previously published articles:

Holland, Curtis and Gordana Rabrenovic. 2017. "Social Immobility, Ethno-politics, and Sectarian Violence: Obstacles to Post-conflict Reconstruction in Northern Ireland." *International Journal of Politics, Culture and Society* 30 (3): 219–244.

Holland, Curtis and Gordana Rabrenovic. 2018. "Masculinities in Transition? Exclusion, Ethnosocial Power and Contradictions in Excombatant Community-based Peacebuilding in Northern Ireland." *Men and Masculinities* 21 (5): 729–755.

Holland, Curtis. 2021. "Identity, the Politics of Policing, and Limits to Legitimacy in Northern Ireland." *Innovation: The European Journal of Social Science Research* 34 (1): 44–68. Copyright © Interdisciplinary Centre for Comparative Research in the Social Sciences and ICCR Foundation reprinted by permission of Taylor & Francis Ltd, http://www.tandfonline.com on behalf of Interdisciplinary Centre for Comparative Research in the Social Sciences and ICCR Foundation.

Introduction

More than two decades after the Good Friday Agreement brought an end to the period of armed conflict known locally as "the Troubles" (1968–1998), the milestones of Northern Ireland's (NI) peace process generally remain intact, including the cessation of lethal political and sectarian violence, significant police reforms, and (partial) paramilitary disarmament and demobilization (Coakley 2008; Mulcahy 2013; Jarman 2004; Nolan 2014). After engaging in a 30-year terrorist insurgency to expel British forces and incorporate the six counties of NI into the Irish Republic, the Irish Republican Army (IRA) put down their weapons, opting to participate in a devolved consociational government in which Irish Nationalists and British Unionists share power. Pro-state Loyalist paramilitaries, who countered IRA violence with their own brand of terrorism against the Irish Catholic community, also demobilized, playing a critical role in the peacemaking process (Shirlow 2012). While internecine paramilitary "punishment attacks" and episodic sectarian rioting continue (Harland 2011; Topping & Byrne 2012; Gray et al. 2018, 106–111), illicit paramilitary groups continue to profit from organized crime, and the threat of Irish dissident republican terrorism remains (Horgan and Morison 2011; Kearney 2016; Reinisch 2019; Knox 2002). Nonetheless, NI did not experience a surge in crime related to the "greed and grievance" of ex-combatants (Rolston 2007), unlike many other societies emerging from conflict (Collier and Hoeffier 2004). Belfast city center, once occupied by British soldiers, now resembles other cosmopolitan urban centers across Europe, becoming a popular tourist site.

Thus, the "security track" of peacebuilding in NI has been generally effective; however, evidence on the impact of other important "peacebuilding tracks," such as, economic development and reconciliation (Byrne and Keashly 2000) is less encouraging. Much research has examined how horizontal inequalities, or overlapping gaps in socio-economic outcomes, political power and social status between ethnic or national groups underscore escalations of political violence (Stewart 2008; Gurr 2000; Horowitz 2000).

1

These important contributions tend to highlight the psychosocial impacts of a group becoming "convinced of its own 'relative deprivation,'" resulting in a consolidation of ethnic boundary activation (Tilly 2003) and conflict escalation (Mac Ginty and Williams 2009, 28; see also, Jacoby 2008, 103–113). Following this perspective, it is often implied that reductions in horizontal inequalities through legislation which increases political representation and socio-economic opportunities for historically marginalized minority groups will alleviate tensions enough for peace to flourish long term. In the NI context, Teague (2019, 698) posits the narrowing of disparate employment rates between Protestants and Catholics as evidence of the overall growth in equality and social integration resulting from the Agreement;[1] and Nagle (2009b) frames improvements in access to city space by Nationalists as confirmation of progress toward a more "equal" Belfast and an early sign of emerging "multiculturalism" in the city.

These frameworks, like most, tend to frame inequality in interethnic terms. This approach is certainly warranted, given the historically horizontal nature of inequality in NI (and most other divided societies in transition). Nonetheless, there is relatively little exploration of the role of class identity and forms of socio-economic inequality which *transcend* ethnonational difference in shaping or undermining peace processes, social integration, and access to "shared spaces" and concomitant institutional avenues of social mobility. A *sole* analytical focus on interethnic inequality risks overlooking the potentially detrimental impacts of class inequalities *within and across* ethnonational blocs on prospects of political and social transformation. Coulter (2014, 773) even suggests that "dismissal of class-based analysis remains akin to a *doxa* in academic accounts of political subjectivities in Northern Ireland." More generally, the "conflict transformation community has so far been reluctant to engage in economic analysis" (Byrne 2011, 1), including, more specifically, the impacts of "post-conflict" class relations on the reproduction of other identities and concomitant trajectories of social and political change. Indeed, notwithstanding notable exceptions,[2] a relatively small number of authors studying contemporary dynamics of conflict and peacebuilding in *post-accord contexts* have placed class at the center of their analyses.

Other critical sociological perspectives remain marginal to the literature on post-conflict social and political reconstruction as well. For instance, feminist paradigms have gained some traction in the literature but are typically resigned to the marginal and bounded domain of "women's issues," and thus left unconnected to other structural and cultural obstacles to a more transformative peace process (Ashe 2008; Zalewski 2005).[3]

Often overlooked more generally is how the limitations of intercommunal integration in transitional societies are ultimately linked to social and economic conditions which become entrenched despite or, somewhat paradoxically, *because* of "peace." To identify these limitations in the empirical literature is not to say that recent work on conflict and peacebuilding has not become increasingly comprehensive. On the contrary; this burgeoning, interdisciplinary field has brought attention to a variety of important issues effecting post-conflict reconstruction, including, most notably, the reformation of political bodies and state institutions (Horowitz 2000; Lijphart 1999; Norris 2008; Barnes 2001) and formal mechanisms of forgiveness and reconciliation, such as truth commissions (Hayner 2002; Rotberg 2000; Hamber and Wilson 2002; Hamber and Kelly 2009). There has also been much research on the functions of interethnic contact and social capital in fostering trust and changing political attitudes (Hewstone et al. 2006; Pickering 2006; Rydgren and Sofi 2011; Rydgren, Sofi and Hallsten 2013; Svenson and Brouneus 2013; Hughes, Campbell and Jenkins 2011), and the productive potential of leadership in "bottom-up" peacebuilding and restorative justice by community-based organizations (Arriaza and Roht-Arriaza 2008; Knox 2010; Eriksson 2009; Jarman 2006a, 2006b; Parver and Wolf 2008; Smithey 2011). Yet how ethnopolitical divisions are *reconfigured, reproduced* or politically *re-activated* following the formalities of "peace" merits further critical and empirical attention.

The relative lack of such attention is likely at least partly due to the inherently optimistic nature of peace studies which examine processes of democratization and transitional justice, or focus on localized, institution-specific forms of intercommunal cooperation. For instance, cases of such cooperation within particular institutions, networks or localities documented in the peacebuilding literature tend to be exceptional, not representative of general trends. Examples include post-conflict research from NI on the impact of interethnic contact and trust on political attitudes (Hewstone et al 2006; Tam et al. 2009) or the promise of integrated education in reducing ethnic or religious intolerance and mistrust (McGlynn et al. 2004). While the findings of such research are no doubt important in both theoretical and policy terms, levels of the segregation of housing and schools in NI remain stark, and such positive developments toward integration exceptional. More generally, effective cooperation among grassroots peacekeeping networks on organizational or neighborhood levels take place within a backdrop of deep polarization between the PUL and CNR communities[4] that persists post-conflict (Shirlow and Murtagh 2006, 33–34; Hughes et al. 2007; Nolan 2014). Research on "bottom-up" community-based and voluntary peacebuilding and restorative justice projects has emphasized the need for a more holistic understanding of peacebuilding which emphasizes the leadership role of civil society groups (Arriaza and Roht-Arriaza 2008; Knox 2010; Eriksson 2009; McCall 2011) and challenges dominant paradigms which tend to implicitly restrict

its meaning to the cessation of violence and establishment of new governance bodies. At the same time, due largely to local, organization-specific
foci, primary scholarly emphasis on community-based initiatives tends to
inadvertently reduce attention to obstacles to peacebuilding rooted in broader
political and socio-economic structures and processes which might mitigate
the transformative capacity of the community sector.

Transformative Justice (TJ) studies have brought increased scholarly attention to the importance of addressing "structural violence" to facilitate effective transition from violent conflict to some version of democracy. Such work
tends to emphasize the "horizontal exclusion" of minority elites from the legislative process (Bell 2018; Hartzell and Hoddie 2003); improving the democratic representation of marginalized groups via reformed "constitutionalism"
(Turner 2015; Bell and Zulueta-Fulscher 2016); or including civil society
representatives or minority interest groups in peace negotiations (Belloni
2010; Herbolzheimer 2019). Much of the TJ literature tends to examine issues
of civil and political participation in the *early* stages of a peace settlement
(see, Gready and Robins 2014). Obstacles to intercommunal integration and
construction of a more shared society remain typically framed in the language
of political and civil rights and democratic participation. Moreover, the lion's
share of the research is rooted mostly in conventional political science and
social psychology paradigms. Critical approaches to the study of nationalism and ethnic relations from sociology and cultural anthropology, and the
nuanced *processes* of political power and identity (re)production they are best
suited to reveal, remain relatively marginal methodologically.

The relatively few important contributions from NI that do center constructs
of class specifically in analyses of political subjectivity in the post-accord
period tend to utilize neo-Marxist frameworks at the macro level (Coulter
2018; Kelly 2012); or geographical analysis of the relationships between
segregation, poverty, and resource competition, and implications of spatial
encounters between and beyond binary identities (Shirlow and Murtagh 2006;
Graham and Nash 2006; Herrault and Murtagh 2019). Notable work has also
examined the role of a progressive movement within "New Loyalism" which
centers class grievances in a rejection of exploitative Unionist sectarian politics and socio-economic injustice (Cassidy 2008; McAuley 2005).

The analyses undertaken in subsequent chapters build on these important
developments in the literature on class, politics, and identity in NI, but also
incorporate a novel approach to peace and conflict studies vis-à-vis a critical
sociological framework rooted in constructivist and intersectionality perspectives (see, Bourdieu 1991; Brubaker and Cooper 2000; Collins 2002) to reveal
processes through which (ethno)political identities and relations of power are
reproduced or reconfigured in distinct ways, and in accordance with the class,
gendered, age-based, and geographical and organizational contexts shaping

and restricting interaction and discourse. Indeed, nation, ethnicity, and other collective identities are visible principally through the processes of their reproduction or transformation (Brubaker 2002; McAdam, Tarrow and Tilly 2001, 157–159; Finlayson 1997, 72). By utilizing such a framework, coupled with recognition of macro-level shifts in the distribution of power and status between and within the ethnonational blocs, the book also intends to bring greater attention to the influence of multiple intra-group inequalities on the reproduction of political identities and ideologies.

A key strength of a critical structuralist approach, in the tradition of Pierre Bourdieu, is its dual emphasis on structure and agency, or the processes in which structures of power constrain intersubjective meanings while also providing space for innovation (Bourdieu 1983; Smithey 2011). In this respect, Bourdieu's framework aligns with Anthony Giddens' interpretation of social structure "as a virtual order rather than . . . a social reality apart from the individual" (Seidman 2008: 137; Giddens 1984). Through an analytical approach based on the principles of critical structuralism and constructivism, institutional, socio-political dynamics are interpreted in relation to "social fields," or "structured social positions" and corresponding forms of "schemes of thought, feeling and action" that emerge through an individual's and group's position within multilayered social hierarchies (Allan 2006, 174). Through this perspective, power is necessarily relational, produced through individuals' subconscious complicity with ingroup practices and ideologies that validate systems of domination, and exercised through ingroup hierarchies and dual strategies of inclusion and exclusion in which a critical reflexivity may gradually emerge.

As Patricia Hill Collins (2004, 539) recognizes, there are at least three levels in which people experience oppression or marginalization: the level of personal biography; "the group or community level of the cultural context . . . and the systemic level of social institutions." In NI, the more dominant community level "cultural context" is typically posited in terms of ethnonational and ethnoreligious membership. In accordance with the social identity perspective, institutionalization of ethnic or national identity centers attachment to such identity as a core psychological mechanism to maintain "positive self-evaluation via . . . group membership" (Coymak and O'Dwyer 2020, 7; see also, Tajfel and Turner 1986). This is especially true in polarized ethnic frontier societies, such as NI, wherein perceived threat from an outgroup magnifies periodically during contentious events and, especially, periods of political or constitutional uncertainty. Under these conditions, according to social identity theorists, individuals are likely to exercise "adaptive strategies (e.g., increase their [ingroup] identification)" to overcome the psychosocial threat from an ethnic or national Other (Coymak and O'Dwyer 2020, 7). Yet iterations of power also shift in accordance with contexts of class, gender, age and place, particularly in locations such as Belfast in which, historically (and contemporaneously, for many) the control of space territorializes identity (Shirlow and Murtagh 2006; Shirlow 2006) and the memories and trauma of sectarian or political violence are largely concentrated within the same neighborhoods characterized as "grinding sites of multigenerational poverty" (Coulter 2018, 2). Some brief examples, discussed further in subsequent chapters, should substantiate this observation. Women, for instance, have historically contributed to the conflict in NI (and many other divided societies), supporting and, in the case of the IRA, directly participating in armed conflict. Later, women in both ethnonational communities played pivotal roles in organizing for peace in NI (Potter 2008; Ashe 2009) but have often been as sympathetic to exclusionary Unionist or Republican ethnonational ideologies as their male counterparts (Little 2002). At the same time, "sectarianism, and the construction of political and social life around [ethnonational] community loyalties, has been a powerful force in maintaining women's subordination" in NI (Sales 1997a, 4; see also, Racioppi and O'Sullivan 2001). The power exercised by former paramilitary prisoners over community-based peacebuilding practices also occurs within a contradictory context, coupling the marginal inclusion *and* broader socio-economic and socio-political exclusion of ex-prisoners and the relatively deprived communities in which they tend to reside. As chapter three will illustrate, such contradictory dynamics shape the thoughts and actions of ex-combatant community leaders in ways which influence both their embrace of traditional ethnopolitical identities *and* rejection of mainstream parties, producing often paradoxical "resistance" narratives and behaviors that obstruct the transformative potential of the community sector. More generally, as the following chapters document, the ongoing polarization between the main ethnonational communities is largely shaped by *intra*-ethnic fields of power, which are mystified by dominant ethnocultural symbology and the discourses of political leaders or "ethnic entrepreneurs" at both the state and grassroots levels. At the same time, as respondents in this study demonstrate, the reflexivity of subjects on the interactions constituting those fields of power can foster a critical political consciousness, potentially providing a foundation for future collective resistance to manipulative political forces and exclusionary social structures. As Allan (2006, 174) observes, "These different structures dialectically exert force upon one another through the strategic actions and practices of people in interaction. And, as with most dialectics, the tension can produce something new and different out of the struggle." Between diverging interactional contexts, the construction of meaning, being spatially and temporally contingent, contains potential foundations for the alteration of identity.

This book also intends to contribute a critical sociological perspective to the literature on peacebuilding and post-conflict transformation by connecting dynamics of structural inequalities to the provocations of eth-nopolitical and grassroots leaders. A central theme emerging from the data is that the coupling of socio-economic marginalization and sectarian threat con-tributes to the reproduction of insular identities promoted by ethnopolitical entrepreneurs, who strategically transition back and forth between a politics of compromise and politics of threat. Yet, the politics that thrive in a given community at a particular time, whether concerning "peace dividends," flags, parades, the past, policing, Brexit, or challenges facing local NGOs—all issues examined in the subsequent chapters—are most adequately interpreted within contexts which recognize the intersectional nature of class/place, gen-dered, and ethnonational identities. Unique gendered identities of particular age groups within each ethnoreligious community differ across space and historical class contexts. Moreover, disparate socio-economic conditions within communal blocs contextualize processes in which political and sectar-ian mentalities shift, are reproduced, or become suppressed. It is within such contexts—or ethnosocial fields of power—where the ethnopolitical character of marginalized communities' collective anger can be located and traced to politicians' and activists' appropriation of outgroup resentment and threat. But it is also within the same contexts in which narratives and practices of "resistance" manifest.

It has been well established that relative deprivation, poverty, and income inequality shape escalations of conflict (Gurr 1970; Birrell 1972; Korpi 1974). But how do structures of inequality, in which some segments of each ethnonational bloc experience increased mobility, whilst others experience status decline or stasis, shape or undermine conflict transformation? The research presented in this volume explores how high levels of economic deprivation and inequity in education, employment, and access to shared spaces do not necessarily have to be "horizontal" in nature to merge with other political, cultural, and historical forces to reproduce divisions which undermine peacebuilding. Rather, such phenomena converge with gendered and place-based identities (among other identities) to reproduce—or, in some cases, reconfigure—insular political subjectivities situated within particular ethnosocial fields of power. Following this theoretical framework, more spe-cific questions are also addressed: How do ethnopolitical leaders connect to heterogeneous and often conflicted ingroup constituencies to reconstitute col-lective ethnonational identity? How do the subjectivities and socio-political emotions underscored (in part) by socio-economic (dis)advantage medi-ate the consequences of ethnopolitical leaders' actions in this respect? In addition, how has the consociational system of governance in NI shaped peacebuilding initiatives and the corresponding subjectivities underpinning such initiatives; and what are the impacts of governance in this respect on community-based peacebuilding organizations? How (if at all) do dominant modes of peacebuilding and the subjectivities legitimating them reflect power disparities between "middle-class" professional Unionist and Nationalist networks, and poor and working-class Loyalist and Republican communities in shaping definitions and prerogatives of "peace"? Furthermore, how does the social, economic and political exclusion of former (male) paramilitary prisoners shape their political attitudes and community involvement; and what are the implications of this dynamic on the power of women and concomitant prospects of more transformative modes of community-based peacebuilding? Finally, how (if at all) are externally imposed crises such as Brexit opening psychosocial spaces for innovative political imaginations and transgressions, even as they somewhat paradoxically reconstitute ethnonational division at the same time? Although the book examines a relatively wide range of contentious issues confronting the NI peace process, the analysis more generally puts front and center processes and discourses pervading intra-communal matrixes of power and their implications on social transformation and peacebuilding at local and national levels.

INEQUALITY AND POLITICS IN NORTHERN IRELAND

The post-conflict situation in NI provides a strategic site in which to examine how matrixes of power along lines of class, gender, place and ethnonational identity shape dynamics of conflict and prospects for transformative iterations of "peace" once the "honeymoon period" of a negotiated settlement subsides, post-accord institutions and structures become entrenched, and long-standing grievances rise again to the center of public consciousness. NI is a society wherein overlapping political and cultural identities within the Protestant and Catholic ethnoreligious blocs are considered especially strong, and myths about ingroup moral superiority are centuries-old and psychosocially powerful (see, Tonge 2002; Hughes et al. 2007). The cessation of lethal violence has at the same time allowed for more open intra-ethnic disagreements over the direction of "peace" (Finlayson 1999). Sustained social order (in most parts of the country, most of the time) has facilitated space for more variable social relationships and an opening-up of political discourse to a greater variety of ideas. Todd's (2018, 315) analysis of NI citizens' personalized narratives about their past and the nation, for example, reveals how such narratives "stretch the conventional boundaries of nation and group," signaling "everyday potential for quite radical revision of conventional constructions of the nation." As put by Neil Jarman, however, it is most appropriate to take a "both/and" approach to analysis of conflict and peacebuilding in NI (conversation with author, Queens University Belfast, May 2014). Indeed, peacebuilding is in reality "temporally disjunctive and dynamic and . . . substantively disaggregated and multi-threaded," in contrast with perspectives that posit peacebuilding as a "singular process whereby 'state' and 'society' move through relatively well-defined phases towards greater tolerance and normalization" (Bollens 2018, 166).

How particular national or religious ingroup narratives are connected to class and gendered identities is an open question, to which this book offers some preliminary answers. In NI, the reduction in horizontal inequalities between Protestants and Catholics has consolidated since the Agreement. In 2014, it was reported that at least 60 percent of entrants to higher education are Catholic and 60 percent female, "rebalancing the communal shares of professional and managerial occupations" (Nolan 2014, 13). Middle-class[5] Catholics have also experienced increases in residential mobility, moving into historically Protestant neighborhoods, and filling private housing vacancies resulting from middle-class Protestant emigration and an aging Protestant demographic (Gray et al. 2018, 177; Shirlow and Murtagh 2006, 101–120). For underserved CNR *and* PUL communities, however, signs of progress are bleaker. With the exception of the Baltic states, inequality levels in the United Kingdom (UK) are the highest in Europe (Center for Opportunity and Equality 2017). And in NI, indictors of spatial inequality, social immobility and intergenerational poverty are particularly troubling. Just 12 of Northern Ireland's 94 postcodes contained over half of all fatalities during the conflict (Fay, Morrissey, and Smyth 1999, 150). Nearly 40 percent of the approximately 3,700 deaths that occurred during the Troubles happened in North and West Belfast, the two parliamentary constituencies wherein 18 of the 20 poorest neighborhoods in NI are located (Devlin, McKay, and Russell 2018, 11). This is not to say that Northern Ireland's economy has not significantly improved since the Agreement. It has, *for some*; but the benefits have not spread evenly throughout the society. The "peace dividend" that was promised as a condition of peace has not accrued to marginalized poor and working-class communities most directly affected by the Troubles; rather, gains in income, educational outcomes and entry into professional careers have increased mostly for the already privileged segments of the population (Coulter 2014). In 2018, before economic problems related to the coronavirus pandemic and UK withdrawal from the EU, the rate of "worklessness"—which estimates employment as percentage of the entire working-age population—indicate that economic activity in NI was 7 percent lower than the other UK countries (Gray et al. 2018, 23). This trend is due in part to the relatively high percentage of the population suffering from conflict-related trauma (Tomlinson 2016; Fenton 2018). The proportion (10 percent) of residents classified as "long-term sick or disabled" is double the UK average, and "the overall trend has been upwards" since 2013 (Gray et al. 2018, 25). But lack of quality jobs is also part of the problem: NI still has the lowest levels of workforce participation in the UK, at less than 70 percent (ibid., 23). Northern Irish people who are able to work "earn gross weekly wages that are 9 percent below the UK average" (Coulter 2018, 5), with many forced into part-time work "and relatively insecure forms of employment (such as zero hours contracts)" (Gray et al. 2018, 23). The price of housing is lower in NI than in other parts of the UK, which provides some degree of poverty alleviation, though this is unlikely to be much consolation to the thousands of families living in areas of concentrated deprivation. Young working-class males in NI have worklessness or economic inactivity rates of over 20 percent, higher than the other UK countries and Ireland (ibid., 152). Underserved by the education system, the same demographic holds the lowest educational outcomes in NI and second lowest in all the UK (ibid., 156–163; Nolan 2014, 98).

Indeed, the boundary between social classes is perhaps marked most saliently by educational record, in ways which generally transcend ethnonational and religious difference. The state transfer exam—which once determined whether pupils would go to a competitive grammar school or a secondary school at age 11—was eliminated in the early post-Agreement period under Sinn Fein's Education Minister. Yet "grammar schools," which prepare students for university at a much stronger capacity than "secondary schools," created new, and somewhat more rigorous "transfer" tests to fulfill the same function. Those who do poorly on the test, or do not take it, face much difficulty pursuing a university education. The General Certificate of Secondary Education (GCSE) exams also serve fundamentally as a mechanism of sorting young people into distinct socio-economic tracks. Pupils take the exam at age 16. If they do well, they may go on to do "Advanced Level" at 17 and 18, which determines their entry to university. The class disparities in exam outcomes, across the PUL and CNR blocs, are quite stark. Borooah and Knox (2015, 84) report that, in 2013, there was a "56 percentage point gap between Northern Ireland's grammar and secondary schools in the proportions of their pupils obtaining good GCSEs and, as worryingly, this gap has shown little sign of reducing over time." The same authors indicate an "absurdly small proportion of grammar schools pupils who are 'disadvantaged'" in terms of parental income and special education needs (Borooah and Knox 2015, 87). State grammar schools are slowly becoming more ethnically and religiously diverse, with an increase in Catholics and those unaffiliated with either religion attending them in the post-Agreement period (ibid., 17). Moreover, more than any other country included in the Trends in International Mathematics and Science Study, the correlation between school pupils' math and science scores and socio-economic status is strongest in NI, where those in the most disadvantaged communities score well below the overall average, and those from advantaged communities outperform most of their counterparts from the other societies (Bradshaw, De Lazzari, and Andrade 2018; DE 2012). Other quantitative measures indicate that distinctions in educational outcomes in NI are now far greater along lines of socio-economic status and gender (with girls having stronger reading scores) than religious affiliation (Gray et al. 2018, 159; see also, Jerrim and Shure 2016).

Earlier in the post-accord period, Coulter and Murray (2008, 17) indicated that "the problems that poorer unionists face are expressed most keenly . . . in their educational underattainment," noting that "of the fifteen districts in Northern Ireland where academic performance is worst, no fewer than thirteen are predominantly unionist." Educational prospects for working-class Catholic males have not fared much better, however, though working-class Catholic girls have seen more notable increases in educational attainment (Nolan 2014, 98). These trends in educational outcomes have generally remained overall consistent.[6] The shifts in class structure across the communal blocs in NI have been in process for decades, and are having complex impacts on the peace process.

Sectarianism was an integral force in the constitution of the industrial NI state prior to the Troubles. The Catholic working class experienced overt discrimination by the Unionist bourgeoisie, who sought to maintain working-class Protestant alliance with the ruling Unionist regime (Bew, Gibbon and Patterson 1979). Consequently, Protestant working-class males were heavily favored by employers for jobs in the shipbuilding, manufacturing and engineering sectors throughout the mid-twentieth century. Women were at the same time highly restricted in their roles in the economy and, while central actors in the shadows of the conflict, often marginalized in the public sphere to maintain the normative role of male masculinities in "community leadership" (Sales 1997; Racioppi and O'Sullivan 2001; Ashe 2009). The decline of Northern Ireland's manufacturing and shipbuilding sectors began shortly after the Second World War (Shirlow 1995), intensifying over subsequent decades. Between 1950 and 1994 manufacturing employment declined by 58.4 percent; and between 1971 and 1991, the unemployment rate increased 14.6 percent and outmigration rose by 12.2 percent (McGovern and Shirlow 1997, 188). The deindustrialization of NI reflected a microcosm of economic transformations occurring across Europe and North America. "[T]raditional heavy industry closed its doors, to be replaced by service industries, and a flexible and feminized work force displaced the male, and mainly Protestant, industrial worker" (Smyth and Cebulla 2008, 176). Their favored position in blue-collar sectors, rather than educational opportunity historically marked working-class Protestant males' socio-economic advantage over their Catholic male counterparts and women, and was key to their political alignment with middle-class Unionism (Smyth and Cebulla 2008, 175). Deindustrialization dislocated many Protestant workers, and their children—especially boys—have struggled to find alternative vocations through educational pursuits.

Following the outbreak of the Troubles and subsequent imposition of British Direct Rule in 1972, the British state would attempt to address the consequent economic crisis and undermine the Republican insurgency by investing heavily in Northern Ireland's professional public sector (Coulter 1997, 118). Most of the funds (almost 90 percent) invested by the British state in NI primarily benefited the privileged classes (McGovern and Shirlow 1997, 192). Eventually, middle-class Catholics benefited from this public expenditure as well, as anti-discrimination legislation gradually improved equity in hiring. The establishment of the Fair Employment Commission in Northern Ireland, under the Fair Employment Act 1976, had a significant impact in reducing religious discrimination and segregation in the workplace (Mitchell 2006, 63; Whyte 1990, 48). Yet, the middle-classes in NI have also benefited from a lower cost of living than their counterparts in other UK countries (Coulter 2018, 119). The British state sought to achieve "greater political consensus" through subsidizing the Protestant *and* Catholic middle and upper classes (McGovern and Shirlow 1997, 192; see also, O'Connor 1994). This goal has been largely successful, particularly in changing Catholics' and Nationalists' attitudes toward the political status quo (Byrne 2011, 175). As middle-class Catholics continue to vote overwhelmingly for Nationalist parties—Social Democratic Labor Party (SDLP) and Sinn Fein (Evans and Tonge 2009; Tilley, Garry, and Matthews 2019)—their ascendancy in socio-economic status has only helped to solidify their acceptance of Northern Ireland's membership in the UK. Since the 1990s, Sinn Fein was able to appeal to more moderate and middle-class voters who previously opposed armed struggle as a means of unifying Ireland (Coulter and Murray 2008) by transitioning its strategy from the pursuit of Irish unification via political violence, to peacefully seeking equality for Catholics within the NI state (Evans and Tonge 2009). Sinn Fein was also effective in transitioning away from militarist symbology in its political communication since the 1990s, adopting language and imagery "to form a vocabulary for peace and national reconciliation" that resonated with more "moderate" Nationalist constituents (Shirlow and McGovern 1998, 171).[7] The two main Nationalist parties are thus now competing for the votes of middle-class Catholics, whose material concerns (house prices, etc.), mirroring those of privileged Unionists, increasingly take precedence over issues of ethnopolitical identity (Coulter and Murray 2008, 17).

At the same time, the confluence of relatively high rates of disability (Gray et al. 2018, 148–151; Powell 2018), educational inequities and limited job availability shape the insecurity felt in many working-class communities. Spatial concentrations of disadvantage are particularly evident in Belfast.

For example, West Belfast has consistently ranked second highest in levels of child poverty among the UK's 650 parliamentary constituencies, with rates in the Colin Glen and Falls areas especially high (over 40 percent of children in poverty) (BBC 2013; Quinn 2018). "North Belfast follows closely behind the West Belfast statistics with 8,433 children" in poverty, compared with just over half that figure in South Belfast (Quinn 2018, 1). According to Nolan (2014, 78) about 20 percent of NI residents live in poverty, a figure that is expected to increase as mitigation of "welfare reform" measures from Westminster are gradually lifted[8] and the social and economic ramifications of Brexit and the Covid-19 pandemic manifest.

Analyses in subsequent chapters suggest that that the dominant mode of social regulation introduced during British Direct Rule—to "consolidate non-sectarian middle-class solidarity" whilst simultaneously "alienating" poor and working-class PUL and CNR communities (McGovern and Shirlow 1997, 190)—has been perpetuated, but follows distinct processes in the post-Agreement era, situated within the logic of the consociational power-sharing system. A gradual consolidation of shared material Protestant and Catholic middle-class interests and political apathy parallel a simmering sense of social and political alienation within working-class Loyalist and Republican communities. Such dynamics present political opportunities for established elites and grassroots ethnic entrepreneurs to exploit, but also pose new challenges to the legitimacy of the consociational regime. The consolidation of inequalities transcending ethnonational difference presents new opportunities for political leaders to appeal to more "moderate" constituencies by upholding policies that support their interests. Yet the same political practices may also reinforce the conditions and narratives that constitute the mentalities of threat and loss pervading poor and working-class Loyalist and Republican strongholds. The politics of ethnopolitical grievance, central to the consociational system's "two party Janus faced" system—wherein "each ethnic champion publicly appeals to its sectarian base for electoral power by blaming the 'Other' for all the Assembly's faults while privately collaborating with the very same 'Other' to ensure" their mutual dominance in the political process (Barry 2017, 3)—may be empowered by the ongoing marginalization of poor and working-class communities, as blame for their social and economic problems is effectively framed in sectarian terms. As subsequent chapters will explore, however, the same conditions and political practices, unresolved over time, may underscore a disaffection from mainstream Unionist and Nationalist party politics across class groups, *potentially* resulting in more inclusive future reconstructions of identity among segments of each ethnonational bloc.[9]

Coupled with the paralysis of local government bodies, signs of the possibility of moving toward greater social integration may elicit an escalation of reactionary, transgressive ethnopolitics. Throughout the post-devolution period, as the NI Assembly struggled with basic processes of governance and subsequently shut down between 2017 and 2020,[10] elected leaders from across the communal divide have doubtless confronted anxiety about maintaining their niches in the political landscape. The possibility of a more pluralist polity brings hope to some but elicits fear and insecurity in others, particularly those who have built public identities and careers on insular ethnopolitical ideologies. Such combined phenomena incentivize strategies of ethnic outbidding which have heretofore proven relatively effective to Northern Ireland's dominant ethnonational parties.[11] For example, the Democratic Unionist Party (DUP) ascended to a hegemonic position in Unionist politics largely by resisting all concessions to Irish Nationalists during peace negotiations in the late 1990s and early 2000s, and charging Ulster Unionist Party (UUP) leadership—who offered concessions during peace negotiations before Nationalists did—of betraying Unionist interests. Specifically, the UUP's cooperation with the early prisoner release scheme, before the official decommissioning of IRA weapons, led to sharp criticism from the DUP, which resonated with many in broader Unionism (Bruce 2007, 127–130). Somewhat ironically, this strategy put the DUP "in an ideal position to increase its popularity within the consociational settlement it had opposed" (McGlynn, Tonge, and McAuley 2014, 280; see also, Moore et al. 2013; Tonge et al. 2014). The DUP has since sought to maintain its dominant position (in part) by stoking fears that "Britishness" is being removed from NI by way of restrictions on symbolic markers and rituals of Unionist hegemony in public spaces (see, chapter 2), and pursuing policies intended to "protect" Protestant Unionist culture, such as resisting the Irish Language Act and increasing funding for the "loyal orders"[12] (McGlynn, Tonge and McAuley 2014, 281).

Ethnopolitical opportunism continues to be a key feature of the NI political process, but is met with significant resistance. As subsequent chapters reveal, such resistance can come in forms which present more inclusive constructions of political identity, as well as others that draw on insular ethnopolitical constructs, undermining conflict transformation.

DATA AND METHOD

The analysis principally utilizes a mixed-method qualitative case study approach, drawing on data retrieved from interviews with community leaders, public officials and politicians, as well as newspaper reports about political disputes and incidents of sectarian violence in Belfast.[13] As Steinhoff and Zwerman (2008, 213) recognize, "the methodological tools of qualitative sociology are particularly well-suited to study of the unfolding of dynamic social processes and interactive meaning-making that occurs in messy, contested real-world contexts," including contexts of violence, conflict, and transition in divided societies.

Most respondents work(ed) across the ethnonational divide in a variety of leadership capacities at the grassroots and public spheres and thus have keen insight into dynamics in PUL and CNR communities relevant to the study. The critical reflexivity of the respondents in this study illuminate the complex and sometimes contradictory realities of socio-political life in NI. Many reflect on experiences they have had working on behalf of their respective organizations when describing challenges to peacebuilding and conflict transformation. Yet, due to their commitment to peacebuilding goals more broadly, members of this group are also likely to have critically reflected on how particular issues may impact politics and peace process outcomes beyond the organizational contexts in which they work.

The open-ended nature of the interview method I utilized is particularly useful to identifying processes in the reproduction or reconfiguration of symbolic boundaries. As described by Lamont (1992, 15), it allows "interviewees themselves [to describe] their standards of evaluation and le[a]d[s] the researcher toward the most appropriate analytical categories . . . " In fact, the open-ended nature of the study in its early phases allowed respondents to identify the importance of intersectional class, gender, place and age-based identities to contextualize perceptions regarding obstacles to conflict transformation. In contexts of everyday social interaction, there is, as Bourdieu (1991, 97) suggests, "a more or less desperate attempt to be correct, or to *silence*" which allows one to maintain some level of inclusion (no matter how limited) while simultaneously reconstituting their marginalization. Yet outside everyday contexts of social interaction, in alternative spaces and contexts, such as, in-depth interviewing, there is the potential for critical reflexivity (see, Hiller and DiLuzio 2004). Most of the respondents who participated in this research strongly demonstrated such reflexivity, lucidly recalling processes of political manipulation and its impact on them and their communities, for example. But many of the same individuals also identify openings of psychosocial space which might potentially facilitate transformations in political culture and an empowerment of those underserved by dominant institutions.

All 41 respondents are from NI; some from middle-class communities from South Belfast, others from interface areas in West, North or East Belfast. A few respondents work in a Protestant working-class housing estate outside Belfast; and three live and work at border regions between NI and the Irish Republic. Approximately two-thirds come from the Protestant, Unionist or Loyalist communities; about one-third are from Catholic and Nationalist communities (though some from both blocs do not identify strongly with an ethnonational or ethnoreligious identity).

There were two sets of in-depth interviews, conducted at two distinct periods. The first phase included 23 respondents, who I interviewed during a visit to NI in late spring and early summer 2014. Specifically, of these 23, 15 respondents (11 men and 4 women) came from community-based or voluntary peacebuilding organizations and 5 (2 men and 3 women) worked in non-elected government positions or public commissions. One elected official serving in the Executive Assembly also participated, in addition to a former elected councillor and a high-ranking PSNI officer (1 woman, 2 men). In addition to being active in peacebuilding, at least 5 respondents (4 Loyalists and 1 Republican) of the 23 are ex-paramilitary prisoners. The first several respondents interviewed in 2014 were recruited through contacts at Northeastern University (USA) and the Institute for Conflict Research in Belfast. Respondents were subsequently recruited via "snowball" or referral sampling. I also took extensive ethnographic field notes during my time in Belfast. This was a time when intercommunal relations in Belfast were on a downward shift in light of a series of contentious events, namely the arrest of Sinn Fein President Gerry Adams for a 1972 murder, and his subsequent release-without-charge; a visit by US diplomat Richard Hass to help design a plan for dealing with the past; and ongoing Loyalist protests over new restrictions on Unionist flags and parades. These events permeated discourses about problems with the peace process, and unfolded at a time when the insecurity felt from the 2009 global recession still lingered, providing a strategic context in which to examine connections between political culture, socio-economic forces and inequalities, and processes of conflict and identity formation.

The second phase of interviews occurred between May 2020 and June 2021. Due to the COVID-19 pandemic, these interviews were conducted via Cisco Webex, a virtual meeting platform. Eighteen respondents participated in this phase of the study. In most cases, I identified potential respondents through the websites of peacebuilding organizations or public bodies, and emailed them requesting their participation in an interview about current problems facing the NI peace process, including Brexit. In five cases, the author reached out to individuals who were already familiar due to their participation in the 2014 interviews. Those who participated in this second round of interviews, like the first, live in NI and work in community-based or government organizations there. In addition to their community work, two also serve in faculty university positions, and at least two are former paramilitary prisoners. Considering the timing of this round of interviews, respondents could provide particularly lucid insight into the implications of Brexit-related events on political and social discourses and community relations. All interviews, in both phases, were audio recorded and coded by the author through NVivo 9 and analyzed using a grounded theory approach (see, Strauss and Corbin 1990).

One slight limitation of the study is that, because most interviewees live in or near Belfast, the findings are not quite representative of Northern Ireland as a whole. Rural-specific dynamics of conflict, peacebuilding, and identity formation in particular are not factored into the analysis. Thus, readers should keep in mind that this empirical study is somewhat "Belfast-centric"; rural-to-urban specificities are simply outside the scope of the analysis.

Whilst certain arguments in the subsequent chapters may be read by some as polemical, they are ultimately the result of the observations and perspectives of stakeholders on the frontlines of Northern Ireland's peace process—some of whom consider themselves excluded from centers of social and political power. Because many of the respondents live and/or work in marginalized communities and feel unheard within dominant political and academic circles, the arguments based on their accounts may be unsettling to some readers who frequent these networks. However, this does not mean that the findings are inaccurate, or that such arguments are not worthy of consideration. As Patricia Hill Collins (2002, vii) recognizes, it is not always necessary or productive to "frame our ideas in the language that is familiar to and comfortable for a dominant group." Collins also teaches us that those marginalized within dominant social orders, whether based on their class, ethnicity, race, gender, or other ascribed social identities, hold standpoints based on experiences of exclusion, which have the potential to demystify systems of power and domination. Members of marginalized groups—and perhaps those who regularly work with them as well—are in this respect particularly well equipped to teach us about dynamics of social and political power.

The analysis also draws on reports about controversial political incidents which escalated intercommunal tensions and violence in Belfast from newspapers based in the UK and Ireland. The reports were retrieved by the author from the LexisNexis database, using a limited set of search terms. The first round of data collection for the content analysis, targeting reports between full years 2008 and 2014, included the search terms "sectarian," "violence," "attack," "paramilitary," "terrorist," "Belfast," "Gerry Adams arrest," "flag protest," "parade protest." A second search was conducted using the same terms, but with the terms "policing" and "politics" added, after the first several interviews in 2014 revealed how grievances over policing were frequently referenced by respondents to rationalize accusations against Unionists or Nationalists as responsible for the decline of intergroup relations they observed. A third search was undertaken, using the terms "Brexit," "politics," and "Northern Ireland," targeting newspaper reports published between January 2017 and December 2021.

Newspaper reports contain interviews with politicians, community leaders, law enforcement, and witnesses to contentious events, and the discourses of such persons give insight into the contexts in which (de)escalations of conflict occur. Incidents that receive significant coverage often indicate which issues and corresponding media narratives are influential in shaping socio-political discourse "on the ground" (Gamson and Modigliani 1989; Sasson 1995). Incorporation of newspaper data also helped contextualize respondents' perspectives and corroborate empirical observations they made which would underscore key arguments of the analysis. Overall, the afore-mentioned mixed method approach allowed for data triangulation and for the capacity to identify how political processes and public events interact to shape political discourses, identities, ideologies.

Throughout the initial coding process, themes were identified as inherent within the transcriptions and newspaper reports, and were not predetermined by the author, following Miles and Huberman (1984). Analysis first went through a stage of "open coding," where each new categorical code was entered into NVivo 9 in language used by respondents or those quoted in newspaper reports. Both "categorical" and subsequent "contextualizing" holistic strategies of data interpretation were then undertaken due to the com-plexity of the data (Teddie and Tashakkori 2009, 253; see also, Mason 2002). Throughout subsequent stages of analysis, I found that this process helped in periodic assesment of the explanatory value of each category and theme in relation to others.

Following the initial phase of open coding, thematic coding was subse-quently undertaken. "Emergent themes" identified through such coding are defined as the "dominant features of the situation or person, those qualities of place, person, or object that define or describe identity" (Eisner 1998, 104). In this respect, "a theme is a pervasive quality," and "Pervasive qualities tend to permeate and unify situations and objects" (ibid., 104). In identifying such "qualities," the author recognized patterns in how each observation is pertinent in shaping the more general views offered by respondents, and how each theme builds on, or subordinates others in this process. Thematic codes referred both to respondents' viewpoints and their more descriptive recall of events, while taking account of patterns unique to particular identity groups. This type of analysis, described by Strauss and Corbin (1990, 96) as "axial coding," through which "data are put back together . . . by making connec-tions between categories" is well established in qualitative research.

THE PLAN OF THE BOOK

The subsequent chapters are organized in accordance with themes generated by the grounded theory analytical method, supporting distinct but inter-connected arguments. With a geographical focus on Belfast city, chapter 1 continues the examination of trends in class inequality within and across the

PUL and CNR blocs, and how these trends shape socio-political interests and practices distinctly within privileged sites of interaction versus areas of concentrated disadvantage and segregation. Particular attention is paid to the function of a culture of silence around contentious issues of ethnonational and ethnoreligious identity in "mixed" upper and middle-class circles, and its socio-political implications. It is argued that everyday "shared spaces," including urban cosmopolitan centers, competitive grammar schools and universities, and professional workplaces, inculcate patterns of interaction which are quite different from those that continue to shape psychosocial conditions of belonging and threat in relatively deprived and segregated neighborhoods. In such neighborhoods, open attempts at physical and symbolic displays of ethnopolitical domination (via flags, parades, murals, etc.) continue to sectarianize the structure of space and corresponding mental maps of those who live in them, marking significations of ingroup belonging tied to insular constructions of nationhood. Observations of respondents which implicate the apparent posturing of political elites intended to appeal to the disparate interests of distinct class segments of their ethnonational constituencies is also discussed, a theme carried over into the subsequent chapters. Unlike later chapters which examine constructions of identity and concomitant processes of domination and manipulation—as well as resistance to such processes—in the context of specific contentious events or issues, chapter 1 examines the more mundane forms of everyday interactions in which identity is produced differently across contexts of class, place and gender. The analysis in this chapter provides a theoretical and contextual basis for analyses undertaken in the subsequent chapters.

Chapter 2 continues the geographical focus on Belfast, examining dynamics linking increases in the incidence of sectarian tensions in parts of the city to conditions of poverty and socio-economic inequity, and the discursive and legislative practices of ethnopolitical leaders. Emphasis is put on the function of the manipulation of ethnocultural symbols by political elites and grassroots actors in promoting heightened tensions which boil over into disorder and (non-lethal) violence. How such leaders manipulate ethnoculturally sensitive symbols (flags, parades, etc.) to promote particular political agendas and reproduce conflict mentalities is critically examined within the context of the post-conflict political economy. More specifically, chapter 2 explores how political provocations which promote sectarian tensions are facilitated by a combination of the economic marginalization of communities historically susceptible to violence, ongoing community influence of neo-paramilitary factions, and disjuncture between the political priorities of the middle-classes and working-classes within and across Protestant and Catholic communities.

Themes emanating from the data also illuminate contradictory processes of ex-combatant community-based peacebuilding, and highlight how the positive contributions of former paramilitary prisoners are paralleled by contemporary neo-paramilitary practices geared toward maintaining power and control on neighborhood levels. The analysis in chapter 3 examines how male masculinities, rooted in legacies of conflict are posited as normative cultural bedrocks of social and political organization. It is argued that this type of thinking risks replicating some of the very same ideologies and interests which contributed to political violence in the first place. Data from chapter 3 also show how such cultural motivations are jointly, inextricably linked to the marginalization of women, and the criminalization of the broader ex-prisoner community, obstructing access to legitimate avenues of social mobility. The chapter argues that elected Unionists' support for policies which permanently criminalize and marginalize former paramilitary prisoners, in line with their intention to punish former IRA militants, also undermines the efficacy of community-based ex-combatant reintegration efforts. Consequently, certain elements within the Loyalist and Republican ex-prisoner communities with few job prospects and limited social legitimacy (Mitchell 2008)—and who experience the broader socio-economic stagnation of their communities—may feel inclined to ratchet-up political hostilities, reproducing the same ethnocultures of semi-militarized masculinities that partially motivate their "community involvement." The voices of women are put front and center of the analysis to identify experiences of marginalization resulting from the partial ex-combatant takeover of community-based organizations, but also to document their agency in facilitating positive intercommunity relations despite the obstacles. How these dynamics impact the scope of community-based peacebuilding more broadly is also discussed.

The ethnopolitics of threat and resentment are also implicated by data which highlight elected leaders' strategic manipulation of policing disputes and conflict over how to deal with the past (chapter 4) and Brexit (chapter 5). More specifically, chapter 4 reveals ontological planes animated by narratives about the so-called political policing of public disorder and disputes over the past which align the identities of otherwise quite different and conflicted intra-ethnic constituencies. Findings illustrate how, when conditions emerge that have the potential to provoke feelings of betrayal and threat in marginalized communities, discourses which implicate the police are especially likely to activate collective mentalities of ethnopolitical victimhood and resistance, subjugating other class-based and place-based identities and grievances. Policing processes which become disputed, due to their historically central role in constituting and reflecting the contested logic of the state provide events or social and organizational "fields" in which opportunistic actors can effectively reconstruct ethnopolitical boundaries. The mixed method, combining thematic codes from in-depth interviews, ethnographic observations and content analysis allowed for the identification of connections between the discourses and actions of political elites, public officials and grassroots leaders in newspaper reports with those of respondents. In this way, the methodology facilitated an analysis of legitimacy as "an *activity* which can be observed" (Barker 2001, 24). The reported findings respond to a criticism of literature on ethnopolitical entrepreneurialism and culturalist approaches to ethnic and nationalist conflict—namely, that there has been little evidence that the fear, grievance, and ethnopolitical belief system promoted by opportunists are internalized by constituents (Brubaker and Laitin 1998, 443); and that researchers have generally failed to "ascertain empirically what the beliefs of those subject to authority may be, and how consistent they are with the legitimacy claims of the powerful" (Beetham 2013, 256).

Chapter 5 will describe how questions about the sustainability of the constitutional status of the North in the wake of Brexit has served to facilitate the politics of fear and resentment by the leading Unionist parties, challenging the gradual emergence of a post-constitutional politics. Yet, I also argue that the hardline constitutional politics facilitated by Brexit in this respect is paralleled by stakeholders' resistance to ethnopolitical manipulation, and by discourses reflecting democratic norms which transcend ethnonational difference. Specifically, the chapter explores how members of the Unionist community challenge DUP representations of supposed negative implications of Brexit for their communities and reject misleading narratives or "official meanings," reflecting a commitment to the principle of consent in NI political society and attachment to European identity in ways which trump traditionally insular Unionist constructions of identity. At the same time, preliminary signs of a rejection of hardline Unionist ethnopolitics occur within a backdrop of simmering tensions within Unionist and Loyalist communities over the terms of withdrawal and perceptions of British betrayal which hold the potential to escalate into disorder and violence. The implications of these combined dynamics are examined with respect to broader potential shifts in dominant Unionist politics and the peace process.

Chapter 6 identifies common discourses about the main obstacles to the work of local leaders in community-based peacebuilding and restorative justice, including structures of funding, support (or lack thereof) from the dominant political parties, competition over resources, and the ongoing marginalization of the concerns of women and economically underserved communities within the broader peacebuilding apparatus. The chapter also documents how innovative community leaders have kept their work going despite these challenges, and what they believe needs to change politically, culturally, and economically moving forward for their work to have a lasting impact. However, many respondents indicate that work focused on fertilization of cross-community capacity building has waned, as political conflict and disinvestment in the community sector requires them to revert focus back to basic peace*keeping*—as opposed to peacebuilding—functions. The socio-political implications of socio-economic inequality, the distinct class cultures it produces, and manipulation by political leaders is examined in relation to deficits in the capacity of the community-based peacebuilding sector to bridge divided working-class Loyalist and Republican communities. Chapter 6 revisits some themes introduced in previous chapters as well, arguing that the positive impacts of cross-community peacebuilding work, disproportionately in poor and working-class communities, is mitigated by segregation as well as "culture wars" spearheaded by ethnopolitical leaders in contexts of under-development. The analysis suggests that only through a substantial transformation in the structure of community spaces and greater state efforts to mitigate ethnopolitical posturing and construct shared institutions can the community sector make a more lasting impact in fostering intercommunal dialogue and trust.

More generally, the subsequent chapters trace reproductions of ethnopolitical identities and conflict to socio-economic and spatial inequalities, gendered relations, the criminalization of politically volatile groups (i.e., ex-combatants, 'anti-social' youth), and the opportunistic behaviors of political elites and grassroots leaders. In doing so, the book illustrates how the coercive force of interlocking class/place, gendered and ethnonational identities are inextricably linked, and how processes in the reproduction of conflict mentalities and practices are underscored, in part, by social and economic inequalities within, as much as between historically divided ethnopolitical communities. Also discussed is how contentious discourses and events surrounding policing, Brexit, and "culture wars" function to subjugate critical political voices challenging sectarian binaries and realign working-class Loyalist and Republican attitudes with the interests and ideologies of the dominant Unionist and Nationalist parties, respectively—stifling resistance to the prevailing system of social regulation and prospects of socio-political transformation. However, while discourses and events are powerful in these respects, the analysis recognizes that they are also subject to the agency of community-based actors whose reflexivity on the manipulation and inequalities faced by their communities may potentially provide new prospects for socio-political transformation in the future.

NOTES

1. Indeed, the substantially increased equity in labor market outcomes between Protestants and Catholics indicates a significant reduction in the horizontal nature of the inequality that contextualized the escalation of violence in the late 1960s and early 70s. Economic deprivation of Catholics set the stage for the peaceful civil rights

protests in 1968, but the escalation of IRA terrorism did not occur until after the state violently repressed these protests. Yet, "in contrast to members of the middle class, members of the working class and student activists are more likely to experience repression, to be available for costly violent protest, and to experience the efficacy of political violence" (White 1989, 1277). As later chapters will explore further, the disproportionate impacts of conflict on poor and working-class communities continues to undermine peace process outcomes.

2. Such exceptions from NI include Tomlinson (2016), Herrault and Murtagh (2019), Kelly (2012), Coulter (2018), Shirlow and Murtagh (2006), Cassidy (2008), Hearty (2018) and McAuley (2015). These important contributions represent a small fraction of the immense scholarship on conflict and peacebuilding in NI, however.

3. There are important exceptions to this trend, however, which this work builds upon. See, Ashe (2019; 2012), Ashe and Harland (2014), Cockburn (2004), Little (2002), O'Rourke (2015) and Gilmartin (2015).

4. The terms "Protestant" and "Catholic" signify ethnopolitical orientations as much as religious affiliations in NI (Shirlow and Murtagh 2006, 15). Although not all Protestants or Catholics are Unionist/Loyalist or Republican/ Nationalist, respectively, almost all Unionists/Loyalists and Republicans/Nationalists are Protestant and Catholic. Republicans have been historically more uncompromising in their call for a United Ireland than Nationalists, and more accepting of the use of violence to obtain this goal. Nationalists have historically been more willing to accept the constitutional status quo if it entails greater equality between Catholics and Protestants. The underlying political ideology of both Unionists and Loyalists is their demand that Northern Ireland remains part of the United Kingdom. However, differences between Loyalists and Unionists are complex. With respect to the Protestant community, Loyalists, who mainly come from working-class neighborhoods, have justified their use of extra-state paramilitary violence by the political objective of maintaining Northern Ireland's place in the UK. While Unionists share Loyalist's constitutional agenda, they believe that the state should hold total monopoly over the use of "legitimate violence" and, consequently, condemn all forms of paramilitarism. See Ruane and Todd (1996), Shirlow (2012) and Tonge (2002) for discussions about the complexities of the binary identities in NI.

5. Class is most basically and universally understood in terms of income and wealth (ownership of assets), occupational status, and qualification (i.e., education level), and these definitions underscore my use of the term here. It is important to note that by using terms such as "middle-class" and "working-class," I do not intend to make overly sweeping generalizations which exaggerate the complex and nuanced reality of class relations in NI. There are various academic definitions of social class, and it is not in the purview of this manuscript to provide an exhaustive discussion of their merits and limitations. When using the term "middle-class," I am generally referring to individuals who have received some university education (a "qualification" definition of class); and work in professional or "white-collar" fields that require specialized training (occupational status), earn medium-to-high level incomes, and/or possess some degree of wealth (most typically in the form of homeownership). When using the term "working-class," I am generally referring to those without third level

education, who tend to work in jobs that do not require specialized training or education, and who have modest incomes (often defined as below the national average) and little or no wealth. Of course, these definitions are not mutually exclusive, and in reality many individuals fall somewhere on a continuum. There are Republican and Loyalist ex-combatants from deprived areas of Belfast who have obtained doctorate degrees, for example, and would fit neatly in neither of these categories. Academic conceptualization is never fully representative of the complex nature of social life.

6. See the more recent NI Peace Monitoring Reports (Gray et al. 2018; Wilson 2017) for additional evidence to support this point.

7. There is still a notable degree of class distinction in terms of party choice within Nationalist politics. Sinn Fein still receives its core base of support from working-class districts, and the Social Democratic Labour Party (SDLP) remains known as the "middle-class" Catholic party. However, the class distinction in this respect has declined significantly in the post-Agreement period, as Sinn Fein has taken many middle-class former SDLP voters and increasingly garners the support of young people who align with neither Unionist nor Nationalist identities by use of inclusive messaging. See, Mitchell, Evans, and O'Leary (2009) and Evans and Tonge (2013).

8. Welfare Reform legislation was passed in 2016, but in NI, "a system of supplementary payments to those experiencing financial disadvantage as a result of some of the changes" was implemented on the advice of Professor Eileen Evason. These payments would act to mitigate the negative impacts on the poorer segments of the society, but expired in March 2020. Income inequality, as well as poverty among children and those with disabilities or chronic health problems, are projected to increase throughout the UK as a result of these "reforms." "Cuts in the real value of working-age benefits are expected to reduce the real incomes of poorer households and housing costs are expected to increase for low income households as a consequence of rising rents" (Gray et al. 2018, 146; see also, Hood and Walters 2017; Barnard 2018).

9. Murtagh and Shirlow (2013, 46) make a similar point when arguing that the "devolved neoliberal structures that sustain social polarization may perpetuate strategies of resistance that could cut across and challenge ethnosectarian politics and deepening social segregation."

10. The shutdown of the Assembly was the result of multiple developments, including rows over an Irish Language Act, the resignation of Martin McGuinness, and controversies over a green energy scheme. Yet, as Coulter and Shirlow (2019, 3) explain, "the collapse of the power sharing executive owes its origins . . . to seismic political developments elsewhere in the United Kingdom" (i.e., Brexit).

11. Ethnic outbidding refers to the process under consociational systems of government in which parties compete for co-ethnic supporters by attempts to depict themselves as the best equipped to defend against outgroup threats (see, Horowitz 2000).

12. The "loyal order," inextricably linked with the Orange Order—named in commemoration of the Protestant William of Orange, whose forces successfully defeated Catholic armies in the Seventeenth Century—refers to a fraternal, Protestant-only organization committed to British Unionism, and considered sectarian by Catholics.

13. Chapter 2 also utilizes PSNI data on trends in sectarian violence as well as quantitative content analysis conducted by the author. These methods are more thoroughly explained there.

Chapter 1

A Tale of Two Belfasts?

Inequality, Segregation, and the Politics of Identity in a "Post-conflict" City

The cessation of violence, coupled with urban renewal in parts of Belfast and Derry (Nagle 2009b) and increased Catholic mobility (Shirlow and Murtagh 2006, 103) has enhanced opportunities for regular cross-community contact. Nagle (2009b) even argues that "multiculturalism" has been advanced as a result of urban renewal schemes promoted by the NI Executive. Within the now cosmopolitan city center of Belfast, people from Unionist and Nationalist communities, as well as those affiliated with neither ethnonational tradition have access to a variety of safe spaces in which to congregate and deactivate ethnosocial binaries. Drissel (2007, 177) identifies how shared public spaces in Belfast "have been utilized by youth to effectively blur schismatic distinctions and at least partially transform their collective identities." Others suggest that "new understandings of shared space can negate territorial identities and facilitate coexistence in the same place" among older Unionist and Nationalist residents as well, including those from traditionally divisive organizations (such as the Orange Order) (Stevenson 2010, 1). At the same time, many young people still fear potential sectarian attack when traveling outside their home neighborhoods, and confront sectarianism regularly (Ruppe 2014; McAlister, Scraton, and Haydon 2014; Harland 2011). The seeming contradiction in the empirical observations of these authors can be better understood through greater analytical attention to the inextricable and often coercive class and place-based dimensions of identity which shape intergroup contact (Murtagh 2011).

As early as the late 1990s, evidence emerged to suggest that the "lifestyles and socio-economic pursuits" of the Catholic and Protestant middle classes were becoming more "mutually agreeable" (Shirlow and Murtagh 2006, 103; see also, Shirlow 1997). Douglas (1997, 171–172) optimistically argued that "new social structures" facilitating the rapid expansion of the Catholic middle class "influenced the process of socialization and the greater diversity of social behavior has led to more subtle definitions of the Self and the Other." Others predicted that increased mobility would reduce middle-class Catholics' sympathy with Irish Nationalist ideology, as material concerns gradually out-flanked those of ethnopolitical identity (Elliott 2007). Shirlow and Murtagh (2006, 122) conclude in their comparison of a mixed, upper-middle-class community in southeast Belfast with the general NI population, that the identities of the former "are less uniform and predictable than those of other people in the province." However, the same authors recognize that this "new socio-spatial class" has not "forged an alternative cultural and, importantly, political identity" (Shirlow and Murtagh 2006, 123).

Findings reported below similarly suggest that it would be misleading to associate the "new socio-spatial [middle] class" in NI with the emergence of a socio-political identity that fully transcends the society's longstanding eth-nonational and ethnoreligious binaries. Yet the qualitative interview findings reported here, augmented by extensive literature review and ethnographic observations, also identify patterns of interaction that function to reconstitute intersecting class and ethnonational identities, in particular gendered and spa-tial contexts. Through analysis of such patterns, processes which deactivate, disguise, or galvanize ethnonational identities are revealed.

More specifically, the following pages document practices of ethnopolitical (de)identification in Belfast's predominantly middle-class "shared spaces." I then contrast these dynamics with analysis of the obstacles to integration and cross-community relation-building experienced most sharply by those residing in areas with high levels of ethnoreligious segregation and concen-trated disadvantage, exploring the implications of these distinct processes on identify formation and the transformative potential of local peacebuilding initiatives. Applying the anthropological concept of "silence" as a mecha-nism of social power, coupled with Pierre Bourdieu's concept of symbolic power, I also examine the suppression of discourse on local issues of ethnop-olitics and inequality in (mostly middle-class) "shared spaces." Specifically, respondents' observations reveal how discourses about interconnected issues of ongoing ethnopolitical conflict and class disparities are repressed within such spaces; and how images of conflict are pejoratively framed as atavis-tic, apolitical aberrations, associated primordially with the "lower classes." Though reflecting dynamics that are gradual and partial, rather than universal or representative of entire class groups, respondents nonetheless reveal the likely ramifications of such phenomena. The chapter concludes by explor-ing how the distancing of segments of the middle classes from Northern

Ireland's ethnopolitics and the class dimensions of conflict in the post-accord era has seemingly informed the strategies of politicians from the dominant parties—but especially Unionists—whose communicative actions appear to be (partially) configured in accordance with the class and place identities of distinct constituencies.

CLASS, SPACE, IDENTITY, AND "INTEGRATION" IN BELFAST

The class dimensions of identity can be identified through dispositions and patterns of interaction, which necessarily emerge from structural social arrangements, allowing connections to be drawn analytically between socio-economic position and cultural practice (Bourdieu 1984). Yet, as structural arrangements change, so do opportunities for alternative modes of social engagement, potentially resulting in the gradual alteration of identity. As Todd (2005, 430) describes, identity change can be linked to "gradual disruptions of cognitive categories over time, underlying concepts which are put in question, inchoate cultural unease, [and] new practices which allow old concepts to fade into irrelevance." Emergent conceptions and performances of self may not come to completely replace others, but nonetheless serve to moderate or subordinate traditional ingroup identifications in particular inter-actional contexts.

Certain members of the society may have greater capacity to access those conditions most conducive to regular intergroup contact, moreover. The increase in middle-class Catholic mobility and access to "shared spaces," for example, provide the conditions for the emergence of a "social field" in which ethnonational dimensions of identity are deactivated, concomitant to emergent forms of *habitus*—"schemes of thought, feeling and action" which recur in accordance with one's "structured social position" (Allan 2006, 174). Bourdieu (1984, 466) explains *habitus* as those "most automatic gestures or the apparently more insignificant techniques of the body . . . engaging the most fundamental principles of the construction and evaluation of the social world." Illustrating emerging forms of *habitus* in ethnically "mixed" settings, respondents describe how youth often initiate interactions with peers without reflecting interest in one another's ethnic or religious identity. For example, a teacher and education reform advocate observes that "middle-class children have more experiences of going outside of their area, so they are involved in a lot more extracurricular activities that expose them more to children from a different background." She further explains how "they begin" interacting without recognizing potential differences in identity, "unless you're doing the discussion with them, unless you're actually deliberately saying, 'we're all different'" (interview with author, South Belfast, May 2014).

Several other interviewees conveyed similar observations, noting that this trend is more apparent among youth from middle-class communities, who can more readily travel outside their neighborhoods and participate in privately-funded activities. A respondent suggests, for example, that "it's mobility" that has helped increase young peoples' connections across the ethnonational divide: "They've got a few pound in their pocket and they can go to the same place of play. . . . The coffee shop culture has a lot to do with it" (interview with author, May 2021). More than half of those I interviewed indicate a significant class disparity in terms of access to these so-called shared spaces. While not representative in a statistical sense, the frequent recognition of this dynamic among respondents (without prodding by the interviewer) is notable.[1] I eventually began to notice firsthand, in the mostly "middle-class" sites I frequented in south and central Belfast, that repression of discussion about identity seemed to underscore meaningful relations in "mixed" settings. In one instance, for example, during a visit to Queen's University, two young women and one young man—all close friends—were at first eager to speak with me about the purpose of my visit, but were clearly discomforted by my answer (i.e., that I was studying the conflict and peace process). The awkward silence was eventually broken when one said, "we don't really talk about that here." One of the young women added: "I don't actually know much about that. We try to just move on from that. It's in the past." After I asked some questions about what part of NI they were from, and their backgrounds, the same young woman answered that she was from a "mixed" family: her father is Protestant, her mother Catholic. "Really? Me too!" proclaimed her friend and dormmate. Clearly, even while sharing the same room, they had never discussed their national or religious backgrounds.[2]

Qualitative evidence from the present study corroborates findings from earlier research, which suggests that ethnoreligious and ethnonational identity is declining as a socially organizing principle within particular social and institutional contexts. For example, several respondents imply that workplace integration has facilitated greater cross-communal relationships among older adults in more informal social settings. One notes, for example, that "because the workplace is now much more mixed, you've got much more social mixing. The city centers and town centers are much more anonymous" (interview with author, May 2020). Shirlow and Murtagh's (2006, 118) survey research showed "high rates of mixing" around professional activities, corroborating this observation. The same authors indicate that interfaith mixing was common in contexts of entertainment and certain sports activities as well.

Even at the height of violent conflict, regular and polite contact between Protestants and Catholics was common in the mundane course of necessary daily interaction in public spaces, in which discussion of religion, politics, and identity is avoided (McAuley 1994, 56). However, the increase in cross-community interaction in the post-accord era is facilitated by a more integral *institutional* incorporation of avoidance strategies or codes of silence on questions of identity. Even discussion about sports teams which are affiliated with Irish or Ulster-Scots identities, for example, is frowned upon. As one respondent describes, "in most workplaces you don't even talk about football, especially the Celtic and Rangers thing, which is a Scottish game. . . . You don't wear any signal or emblem that would identify you as one side or the other. It's these polite conversations and we do a lot of dancing around each other" (interview with author, June 2020). A woman involved in promoting integrated education in Belfast explains how young people in "middle-class" and "mixed" areas "work together, they shop together, they go to concerts together—they're just not having those conversations [about identity and history] that they need to have." She then admits, "I live in a middle-class area and my area is mixed. But I don't have that conversation with my neighbors" (interview with author, May 2020). Even as this respondent is actively involved professionally in promoting cross-community dialogue on contentious issues of politics and identity, silence on such issues outside that context is a cultural expectation in her middle-class South Belfast neighborhood which apparently facilitates "good relations." In more privileged sites of interaction, formation of relationships across the traditional communal binaries—facilitated by repression of discussion and displays of ethnonational identity, and a culture of silence on contentious issues related to the conflict—seemingly cross over into multiple social spheres, and carry on due to the few spatial and economic barriers imposed on agents within these environments. In this respect, silence is a marker of a "middle-class" identity negotiation process—a "code of spatial performance" (Drissel 2007, 178; see also, Gotham 2003, 724).

Many respondents acknowledge that the cross-community interactions and friendships they have, and those they witness among younger people in the "global village" of Belfast—including their children and extended relatives—have increased both in frequency and quality, marking a significant generational shift. One self-described middle-class participant in the study recalls that, as a child, "I didn't have much experience of being able to communicate or engage [with Protestants] and I perceived the other to be strange. But my nieces or nephews are living in a global village and they're able to engage. It's there for them." At the same time, official restrictions on political or cultural discourses in professional and educational organizations has further entrenched codes of silence on related issues of identity. As the same respondent explains, the sharing is governed by a series of policies and procedures which zone out your identity. They [organizations] try to make a neutral space. So what I see with them is that they're not allowed to have a conversation with the Protestant or Unionist or Loyalist that they know, that says, "why is that Red Hand important to you?" They'll be sacked for that. We have policy which says, you can't discuss flags, emblems, politics. (Interview with author, Belfast city center, May 2014)

Such policies exist in workplaces as well as universities. Yet the lower rates of employment among poor and working-class residents, and the greater difficulty they face accessing more "open" or "anonymous" areas of the city—due to both economic barriers and fear of sectarian harassment when traversing ethnosocially prescribed routes—corresponds to comparatively less workplace "mixing" vis-à-vis their middle-class counterparts (see Shirlow and Murtagh 2006).[3]

Respondents describe how discursive practices of silence and avoidance, characterizing what one terms "the polite culture," preclude not only discussion of ethnonational and religious identity, but *class* identity as well. One woman, employed by a prominent NGO stated that "the middle class can have meetings and organizations and things and the way they keep it safe is by not talking about things. Not going into any of those difficult areas" of identity. She also notes that "class is the big white elephant in the room we're not allowed to talk about" (interview with author, South Belfast, June 2014).

While facilitating non-political cross-communal interactions which ease the development of a broader range of relationships, official *and* informal codes of silence on ethnopolitical identity, in the fear of many respondents, may also undermine efforts at inculcating a willingness and ability to engage across communal lines about issues that continue to politically divide the broader Unionist and Nationalist communities. Such issues, moreover, have disproportionate affects in areas of concentrated disadvantage and conflict related trauma, which also contain more structural impediments to cross-community interaction. Although adherence to codes of silence on national and religious identity are not restricted to any class grouping, the greater levels of segregation and exclusion experienced by poor and working-class residents across various social spheres (housing, education, workplaces, and even leisure and shopping centers in some areas) (Shirlow and Murtagh 2006; Murtagh 2011; Herrault and Murtagh 2019) obstruct the extent to which contact translates into long-term relationships with outgroup members. Several interviewees explained how structures of segregation and sectarian territorialization continue to obstruct cross-communal interactions, shaping a very different reality for less privileged young members of the society. A respondent indicates that "middle-class people feel it's very comfortable here," and points to examples from Derry, such as its success in hosting the City of Culture, to suggest that there is "great confidence [in urban development] and people love it." Yet, she also acknowledges that for those from lower-income backgrounds, there is a "sense of hopelessness" (interview with author, Belfast center, June 2014). An older respondent, from a working-class Republican community in Belfast, similarly identifies a "class division" in terms of cross-communal interaction. In his view, "the younger generation don't have the barriers that we had about where not to go to. That's better in a lot of ways but it might be a class division, too. . . . The working-class communities still feel like they're less free to move" (interview with author, East Belfast, June 2014).

I witnessed such a "class division" firsthand during my time in Belfast. The longer my stay, and the more time I spent with some key informants in the study, the more I began to observe how the physical structures of segregation in working-class Belfast shaped the consciousness of its residents—the mental maps that structure travel and interaction, and the emotions (i.e., fear) that come with diverting from an ethnosocially prescribed route. An illustrative example was provided during a private tour I received from a key Nationalist informant in the study, whom I will call Colin. As we approached the Shankill Road—a notorious flashpoint of violence during the Troubles—he stopped, and I sensed his nervousness as he stood and glanced toward some residents looking back at us suspiciously. He asked if I was okay with going "the long way" around the Shankill, rather than through it. Being tired already from the miles-long walk from the city center, I showed hesitation. Being a courteous guide, Colin withdrew his question. Before resuming our walk, he set down some important guidelines for this phase of our journey, careful to speak quietly. Most importantly, he indicated that if anyone talks to us, I would have to answer, because my American accent would likely eliminate their suspicion. He then borrowed my jacket, to cover up his green Celtic jersey. (Celtic is the regional soccer team supported predominantly by Irish Catholics, and green is a color more generally marking one as a target from sectarian elements of the PUL community.) As Colin's demeanor changed from happy-go-lucky and talkative to stoic and silent, my awareness of the dynamics taking place around me sharpened. The suspicious looks toward me, I now realized, were not due to me being a suspected tourist, but a suspected Catholic. (I experienced this again later, when a motorist, assuming that I was a Catholic resident, yelled "fucking Taig"[4] at me while I walked down the street. I was told later that this was either because I was holding an issue of *The Irish Times* newspaper—which is read predominantly by Catholics—or simply because I was an unknown person walking through a tight-knit Protestant area.) The tensest moment for us both came when we approached a group of adolescents and young men building a massive pile of wood pallets and discarded tires in preparation for the upcoming July 11th bonfires, which occur on the eve of Unionist parades celebrating Protestant William of Orange's victory over Catholic forces in 1690's Battle of the Boyne. As we then neared the exit and approached a Catholic neighborhood, my guide, now visibly relieved, notified me that this was the first time he had ever traveled down the Shankill in his 23 years, even though it was just a short distance from his home.

This experience mirrors those of countless other young people residing in segregated, poor, and working-class communities of Belfast, who often "consider themselves imprisoned within their neighborhoods" (McAlister, Scraton, and Haydon 2014, 300), fearing the prospect of sectarian harassment and violence when venturing beyond sectarianized territorial boundaries, and lacking the means to relocate. Shirlow and Murtagh (2006, 102) explain how, in these highly segregated parts of the city, "peace walls,"[5] paramilitary murals, national flags, and other ethnopolitical imagery homogenize the identity of a place and act as "the mediums through which Belfast's residents transform daily occurrences and emotions into a symbolic system of territorial attachment." To my surprise, even Colin, employed by an organization that brings young people together from across the ethnonational divide, was significantly influenced in his movement by this symbolic system and fear of sectarian attack. A young woman reflects on her experience working with youth in a working-class PUL Estate to explain the extent fear plays, in combination with a more general "lack of confidence" in restricting young residents' mobility: "I had a group of young men who were saying that they wouldn't be leaving to go anywhere, and it took me two years before I managed to get them to head out just on the [predominantly Catholic] Falls Road for a tour. It was two years before we got them to that point" (interview with author, May 2020).[6]

The neighborhoods most affected by the legacies of the Troubles remain among the most socio-economically deprived in NI. Fay, Morrissey and Smyth (1999, 150) indicate that approximately 13 percent of postcodes in Northern Ireland experienced more than half of fatalities during the Troubles. Residents of these highly segregated neighborhoods suffer disproportionate levels of poverty and ill-health, and have limited access to public services (Shirlow and Murtagh 2006, 81–100; Nagle 2009a, 328). Eighteen of the twenty poorest wards in NI are found in North and West Belfast (Devlin, McKay, and Russell 2018, 11), the same areas where most killings in the city occurred (Mesev, Shirlow, and Downs 2009). North and West Belfast have continued to suffer from some of the worst deprivation indicators in the UK throughout the post-Agreement period (Coulter 2014; Tomlinson 2016). Clearly, in much of Belfast, class identities are also identities of place.

I discovered that the dual persistence of segregation and poverty in urban, working-class Republican and Loyalist strongholds symbolized to respondents the broken promise that the Agreement would bring "peace dividends" to revitalize these communities. To one respondent—a former UVF prisoner and current community-based restorative justice advocate— "It's very obvious they spend money on the city center, for all the tourists, but forget about the places that count" (interview with author, West Belfast, June 2014). As a respondent from Loyalist West Belfast similarly describes, "When you go into the center of town there's a bunch of new buildings up and lovely new infrastructure all about the place. But when you come into the hearts of communities, there's nothing. Its people living the same way that they did 30–40 years ago, and sometimes worse" (interview with author, West Belfast, June 2014). The development of Belfast city center into a cosmopolitan site hosting much of the city's economic activity, and frequented by visitors from outside the UK, contrasts with the segregated parts of Belfast, especially North, West, and East Belfast where sectarian territorialization is most evident. Respondents corroborate a phenomenon indicated earlier in the devolution period, that "processes of urban regeneration act as a 'mask' to cover the intensification of poverty, segregation and exclusion that affect working-class urban districts" (Nagle 2009a, 173). Various grassroots community leaders note the increasing, detrimental impact of economic strain on relations between working-class Republican and Loyalist communities, moreover. *Every respondent* interviewed in 2014, and several others interviewed in 2020 emphasized poverty, socio-economic inequality, or educational under-attainment in working-class Loyalist *and* Republican communities as among the greatest obstacles to peacebuilding. When asked if he thought that relations between young people from Protestant and Catholic backgrounds were improving, a Loyalist respondent who works with at-risk youth answered that

> It depends where you're coming from. It depends on the background of those young people. There are a lot of young people who just get on with life, because they've had an opportunity, and maybe they've gone to a better school, and they're going to university and moving on and doing things properly. But in the broad Republican and Loyalist areas where younger people aren't getting that opportunity, it's just making things worse. Things are as bad now as I ever remember them to be, in terms of cross-community culture, getting together, speaking to each other. It just doesn't happen. (Interview with author, West Belfast, June 2014)

The class distinctions recognized by respondents with respect to the frequency of contact between residents from Protestant and Catholic communities, and its impact on identity speaks to the ongoing structural and political obstacles to relation building facing underserved communities most sharply. Several respondents contend that representatives from Loyalist and Republican communities, including former combatants, have engaged with each other in substantial discussions about history, conflict, and identity more regularly than political leaders, and in ways rarely observed in "polite," "middle-class" settings (see chapter 3). Some community leaders in the same neighborhoods also engage in various projects which bring at-risk youth from Loyalist and Republican communities together for play, as well as to discuss difficult issues of identity. Furthermore, while state grammar schools are somewhat more integrated than secondary schools (Borooah and Knox 2015), allowing "more opportunities to mix" (as put by one respondent, in a May 2020 interview) there is no evidence to suggest significant socio-economic difference on average between students who attend officially integrated schools and those who do not. While serving only about 7 percent of NI pupils (Borooah and Knox 2015), these officially integrated schools are characterized by proportional representation of Catholic, Protestant, and unaffiliated pupils, and envisage conversations about ethnonational and religious identity and Irish and British history in efforts to facilitate mutual understanding and trust (see, McGlynn et al. 2004). Thus, parents who choose to send their children to these schools make a conscious effort to inculcate tolerance and promote cross-communal ties. Sixteen families decided to send their children to the first integrated Irish language pre-school—Naiscoil na Seolta—in the heart of Loyalist East Belfast. The school was established through the leadership of Linda Ervine, who had for years prior run Irish language classes for adults in East Belfast. Yet, the location of the school had to be changed weeks before its planned opening "due to an ongoing social media hate campaign" (McCambridge 2021) led by a former Red Hand Commando (Jordan 2021).

Even those who attend integrated schools struggle to construct an environment conducive to multiculturalism more broadly. Grassroots leaders and education reform advocates emphasize the point that integrated education, like community-based peacebuilding projects, while important, tend to have limited impact on young people residing in more isolated and segregated communities, where the sectarianization of space is most acute. A Republican who works with young people at an East Belfast interface explains how there are

> integrated schools in Northern Ireland where kids enjoy each other's company and it works well, but they're going back into segregated communities, so it doesn't work because they're getting the old traditional, "we hit them and they hit us," or "they're Prods and we're Fenians" . . . once they're getting [back] in their own community. So things like that put a stop-gap in community co-operation and it's the same with community projects. (Interview with author, East Belfast, June 2014)

When asked if contact between young people from Protestant and Catholic backgrounds through integrated education leads to lasting relationships outside of school, an integrated education advocate answered that "it depends where the school is. I know for example in Hazelwood, that can be very difficult until they can go into town" (i.e., Belfast city center). Young people from different ethnoreligious backgrounds tend to get along successfully inside integrated schools; however, "when they leave the school, they can't socialize. If they live in segregated areas, it's beyond safe to go into the other's neighborhood" (interview with author, May 2020; see also, Harland 2011; Lysaght 2002). The combined pressures of poverty and threat of sectarian harassment in segregated working-class wards undermine the development of interethnic friendships fostered in integrated schools and community-based peacebuilding projects (see also chapter 6). Although the city center provides some refuge from the threat of sectarian intimidation, accessing this part of Belfast is much more difficult for relatively poor young residents from segregated neighborhoods and single-community estates who must travel far distances while lacking access to reliable transportation.[7] These combined challenges to mobility throughout the city undermine the frequency of intergroup contact that can facilitate lasting friendships and subordinate ethnopolitical loyalties to supranational identifications.

For young people from segregated poor and working-class areas participating in cross-community projects or attending integrated schools, the need to "live double lives" brings additional stress. A former city councillor and current youth advocate explains that "if you are asking children to integrate in school, and then go back into their segregated community, you're actually asking them to live double lives, because they're going to go back into the culture of the community even though they know it's wrong." As one respondent elaborates, "to some degree" relations between Nationalist and Unionist young people

> may be getting better, but I'm not so sure about that. And I suppose when it comes to my role here is the worry of the number of mixed messages that we give our young people. So for instance we say to them on one side of the road, particularly around flag protests, and others—"it's Thursday night, go across to the other community and do your cross community work, but remember on Friday and Saturday night you have to be on this side of the road, and you have to be loaded with bricks and bottles and stones, and call them all the names of the day." (Interview with author, Belfast city center, May 2014)

Moreover, it is important to point out that when respondents discuss violence, they are primarily discussing the actions of *boys and men*, in whom sectarian rituals and events function to re-center the ethnonational and ethnoreligious dimensions of self—a phenomenon reflecting one process in the compart-mentalization of distinct place-based identities.

The Gendered Dimension of the Social Construction of Working-class Ethnonational Identity

For young men in marginalized, segregated communities, ethnopolitical dimensions of self are inextricably linked with their identities *as* men. In contrast to the polite secularism more visible in cosmopolitan, "middle-class" urban locations, "tribalism" in segregated working-class communities, under-scored by more open displays of ethnopolitical membership—and taking inherently gendered forms—remains relatively strong. Displaying symbols of ethnopolitical belonging serves the function of a "statutory assignation"—to use Bourdieu's (1991, 121) terminology—marking conformity with one's presupposed "social essence" in ways distinct from those whose everyday interactions occur largely within cosmopolitan or professional settings. As one respondent observes, for

> the lower class, the working class, the issues remain the same. Tribalism is still fervent, albeit that it might manifest itself with softer symbology; it might be much more about the sports teams you support, rather than the paramilitary you support. You might get a tattoo for Celtic or Rangers rather than an IRA tattoo or UDA tattoo. You still get a tat because you're working class and you're from a tribal area. You want to have that tat that says, "That's who I am. These are pubs I drink in and not in the new Protestant pubs" and so on and vice versa. That's the lower class. There's not that much mixing going on there. (Interview with author, June 2020)

Indeed, one study found that 68 percent of 18–25-year-olds from relatively deprived neighborhoods of Belfast separated by "peace lines" had never had a meaningful conversation with someone "from the other community" (Smithey 2011, 16). Considering that levels of segregation in social hous-ing remain high, it is hard to imagine that these numbers have significantly changed since. The Northern Ireland Housing Executive (2016) reports that 94 percent of those residing in social housing in Belfast live in segregated or "single communities," where over 80 percent of residents are from the same ethnoreligious group (see also, McClements 2018).

In NI overall, however, residents are less segregated residentially along religious lines than they used to be.[8] One indicator of this trend is the decline in the proportion of "single-identity wards" from 55 percent to 37 percent. In Belfast specifically, the decline in segregation is mostly the result of increased immigration coupled with an influx of middle-class Catholics into once Protestant-dominated areas (Gray et al. 2018, 177; Shirlow and Murtagh 2006, 105). Nonetheless, in those segregated areas also characterized by high levels of deprivation and limited mobility, a sense of ongoing threat from the outgroup and drive for positive ingroup reinforcement[9] underscore the centrality of ethnonational affiliation for younger residents especially, helping to drive an emotive attachment to ethnopolitical identity, and establish a "social essence" and sense of belonging or "home" it provides. Following Rothschild's (1981, 5–6) analogy, ethnicity "defines and accepts them for what they are, rather than what they do—an entity analogous to Robert Frost's definition of home, 'the place where, when you have to go there, they have to take you in' (from the poem 'The Death of the Hired Man')." For young men in this social milieu, claims to "home" are often predicated on ritualized performances of ethno-masculinity. Although middle-class young men (and young women) may demonstrate hyper-masculinist attitudes and practices on occasion, such practices, due to distinct socio-environmental conditions, are generally less coercive, or less central to everyday productions of self. In segregated neighborhoods, memories of the Troubles remain especially central to collective identity, since these neighborhoods experienced disproportionate levels of the political and sectarian violence of this period. A systemic sense of collective threat from neighboring outgroup communities, and periodically escalating tensions emerging from political mini-crises provide a locus of community activity where young people (or, young men) can perform valued roles as "protectors of their communities." As a woman working in restorative justice in a Loyalist Belfast community explains, "Young people get it into their heads in the interfaces—they're not there just to fight the other side; they're there to protect their community" (interview with author, West Belfast, June 2014). Although young men risk being criticized and excluded from communities when exercising agency in this way (Harland and McCready 2007), respondents suggest that some continue to follow such scripts, as they are provided with few other avenues to identity formation. "Protecting the community" brings with it a reliance on ethnocultures of hyper-masculinity for the construction of self, where aggressive behavior, rationalized by the need to "protect" one's local ethnoreligious space is inextricably linked with narrow constructions of manhood. As Nagel (1998, 750) says, "terms like honour, patriotism, cowardice and duty are hard to distinguish as either nationalist or masculinist, since they seem so thoroughly tied both to the nation and to manliness."

Although women played central roles in the armed Republican campaign, the contributions they made are often overlooked due to their transgression of a gender order where political violence is legitimated by normative, militarized male masculinities (Ashe 2009; Arextaga 1997; Dowler 1998).[10] Due in part to the association of feminism with Nationalism in NI, Unionist women, across organizational contexts, have been even more marginalized from ingroup positions of social power[11] (Sales 1997b; Racioppi and O'Sullivan 2001).[12] While acting to replicate sectarian divisions, respondents envisage how a sense of threat from the Other, validating the persistence of "gangs" (or paramilitaries), and the ethnocultures of masculinity they embody, also help constitute a "sense of community." A young woman from a PUL community refers to the insights of an American colleague that helped inform her perspective on this dynamic:

> He was from Washington and he'd been working before in the ghettos [in the U.S.] and he made the very good comment of whenever he's been in working with gangs [there], there's no real sense of community. Whereas, for a lot of the people that we would be working with [in Belfast] that may have got involved in gangs [or paramilitaries] over the years, they have always had some connection to their community. For a lot of people, they genuinely did believe they were protecting their communities. There is a real desire to make sure your community is safe. (Interview with author, May 2020)

While many girls and women are excluded from both formal and informal modes of community leadership as a result of ethnomasculinist attitudes and behaviors, some connect with constructs of "community" which reify and normalize such attitudes.[13]

Decline of Middle-class Ethnopolitical Fixations?

In contrast to the gendered dynamics of collective identity formation in the segregated wards of working-class Belfast, collective emotive attachments to ethnopolitical entities rooted in the legacy of conflict is less apparent in middle-class and upper-class networks. Recent survey research corroborates the view of many respondents, who describe a decline in ethnonational identification in some relatively privileged sections of the society. Hayward and McManus's (2019, 148) analysis shows that a higher proportion of those identifying as neither Nationalist nor Unionist tend "to be either in full or part-time employment or in education, compared with Unionists and Nationalists—a finding which correlates with this group tending to have higher educational qualifications." Those identifying as "neither" are also more likely to have lived outside NI, an additional marker of class privilege in most cases[14] (Hayward and McManus 2019, 148). In addition, the gap between the proportion of individuals identifying with neither ethnonational tradition "in paid employment compared with Unionists and Nationalists . . . has grown steadily in the past 20 years" (ibid., 147).

Differences in the political fervent of segments of middle-class Unionism and working-class Loyalism are particularly salient. As early as the mid-twentieth century, the improvement of living standards brought with the creation of planned suburban communities, such as Glengormley, "while not displacing traditional [ethnopolitical] fixations . . . drained them of some of their emotional centrality" to middle-class life, and ultimately "weakened traditional allegiances with the Unionist party" (Patterson 2006, 182; see also, Legg 2018, 59–62). Other cultural differences seem to be emerging within the broader PUL community, creating internal cultural fractures. John Brewer (2013, 1) indicates how "middle class [Protestant] denominations commute into inner city churches but are disconnected from the evident problems in the vicinity." However, many other middle-class residents "abjure religion entirely, with the growth of non-identification and decline in observance rife among the suburban affluent, both Catholic and Protestant (but especially the Protestant middle-class)." For decades, Protestantism functioned to culturally bond middle-class Unionist and working-class Loyalist communities, and was integral to the constitution of a shared Protestant/Unionist political consciousness.[15] Yet, some segments of middle-class and working-class Unionist communities now share little in common outside their resistance to a united Ireland. "In cultural terms," the Protestant middle-classes have increasingly removed themselves from the Orange Order and Masonic lodges, "as linkages with such organizations no longer upholds the same status within a professional community detached from traditional industries" (Shirlow and Murtagh 2006, 106).[16] Non-voting is an "important facet" of the middle-class Protestant community as well, corresponding with its lack of spatial awareness of the problems of sectarianism that persist, and issues of ethnopolitical parades and state and paramilitary violence. In addition, many "have located material affluence and cannot identify reasons why voting is important to them" (Shirlow and Murtagh 2006, 106). Research from the post-accord era also shows that Protestants tend to identify with a wider range of identities than Catholics (Loyalist, British, Northern Irish, and even, to a lesser extent, Nationalist) (Muldoon et al. 2007)[17]; and that "ethno-nationalism has become less important in predicting vote choice for Protestants, but not Catholics" (Tilly, Garry, and Matthews 2019, 1).

Respondents imply that the depletion of the emotive ethnopolitical energy noted above is especially evident in more privileged Protestant communities, but is apparent to some degree among upwardly mobile Catholics as well. As one participant in the study describes,

> For upper-class Catholic Republicans, they will probably go to Trinity in Dublin, do their degree there, maybe take work in Dublin or head for London or New York, some of that. They are a very, very strong diaspora as you know,

and they're coming back home. Not to be politically active; they're coming back home because it's home. The property's cheap; they can fly every Monday to London and get their work there, or they can drive down to Dublin and work there and take a flat. The Protestant upper class, no change. Even less plugged into reality than before. They live in Northern Ireland, but they don't live in the Troubles. . . . In my head, I've become one of those. I've become one of those for different reasons. I was away for years and when I came back, I didn't need to join a tribe. I came from a tribe. Everybody knows what that tribe is . . . I didn't even have to live that reality; that's done for me. It's no longer a big thing to me. I am now a global citizen. Northern Ireland is literally . . . an economically sensible home. (Interview with author, June 2020)

Apathy is increasingly evident among young, middle-class Catholics who have little connection to Irish nationalism, as indicated in their relatively low participation in the polls (Delargy 2017). Of course, the "middle classes," like any socially constructed group, contain members who display various and often inchoate attitudes and behaviors (Graham and Shirlow 1998). For example, both the DUP and Sinn Fein have produced an increasing number of middle-class representatives in the post-Agreement period who are quite vocal on contentious ethnopolitical issues. A shared history of social and political oppression remains somewhat influential within the rising Catholic middle class, as some still connect with the legacy of minority status and resistance against a sectarian state. Higher rates of involvement with the church in cultural activities also maintains a Catholic/Nationalist collective identity that transcends class position to some degree (Goeke-Morey et al. 2016; Economist 2021). Moreover, while a decline in identification with Catholic identity in the traditional, religious sense is more noticeable in middle-class CNR communities, many working-class Catholics, on both sides of the border, have lost confidence in the church due to the various institutional child sex abuse scandals (New York Times 2010). There has developed a cross-class, cross-ethnonational alliance to promote reproductive rights, same-sex marriage rights, and redress for historical institutional abuse by the Catholic church. Nonetheless, the compartmentalization of ethnonational, religious, and class identities is particularly evident among a segment of the Catholic middle-class. This is not surprising, given the fluid and often contradictory nature of identity in general. Similar to constructivist conceptualizations of ethnic, racial, and nationalist identity, class identity can also be identified as an identity *in motion*, as "a category of practice . . . used by 'lay' actors in some (not all!) everyday settings to make sense of themselves, of their activities, of what they share with, and how they differ from, others" (Brubaker and Cooper 2000, 4). Just because a section of a particular class group still connects with traditional ethnonational loyalties or ideologies in some instances does not preclude the same members departing from certain conventional ingroup positions, or showing support for the particular class interests it shares with members of an outgroup.

The Catholic middle-class has demonstrated a willingness and capacity to subvert traditional ingroup ideologies when it suits (doubtless like most upwardly mobile populations). For example, in opposition to Sinn Fein and SDLP's position opposing the 11-plus transfer test (due to long-standing concerns of these parties about educational equity) Catholic grammar schools across the North devised their own private transfer exams, as a result "of pressures from middle-class Catholic parents" (McDonald 2009). As a teacher and education reform advocate I interviewed explains, "parents send their kids to grammar schools because they get a better choice and better preparedness if they want to go into university," as secondary schools in general have more limited academic offerings. However, she also notes how "it's a catch-22 because you're not funding—the secondary schools aren't getting the kids, so they're not getting funded in the same way" (interview with author, South Belfast, May 2014). Recognition of "a large number of Catholic middle-class children attending some of the top state grammars in Northern Ireland" corresponds to a growing disparity within the CNR community with respect to attitudes about educational policy. Middle-class Catholics "are actually with the Unionists in wanting to maintain the grammar/secondary school divide," though most would never vote for Unionist parties (McDonald 2009). The more competitive grammar schools, which prepare pupils for enrollment at university, have few students from low-income families (Borooah and Knox 2015, 9–10). As another respondent explains, "There's a very early embedding of two streams of experience . . . in our public schools. The consequence of that is that the culture between the so-called secondary schools and the grammar schools is quite sharply divided, particularly around expectations of where people are going" (interview with author, North Belfast, June 2014). This cultural and educational divide now looks increasingly similar within Unionist and Nationalist communities (see introduction). Importantly, despite the messiness of class identity in NI rooted in the power of its national and religious binaries, the withdrawal from ethnopolitical affairs by some members of *both* the Nationalist and Unionist middle classes who hold significant resources to effect social change, may weaken resistance to the divisive politics that impede transformative modes of peacebuilding.

CLASS, SILENCE, AND SYMBOLIC POWER

Although the power to name—a defining feature of *symbolic power*—is most recognized in those bestowed with a position of legitimate group authority

(Bourdieu 1991), no such dominant authority exists to represent purely class interests in NI. Indeed, if one looks to political elites to represent a supranational class identity, it is unclear which party or parties could fill this role. Alliance Party, supported predominantly by middle-class voters (Tonge 2008, 64), experienced notable gains in the 2019 elections at the expense of DUP and, to a lesser extent, Sinn Fein (Tonge 2020; Hayward 2020b). Yet overall, DUP and Sinn Fein remain the two largest parties in the Assembly, having gained a notable degree of support from middle-class voters post Agreement (Evans and Tonge 2009; Tilley, Garry, and Matthews 2019). At the same time, UUP and SDLP maintain relatively strong support from middle-class Unionist and Nationalist constituencies, respectively. Because neither an alternative, supraethnic class culture nor class politics has emerged in NI at a large scale, a symbology that represents a shared class identity remains virtually absent. Largely for this reason, *silence* is a particularly strategic concept which can be applied to reveal manifestations of power, and how social actors navigate systems of power. As findings reported above indicate, a culture of silence on issues of identity and history largely constitutes the cordiality that makes "shared space" possible. But silence in this context serves additional functions as well. Since class identity in NI is an identity with no "language"—that is, in Bourdieu's terms, a language that represents an authority that "speaks for the group"—silence serves a particularly significant function in the everyday constitution of supranational class "identity." Silence, in this way—at least in certain contexts—is a "ritual form . . . of expression," or "ritualized strategy" reflecting the actor's attempt to "impose a certain vision of the social world, i.e., of the [class] divisions of the social world" (Bourdieu 1991, 106). Silence acts in this respect not necessarily as a strategic, willful (in)action, though, but may also function as a type of automatic iteration of the coercive power of class positionality: a process of social power that works subconsciously *through* actors situated within the particular social field occupied by the "middle classes," regardless of their particular politics.

In conflict societies, the concept of silence has most commonly been applied to understand how individuals negotiate violence, or forms of "agency that can be related to purposefully forgetting or a practice directed toward not remembering" (McCormack 2017, 50; see also, Sheriff 2000, 122). As an anthropological construct, the concept of silence has revealed, for example, how ethnopolitical commemorations act to repress recognition of "alternative histories and memories," the "ethnic identities in which these are rooted," and corresponding imaginings of territorial belonging (McCormick 2017, 50). The socio-political implications of silence are most obvious when it exists between opposing national, ethnic, or religious groups, such as between Protestants and Catholics throughout most of twentieth-century NI, when the latter held a subordinate social and political position of power, and speaking in defense of this identity in mixed settings threatened the dominant logic of a sectarian state (ibid., 54–55). The fear to speak "from within" against a community's dominant ethnonational ideology, due to threat of violence from ingroup hardliners, is also a well-recognized form of silence which reproduces relations of power in divided societies (Shirlow 2003a). However, other identities, such as those of class, gender, or place, demand their own unique functions of silence, with quite different yet significant political implications. Silence can also function in the form of simply refusing to acknowledge, in any genuine way, forms of social difference that transgress historical national or religious solidarities. Indeed, "different groups . . . have markedly divergent interests at stake in the suppression of discourse" (Sheriff 2000, 114) depending on their locations within overlapping social hierarchies. For young people who are forced to regularly navigate sectarianized structures of space, silence more often reflects a "navigation of violence," or a mechanism of self-preservation which acknowledges the historical territorial power exerted by the Other. Sheriff (2000, 114) recognizes that customary silence, or "cultural censorship . . . demands collaboration and the tacit . . . understandings that such collaboration presupposes." Yet silence within homogenous spaces—specifically, for purposes of the present analysis, *homogenous class settings*—can function to obscure recognition of shared interests among historically conflicted ethnic or national groups, reconstituting in particular the social location of actors in relatively privileged social positions. In this way, silence "is a relational category that draws attention to the co-implication of body and power and, in particular, to the way in which certain types of oppression are rendered politically invisible by being internalized as corporeal dispositions" (McNay 2012, 230). On the surface, silence is indicative of "the polite culture" described by several respondents. Yet it also functions to preclude recognition of the fracture(s) that would demystify the contingent nature of ingroup ethnonational or ethnoreligious solidarity, thereby acting to maintain dominant political constructions of identity. As the Unionist and Nationalist middle-classes have become increasingly aligned in their material interests, so too has a shared exercise of silence come to constitute the reproduction of class "identity." For some, it can simultaneously serve to sustain images of ethnonational ingroup solidarity to which an emotive attachment remains; for others, it allows a dissociation from ethnopolitics without risking ethnoreligious ingroup exclusion. In any case, silence in ethnically heterogeneous "middle-class" or "cosmopolitan" spaces allows a shared class position to function without violating the dominant binary structure of collective political representations which constitute cultural attachments and the concomitant logic of the power sharing system of governance. And it is likely for this reason that politicians have embraced this silence on certain contested ethnopolitical issues when communicating with constituents in more privileged and ethnically heterogenous areas (documented below).

A shared perspective among several respondents suggests that silence on not only issues of political and sectarian violence, but also on how poverty and inequality underscore such problems is rooted largely in the mutually agreeable lifestyles and socio-economic interests of the Unionist and Nationalist middle-classes. Based on respondents' observations, discourses and practices within predominantly upper- and middle-class Protestant/ Unionist *and* Catholic/Nationalist communities, denoted by silence about, or social distancing from, images of conflict and sectarianism, reflect forms of "post-conflict" symbolic capital which reify class identity. In this vein, a scholar and long-time peace activist in a cross-community NGO implies how the silence among those with vested interests in the social and economic status quo undermines political transformation. In his view

> The peace dividend hasn't really hit poor communities in the way that we imagined in the wake of 1998. Secondly, the middle-class people in Northern Ireland have less recurrent costs in terms of water rents and housing rents then people living in England and Wales.[18] So, the middle classes have been cushioned in this society by the current political parties. Sinn Fein and DUP, who have historically presented themselves as an advocate for the poor and the disenfranchised, have, in my view, looked after and sought to maintain the support of middle-class voters. You've got a middle class that conspires in silence to avoid contested issues. Everybody first of all assumes that they're the people who are sectarian—the poor and working class—which I think is rubbish; and that they're the people who should move first, which I think is ridiculous. Those who have position, those who have power, and those who have money, though, often don't want to move because they would threaten those positions of power and money. They are the ones who have a place in this society, and they are the ones that tend not to use it. (Interview with author, Co Antrim, May 2014)

Although "conspire" may seem like a polemical term, it is qualified, for this person (and some other respondents) given the historical contexts of ethnonational solidarity. Since the fault line of political difference in NI has historically been, and continues to be, ethnonational identity, it is assumed that to not speak on issues facing some segments of one's ingroup (such as poverty, segregation, and violence) signifies some degree of awareness of how one's social position is aligned with certain members of "the other community." It signifies a class consciousness that must be kept silent, since it may undermine constructions of ethnopolitical "groupness"[19] to which many are still attached. Given the class dimensions of sectarian and political violence in NI, historically and contemporaneously, repression of discourse on "contested issues" of ethnonational and ethnoreligious identity also functions to preclude recognition of socio-economic inequalities implicated in contemporary manifestations of conflict. One respondent intimates how the potential negative consequences of avoiding "difficult areas" of identity should have been learned from similar, past dynamics of "polite culture" that led up to the Troubles. This former teacher explains how, "here [in middle-class South Belfast] you have the more polite culture. There's one who's quite prominent in education circles and according to her, everything was fine until 1969 [when the Troubles broke out]. People think 1969 happened in a vacuum. 1969 happened because people were having polite conversations and nobody was challenging anything" (interview with author, May 2020). In the lead-up to the Troubles, the social and economic marginalization of Nationalist communities, coupled with their political disenfranchisement, was ignored by most in the Unionist community until peaceful civil rights protests resulted in violent repression by the Unionist regime, accelerating the IRA insurgency (White 1989). In the post-Agreement period (as chapter two will more fully examine) the dual marginalization of poor and working-class Loyalist and Republican communities has contributed to sectarian tensions and rioting.

According to respondents, the opening up of more "shared spaces" has also normalized other discursive strategies of (de)identification in which actors distance themselves from images of conflict, reflecting a dimension of class identity that deactivates or mitigates emotive ethnonational solidarity. To illustrate this phenomenon, several respondents refer to discourses about the "Flag Protests" in 2012–2013, when the decision of Belfast City Council to fly the Union flag on City Hall for holidays only, led to Loyalist rioting. One respondent, an integrated education advocate, notes how "we would have schools that are in the nice part of Northern Ireland and they would say that the Flag Protests would have nothing to do with them" (interview with author, South Belfast, May 2014). A respondent who works with at-risk youth similarly describes how, among the middle-class networks he frequents,

> there's almost this thing of saying "Well, that's what they do" during the Flag Protest . . . Middle-class communities said, "That's not our issue. We don't need to talk about that. That's a working-class issue. To be honest with you it's just these under-educated yahoos who are throwing rocks at the place. This is a criminal issue rather than a social issue." It's interesting how working-class communities can be dismissed very readily by people. (Interview with author, June 2020).

Several respondents, who grew up in relatively poor Loyalist or Republican backgrounds, and are now highly educated and have regular access to "middle-class spaces," are particularly reflexive on this point. As they describe, images of violence and street disorder are shrugged off by *some* middle-class residents as "criminal" matters or as isolated issues that are of no concern to the "normal" segments of the society. Recognition of the struggles of residents living in areas with high levels of segregation and concentrated disadvantage are also precluded in more privileged circles through discourses which frame images of violence and disorder pejoratively as aberrations inherent to poor and working-class communities. In this respect, actors impose and validate "a certain vision of the social world" along class lines (Bourdieu 1991, 106), obscuring, if not defusing ethnonational solidarity. As a mechanism of symbolic power, this discursive construction of class difference, similar to the function of silence, allows actors in more privileged sectors of the society to avoid recognition of some of the complex causes of ongoing ethnopolitical conflict rooted in a social structure to which they've become accustomed.

Even *some* from the middle classes, who *are* vocal on ethnopolitical issues and active in peace process initiatives, are perceived by a section of grassroots leaders from poor and working-class wards I interviewed as keeping conversations relatively "safe" by excluding the voices of practitioners who may challenge dominant discursive frameworks. Some respondents also perceive that middle-class peace sector participants, who tend to head the largest peacebuilding organizations, ensure dominant frames which exclude recognition of class dynamics are followed in organizational proceedings, such as peacebuilding conferences and workshops. Such practices can be considered exercises in symbolic violence insofar as those perspectives reflecting experiences of marginalization, in ways which do not neatly align with images of two narrowly defined ethnonational "communities," are excluded, and thus rendered incapable of underscoring a transformative class politics. Exclusion of leaders in the community sector who live or work in areas of concentrated disadvantage act accordingly to structure "instruments of communication . . . which help to ensure that one class dominates another (symbolic violence) by bringing their own discursive power to bear on the relations of power which underlie them" (Bourdieu 1991, 166). While this is not a universal phenomenon, of course, it was an experience noted by several interviewees. The statement of a PUL leader in ex-paramilitary reintegration efforts is a case in point:

> In Northern Ireland you have to understand that if you're not in that little circle, you don't get invited to anything. When there's a conference or someone wants to talk to people, it'll invariably be with the middle classes, because you know what you're going to get. It manifests itself in people who don't have a problem judging their own working classes, but would stand up for people from countries on the other side of the world and fight for their right to say what they have to say. But they won't let their own people say that, either Protestant or Catholic.

The only way people are going to learn is if you let them express how they feel rather than judge them. . . . Unfortunately here, if someone does—I work in the [redacted] public housing estate—if something happens in this estate, all . . . people are labeled with the same thing that [that] one person did. It's so, so hard to bring people back from that or to say to the people who are labelling them, "They're not all like that." The middle classes do it very subtly, but very, very effectively. They close ranks—won't let you in; you can't work in certain places. (Interview with author, May 2020)

Statements describing a sense of alienation from mainstream peacebuilding networks was articulated most frequently by Loyalist respondents. This is not surprising, given the greater disconnect culturally and politically between middle-class Unionist and working-class Loyalist communities.[20] Unlike Sinn Fein, with many of their elected officials being former IRA associates—coming from, and often still residing within, relatively deprived working-class communities—most Unionist politicians come from middle-class areas less affected by legacies of conflict, wherein former Loyalist paramilitaries are generally treated as pariahs. Unionism has historically believed in the state's monopoly over the use of legitimate violence, corresponding not only to their claims of moral superiority over Republicans, but also their disdain for working-class Loyalism and its association with paramilitarism.[21] Thus, the criminalization of Loyalism from across the political spectrum (Shirlow 2012, 1–10) compounds the exclusion of working-class urban PUL communities, apparently even from some sites of "peacebuilding" in which they are central stakeholders.

Some respondents also indicate a frustration about the tendency of recurring discussions about long-standing issues to reify ethnoreligious binaries and prevent cross-communal agreement that could propel forward solutions to problems faced predominantly by the poor and working classes within the PUL and CNR blocs. One respondent describes, for example,

one of our symposiums a couple of weeks ago [which] was around underachievement of young Protestant males. Now, this has been going on 25 years, that statistically . . . [researchers] have proven that this is the case. Even a Sinn Féin minister at the time admitted it [that working-class Protestant males have the worst educational outcomes]. He was the Minister for Education and he admitted that it was the case, but they've never done anything about it. Two days ago, they announced they were going to set up a panel to have a look into it again. In 25 years, look how many young people have missed out on school, on education, on anything, while the middle classes decide, "Is that true or not?" Then of course, there's always the counterbalance of, "But there are young Catholics who don't achieve." (Interview with author, May 2020)

In some instances, even when problems of inequity are discussed, it is in ways which avoid unequivocal recognition of the causes and consequences of such problems, and in manners which preclude recognition of class difference as such by framing the issues in ethnoreligious terms.

POLITICAL IMPLICATIONS

Middle-class silence on sectarianism and ethnopolitics is interpreted by several interviewees as having implications on the multifaceted and sometimes contradictory campaigns and legislative agendas of Northern Ireland's main ethnopolitical parties. Some parties who rely largely on voters in areas of concentrated disadvantage are complicit in socio-economic policies which disproportionately serve the interests of the middle classes—social milieus with a tendency to withdraw from contentious grassroots politics. Ethnopolitical parties are thus able to gain support from middle-class residents from their respective ethnonational communities in elections to maintain their hegemony in the Executive, while the relative disengagement of the same constituents from issues that drive sectarian strife only helps to sustain narratives of loss and threat that politicians appropriate to rally their bases in working-class locations. Not coincidentally, the more divisive Unionist and Nationalist parties—DUP and Sinn Fein, respectively—have received strong support since the signing of the Agreement (1998), as more "moderate" parties have struggled to gain influence in the Executive. The disjuncture between who is generally supported in terms of economic and social policy, and whose interests are reflected in the discourses of political leaders, likely contributes to the domination of these more "hardline" parties. Tilley, Garry and Matthews (2019, 1) find that "vote choices are largely independent of people's policy stances on economic or social issues" in NI. However, this does not mean that parties will not attempt to maximize support from various intra-ethnic constituencies by developing a hybrid identity coupling ethnonational affiliation to alignment with other social interests and cultural significations; or that such strategies will not have cascading effects on collective identity formation.

With the exception of the Progressive Unionist Party (PUP), which has minimal presence in government, Unionist parties tend to support neoliberal approaches to "development," including austerity measures. DUP combines this ideological position with an ultra-conservative evangelical Protestant identity (author interview with Unionist government official, 2020).[22] Unlike Nationalist frames which promote a type of collective solidarity around calls for equality on various issues, Protestant/Unionist socio-economic ideology is based more so on principles of liberty, individualism, and personal responsibility (McAllister 2005). Since the Agreement, DUP political strategy has been somewhat ambiguous, combining "dogmatism" and ethnic outbidding with a "pragmatist" governance agenda rooted in neoliberal principles of "modernization" (Murphy and Evershed 2019, 8; Gormley-Heenan and Mac Ginty 2008). Yet historically foundational to the DUP platform is its interest in consolidating an identity as *the* party of resistance against Nationalist threat and "Papism" and protector of Ulster Loyalist culture[23] (McAuley 1997; Bruce 1986; Moore et al. 2013).

Although the DUP did gain some degree of support from middle-class voters in the years following the Agreement, overall it has had more success mobilizing PUL constituencies living in interface areas surrounded by Catholic neighborhoods, who "demonstrate their loyalty to the DUP amid a sense of siege" (Evans and Tonge 2009, 1027). Affluent Protestant areas of NI have recorded relatively low voter turnouts in comparison with privileged wards in other UK countries (ibid, 1027). Nonetheless, the DUP, which has historically positioned itself as a working class Loyalist party, has done little to serve the material interests of economically marginalized PUL communities. For example, even while many working-class PUL residents are economically reliant on state entitlements, DUP officials have used the language of welfare dependency and personal responsibility to justify their support for British austerity measures. Party leaders were able to do so with minimal political damage by also framing the debate in "Orange and Green" terms, criticizing Sinn Fein in 2014–2015 of using its rhetorical support for a strong welfare state to appeal to their Republican base.[24] This example illustrates how the party intends to balance its appeal to quite different constituencies, using an ethnopolitics of grievance to connect with Protestant working-class elements who feel particularly "under siege" and left behind to the benefit of nationalists (see, Hayes, McAllister, and Dowds 2005), while acquiescing to an austerity agenda favorable to its neoliberal wing and compatible more broadly with individualistic Protestant culture.

Describing a phenomenon more common in Unionist than Nationalist communities, respondents note one way politicians "connect" to middle-class constituencies is through "distancing themselves" from identities and concerns associated with the poor and working classes, while appealing to voters from less advantaged segments of their ethnonational community through discourses which express socio-economic insecurities in the language of ethnopolitical loss and resentment. What Gormley-Heenan (2006, 54) calls the "chameleonic" nature of political leadership in post-Agreement NI—that is, the "inconsistent form of political leadership which shift[s] . . . according to the opinion of others and the climate in which it exist[s]"—not only shifts with public attitudes about the peace process, but also takes distinct forms in accordance with the particular class identities within the ethnonational constituency for which co-ethnic parties compete for support. One respondent, for example, references observations she made during the period of the Flag Protests to suggest that DUP tactics used to garner appeal from a particular sub-constituency appear contingent upon the socio-economic make-up of the area:

> What I find difficult personally is when people like Peter Robinson and Ian Paisley . . . incited people to hatred. That's what they [some DUP representatives] still do. [Then] they step back. They've stirred it [flag protest] up and they're all at it in certain areas. The way they go about their business in North and West Belfast would be different to how they go about it in [mostly middle-class] South Belfast, for example. It's what they do. (Interview with author, Belfast city center, May 2014)

As implied by this respondent, among others, DUP leaders moderate discourses promoting ethnocultural resentment when targeting communications toward constituents in more privileged wards. The party's policy positions on socio-economic issues also indicate a catering to middle-class interests. At the same time as its party agenda under devolution continued to be centered around "ethnic entrenchment and populist loyalism designed to reassure its urban base," the DUP continues to "pitch on the territory of middle-class former UUP voters, perhaps most notably in the party's strong support for the retention of grammar schools" (Evans and Tonge 2009, 1027). A few respondents also view DUP support for transfer—the selection at age 11 of young people into distinct educational tracks—as an example of the party prioritizing middle-class interests over the concerns of its traditional working-class base. One describes how the "transfer . . . suits, in the main, middle-class parents because they can get them [their children] tutored. But if you look at the statistics, working-class Protestants, especially boys, do not do well at that test and yet the two main [Unionist] parties support that test" (interview with author, May 2020).

In efforts to appeal largely to underserved PUL communities, quite different messages are often conveyed. Economic anxieties are often translated in sectarian terms. At the same time, social distancing mechanisms employed by middle-class residents are seemingly appropriated by representatives of the same Unionist parties. One PUL respondent contends, for example, that local politicians

> perpetuate a myth that other working-class people are getting more than some other working-class people. For instance, there's this whole notion of [unintelligible 00:40:21] and it seemed to be that there would be more infrastructure in working-class Catholic communities than in working-class Protestant communities. Working-class Catholic communities were getting new medical centers, were getting better schools, are getting more money spent on schools, getting

libraries, getting leisure samplers, and Protestants were saying, "We're not getting any of that." I don't know if any of that was true, but it was a myth that was peddled to communities to say, "They're actually getting more than you. We need [sound cut 00:41:01] for what we want because they're getting it all and you're not getting anything." I don't think that was true but it certainly was a strategy used by politicians. The hard part of this is that politicians can then distance themselves from working-class communities because middle-class [Unionist] communities like my own often do that. They look at these working-class communities and say, "They're undereducated. They've got no aspiration in life. They're all junkies and terrorists," and they're often dismissed. (Interview with author, June 2020)

An additional example of the more divisive political strategy used by some Unionist politicians to appeal to disadvantaged, rather than more privileged ethnonational constituencies via appropriation of status frustrations and sentiments of cultural loss is illustrated by the politics of housing in North Belfast. Amid a growing Catholic, and declining Protestant, demographic, the DUP motioned to dismantle the Northern Ireland Housing Executive, which "is widely credited with the depoliticisation of housing" so that it is allocated purely on the "basis of need." Even as numerous buildings in working-class neighborhoods in Belfast stand derelict, "the shortage of public housing is acute," exacerbating insecurity among poor Catholic families, who are in greatest need of affordable housing (Nolan 2014, 114). The NI Equality Commission (2015) even charged the NI Executive's Department of Social Development with failing "to comply with its commitments" to equality of opportunity with respect to housing practices. Peter Osbourne indicates in an *Irish Times* interview how "In 10 years our [government] policy is to build 487 shared housing units, in the same ten-year period in Northern Ireland in which about 60,000 houses will be built in total" (McClements 2018). Of course, the lack of progress with residential integration in Belfast is in part the result of many residents living in communities divided by peace walls for over 50 years, as well as paramilitary intimidation of outgroup residents attempting to move into "single-community" areas (McClements 2018; Nolan 2014, 11). Yet acknowledgement of the complex nature of the issue does not require a downplaying of the role of ethnopolitical leaders in perpetuating structures of segregation. Rather, diffuse social and ideological forces function in tandem with leaders' political practices to (re)shape the sectarianization of space (Shirlow and Pain 2003).

Shirlow (2003a, 77) describes how "the relationship between fear and residential segregation is contingent upon a series of relations such as the environments of everyday life, violence (both imagined and real) and political manipulation." A similar series of relations is at work in reproducing the integral link between ethnopolitical *resentment* and residential segregation. Several respondents in 2020 interviews observed that the competition for votes in North Belfast—the district of the city containing the most sectarian interface areas—underscores Unionist opposition to fair housing practices and integrated housing initiatives. To them, the loss of influential and divisive DUP figure Nigel Dodds's seat in British parliament representing the North Belfast district to Sinn Fein indicates that PUL fears of a gradual Nationalist state takeover via demographic shifts (i.e., relatively high Catholic fertility rates amid a decrease in the Protestant population) are coming true despite Unionist attempts to restrict the expansion of Catholic residences in the area.[25] Dodds was a leading figure in the DUP for decades, with a long history of politically appropriating intercommunal tensions over housing in North Belfast. In one instance, he even framed "Nationalist expansionism in north Belfast as comparable to Hitler's ethnic cleansing policy, *lebensaraum*" (Nagle 2009a, 187). A government official from a Unionist community, who has worked on public commissions to advance equality in various social sectors, implies how interpretations of lived experience vis-à-vis housing opportunities for working-class Protestants is shaped by ethnopolitical heuristics rooted in official Unionist discourse associating "equality" with Nationalist threat. He explains how those with

> The biggest need [for social housing] in West Belfast are Catholics, and therefore if a house comes up in West Belfast, the Catholic will get it. There's a disproportional, probably two or three to one need for Catholic houses over Protestants. You can see why Protestants feel when Catholics get houses over them, that this is disproportional and that feeds the agenda, that "equality works for them." . . . This is their [DUP's] delivering approach and then the young people growing up in those traditions, they have bought into this notion that Catholics have better houses, they get on the housing market more quickly, that their education system is better, that equality has worked for them, but not for us. That then fills into the [PUL] community narrative that stops the growth of equality. (Interview with author, May 2020)

Housing accommodations for the growing Catholic population apparently contributes to PUL perceptions, corroborated or shaped by DUP discourse, that the "equality agenda" associated with the peace process supports Nationalism over Unionism and Loyalism. The association of "equality" with Nationalism in PUL communities, and its manipulation by Unionist politicians, is situated within a particular historical context. Members of the PUL community apparently recall when "Gerry Adams [was] saying, equality was basically the Trojan horse by which they [Sinn Fein] were going to win . . . Sinn Féin, by the way, they know the buttons to push" to incite Unionist backlash and re-center ethnopolitical grievance in public political discourse.

"They just drop the equality word in there every now and again and then walk away."[26] According to this respondent, "all of that has helped this notion of zero-sum" Protestant/Unionist loss felt most sharply in neighborhoods with relatively high levels of material need. In his view, such "zero-sum" thinking constitutes a

> real lack of [government] investment in shared housing. If we continue only to expand in areas that are Orange or Green, the housing will continue to be segregated . . . If people want the equality assured neighborhood, you do that voluntarily. There isn't a government incentive to do it. That's very small. The DUP certainly wouldn't be supportive because it's about voting patterns. If you let more Catholics into some areas that are marginal, the voting patterns could change. There's a vested interest going on there. (Interview with author, May 2020)

For those who have access to private housing markets, where residential integration is increasingly common, lack of proactive government initiatives to promote integration is less of an issue. This is not to say that middle-class Unionists do not espouse notions of cultural loss or threat, but such notions are less applicable to negative interpretations of their lived experience in socio-economic contexts, in comparison with poor and working-class PUL communities suffering high levels of unemployment, underemployment and poor educational prospects. Shared private housing markets and "school choice," available mostly to the privileged segments of the NI population, have facilitated some degree of increased interaction across the traditional binaries. For more deprived residents living in social housing communities divided by peace walls, and with limited avenues of mobility, however, the failure of elected leaders to facilitate a path toward reconciliation and gradual integration at a systemic level is signified by the everyday experiences of fear and threat that undermine the potentially transformative contributions of integrated education, community-based peacebuilding, and other works dedicated to interethnic relation building.[27] Experimental research in social psychology suggests that ethnic or religious segregation "ensures the long-term prevalence of . . . negative emotions by reinforcing mutual ignorance" (Hughes et al. 2007, 36), functioning as a major impediment to peacebuilding, and perpetuating a system of segregation and separation that helps sustain the fear and resentment appropriated by ethnopolitical entrepreneurs. Whilst a culture of silence on divisive intercommunal issues has potentially "moderated" or "de-ethnicized" the dominant parties' narratives in some contexts, an ethnopolitical entrepreneurialism—especially by Unionists—is particularly evident in communication with residents in segregated, underserved neighborhoods who feel left behind by the peace process.

NOTES

1. Future quantitative survey research should examine the extent of these dynamics observed by respondents. Thus far, there are no data available to test the generalizability of these observations in a statistical sense, and conspicuously few surveys examine social class distinctions in political and social practices in NI, more generally.

2. It is worth noting that some universities, such as Queen's University Belfast, have increased efforts at recruiting first-generation students from disadvantaged backgrounds, and have seen a growth in enrollment and retention of these students (Dahanayake 2020). Nonetheless, significant class disparities in university enrollment persist, as is the case across the UK.

3. Previous research suggests that sectarian harassment is at least less overt in white-collar, professional workplaces as well (Dickson and Hargie 2006).

4. "Taig" is a derogatory, sectarian term used against Catholics in NI.

5. In total, 97 barriers or "peace walls" stand along the "interface" areas separating Protestant and Catholic neighborhoods in Belfast, up from 18 in the early 1990s (Belfast Interface Project 2017).

6. Apparently, a trend indicated earlier by Harland (2011, 423) in the peace process continues: fear of getting involved in violent incidences makes young men "highly suspicious and distrusting of those outside their immediate peer group" and reluctant to venture outside their neighborhoods and meet people from different backgrounds (see also Harland 2000).

7. See Harland (2011, 423) on restrictions to accessing the city center and other "safe spaces," including fear of sectarian threat when riding buses.

8. This dynamic has been slow and partial, though. Research shows that Catholics and Protestants across social classes prefer to move into areas where most of the neighbors will share their religious identification (Shuttleworth et al. 2020). For many, the choice to move into a more "mixed" neighborhood is often based on various other "practical" considerations that have little to do with religion or politics.

9. For a description of the psychological mechanisms at play in reinforcing ingroup identification, see Tajfel and Turner (1986) and Coymak and O'Dwyer (2020).

10. There is also intriguing work from the United States on the precarious gendered positions women non-state combatants face during and after an armed campaign. See Zwerman (1994).

11. Although there seemed to be a glimmer of hope that the emergence of progressive female leaders, such as Dawn Purvis, Julie Anne Corr Johnson, and Sophie Long could transform loyalist politics, none of these women are still active in the Progressive Unionist Party (PUP). See Irish Times (2010).

12. Gender disparities linked to the masculinization of perceived leadership qualifications persist on a broad societal level as well. Women are under-represented in public bodies and elected office, as well as in managerial positions, contributing to a persistent gender pay gap (Potter 2014, 1).

13. This dynamic will be discussed further in chapter 3.

14. More Protestants than Catholics leave NI for university, and the proportion of Catholic enrollees in NI universities has increased relative to Protestants. Most

students remain in the location where they received their degree, and thus there is a greater level of permanent outmigration among young educated Protestants. This trend has been developing for decades. For data on trends in university attendance and outmigration, see: O'Connor (1994) and McQuaid and Hollywood (2008, 9–10).

15. As McAllister (2005, 851) indicates, the adage "no surrender," which Ian Paisley made synonymous with DUP resistance to greater influence of the Irish Government in NI affairs, is associated with Free Presbyterian theology. See also, Morrow (1997) and Bruce (1986) on the influence of Protestant theology on Unionist political consciousness.

16. Orange Order created socio-economic networks across classes in the Protestant community (Tonge 2002, 102).

17. Apparently, a decline in perceived group status satisfaction has led some Protestants to explore alternative identifications (Goeke-Morey et al. 2016).

18. This has been true for decades. See Coulter (1997, 119).

19. Here I refer to Brubaker's (2002, 167) plea to think of "groupness as a contextually fluctuating conceptual variable," as a process identifiable in "cultural idioms, cognitive schemas, discursive frames, organizational routines, institutional forms, political projects and contingent events."

20. Evidence of this phenomenon is documented in chapters 2 and 3.

21. This phenomenon is documented in more depth in chapter 3.

22. As Mitchell and Tilley (2004, 586) identify, there was "an increase of importance between 1991 and 1998 of a moral conservatism-liberalism dimension as a source of party choice in Northern Ireland," with the "most morally conservative Protestants . . . now more likely to vote for the DUP" over UUP.

23. Ulster Loyalism, according to Jennifer Todd, holds primary allegiance to an imagined community of Northern Protestants, and a secondary and conditional loyalty to the British state. It is ritually reproduced by "dominatory" street parades and marches, and supportive of democratic principles only insofar as they uphold Northern Ireland's political and cultural separation from the Irish Republic (Todd 1986, 1).

24. Sinn Fein MPs refuse to sit in British Parliament in protest of what they view as the ongoing illegal British occupation of Ireland.

25. The 2011 census indicated that, for the first time in Northern Ireland's history, Protestants were not the majority of Belfast's population (about 48 percent). In NI as a whole, approximately 20 percent of Protestants are 65 or older, compared with just 11 percent of Catholics, and 51 percent of Catholics are aged under 35, compared to just 40 percent of Protestants. Northern Ireland has the second, fastest-growing population in the UK, the youngest population, and the highest fertility rate—disproportionately Catholic—suggesting that the Nationalist electorate will soon outnumber the Unionist electorate (Gray et al. 2018, 30).

26. This dynamic occurred, for example, when DUP leaders responded to Sinn Fein's call for Unionist "celebrations to mark the Queen's Jubilee to be equality screened." As put by one DUP representative, Sinn Fein "are a party that uses lightly the word equality when it comes to them marking or remembering certain events, but whenever it comes to unionists doing it, they have a real problem." Other Unionist commentators implied it was unfair that Sinn Fein was trying "to prevent Belfast City

Council from marking the Queen's 70th Jubilee" while at the same time "trying to have the Irish Language imposed on us" (Campbell 2021).

27. Further evidence of this phenomenon is documented in chapter 6.

Chapter 2

Social Immobility, Ethnopolitics, and the "Culture Wars"

Contextualizing Violence and Disorder in Belfast, 2008–2014

On December 1, 2012, hundreds of Loyalists gathered outside Belfast City Hall to protest the City Council's vote to reduce the number of days the Union Jack flag will fly there, from 365 days a year to 18, and for British holidays only.[1] Protests turned violent as men forced their way inside and riots subsequently ensued in surrounding areas, injuring police officers and shutting the city center down for several days. Elected officials of the Alliance Party—the largest party in NI with no ethnonational affiliation—had their homes attacked, as some Loyalists blamed the party of accommodating a "Nationalist agenda." By the spring of 2013 more than 100 police officers were injured, and millions of pounds of property damage reported (Nolan 2014; Nolan et al. 2014).

Shortly thereafter, in the summer of 2013, tensions that had been simmering since December 2012 again boiled over during the July 12th parades in North Belfast. Some Loyalists attacked police after the PSNI, enforcing the ruling of the Parades Commission (PC), restricted Orange Order bands from marching through the Ardoyne interface that crosses into a Catholic neighborhood. The marchers were restricted from returning home through the interface in the evening, as excessive alcohol consumption among Loyalist marchers and the presence of Republican protesters in the past often resulted in violence. Angered with the police over their enforcement of the PC's ruling, Loyalists attacked police, and riots subsequently ensued over several days throughout Belfast. Blast bombs and petrol bombs were used against police and exchanged between Loyalists and Nationalists. Dozens of police officers were again wounded throughout this stage of disorder.

Investigation of the violence led to the arrest of over 100 people later that year—mostly young, male Loyalists (Nolan 2014, 11–12, 154)—deepening the alienation and frustration toward the state that had been simmering in PUL communities for some time (Hayes, McAllister, and Dowds 2005). The flag and parade crises, which continued to inflame intercommunity division long after the violence subsided, pointed the world to the fragility of the NI peace process.

As indicated in chapter 1, conflict over flags and parades are seen pejoratively in some circles as "lower-class" and "criminal justice" issues, rather than manifestations of legitimate political grievances warranting widespread public attention. Many middle-class residents disassociate themselves from the images of disorder and violence that these events have come to symbolize in "modern" Belfast. For many politicians, disputes over policies concerning flags and other "culture war" issues have taken priority in their public discourses and legislative agendas (Nolan 2014, 14). Yet the overall trend analytically has been to implicitly downplay the role of manipulation in the ethnopolitics that contributes to protests, rioting, and other violence in *post accord* contexts. More generally, though research on initial escalations of mass violence emphasizes the integral roles of self-interested political and community leaders in mobilizing armed actors (see Brass 1997; Tilly 2003; Gagnon 1995; Wilkinson 2002), surprisingly little empirical work has examined the potential for similar (albeit less extreme) processes in post-accord societies in transition.

Certainly, "both leaders and followers are involved in a circular process of motivation and power exchange that is often difficult to break up into a causal sequence" (Masciulli, Molchanov, and Knight 2009, 2; see also, Wildavsky 2006). The capacity of a leader to appeal to a targeted constituency through discursive manipulation of cultural symbols presupposes a shared ontological orientation (Kapferer 1988; Fearon and Laitin 2000). In this way, "leadership"—or, identity entrepreneurism—is a "symbolic activity mediated by culture" (Masciulli, Molchanov, and Knight 2009, 2). Research has established that partial memories of intergroup violence factor substantively into the rationalization of myths of ethnocultural superiority (Rydgren 2007). However, exclusive focus on such phenomena, without simultaneous attention to ongoing dynamics of political and economic power risk inadvertently constituting neo-primordial arguments which implicitly frame limitations of peace processes as consequences of "inevitable" divisions between polarized ethnopolitical constituencies. Attention is put on the attitudes and interests of the "masses," as if they develop organically, analytically marginalizing the role of ethnopolitical leaders at both state and grassroots levels in constructing such attitudes and interests. Certainly, "ordinary folk (not just elites) strategically construct ethnic boundaries" (Fearon and Laitin 2000, 846) in pursuit of various collective and individual interests; however, to frame the discussion in such a way risks masking the socio-political implications of disparate levels of power held by distinct actors in shaping discourse, behavior, and policy. As Tucker's (1995) "politics as leadership" thesis suggests, political leaders mobilize a substantial number of followers to accept their vision of reality and the policy prescriptions to social problems they advocate, wielding disproportionate power in shaping collective consciousness. In doing so, political leaders also direct the attention of the population to particular issues while distracting from others.

Moreover, evidence exists which suggests that mutually exclusive ethnic and political identities and attitudes are capable of flux when the conditions of intergroup relations are altered (Fearon and Laitin 1996; Sonnenschein et al. 2010; McGlynn et al. 2004; Pickering 2006; Hewstone et al. 2006). Given that few survivors within societies emerging from conflict desire a return to the violence of the past, provocative political strategies might be *especially* instrumental in explaining escalations of ethnopolitical hostilities during periods of "peace." In Northern Ireland, the relative stability brought with political reform has facilitated more variable intra-community political debate. This dynamic can be viewed as enabling the development of a greater variety of political relations and goals (Finlayson 1999; Smithey 2011), but also as a potential threat to the electoral security of ethnopolitical leaders. In addition, attention to how elected leaders respond to, or incite, provocations that turn violent helps illuminate their more general political strategies. Citing Zartman (2005, 268–273), Mac Ginty and Williams (2009, 30) indicate how the transition from "latent tensions" to collective violence requires "instigation agents" such as political leaders or ethnic entrepreneurs "who purposively inflame and mobilize their supporters, or circumstances" which heighten hostile, reactionary collective emotions. Even in societies such as NI, which have achieved key peacebuilding milestones, leaders who have based their careers on ethnopolitical ideologies rooted in conflict are likely to periodically reconstruct identity in contentious ethnopolitical terms, as such efforts provide a predictable way to transform "politics from an issue on which they are likely to lose power into one on which they can retain power" (Figueiredo and Weingast 1998, 262).

At the same time, it is important to identify the specific *structural conditions* which facilitate or hinder such (ethno)political strategies. Styles of political opportunism are not uniform, but differ across contexts, and in particular, contexts of *class* and *place*. Likewise, the consequences of manipulation depend largely upon the everyday living contexts of those subject to it. As Van Dijk (2006, 362) explains, the nature of the social environment is pertinent to the relative efficacy of symbolic manipulation by elites; "the same recipients may be more or less manipulatable in different circumstances . . .

[and] states of mind," including, I argue, circumstances of poverty, poverty-induced anxiety, and conflict-related trauma.

As findings of this chapter suggest, the flag and parade disputes illuminate the incendiary impact of divisive discourses and legislative (in)action of ethnopolitical elites on the conflict mentalities within working-class Protestant and Catholic communities, compounding underlying communal tensions exacerbated by poverty and inequity. Opportunistic elites do not simply appeal to ingroup interests; they also preeminently manipulate culturally sensitive ethnopolitical symbols to elicit fear and reconstitute their niches in the socio-political landscape. The present chapter argues that, while it is evident that DUP and UUP did not benefit from the protests in any immediate or tangible way (Nolan et al. 2014), their roles in promoting discourses which reconstruct polarized identities nonetheless reproduce the broader ethnopolitical fields in which their party platforms are most reliably sustained. In this vein, this chapter offers an empirical account of the ways in which inopportunity and class inequalities, operating across Protestant and Catholic communities in NI underscore or facilitate the ethnopolitical provocations of political elites and hardline community leaders. Findings suggest that rising intra-group class divisions sharpen social and political anxieties and mentalities of loss in underserved, working class communities. Some political leaders channel such anxiety toward the historical Other, framing their discourses around culturally contentious signifiers (flags, parades, etc.) that activate ethnopolitical and sectarian schemata. Predictably, manipulation of such symbols elicits emotionally-charged, hostile responses which risk boiling over into violence. By identifying such a dynamic, I offer a rare empirical example of a "*specific process* by which identities are produced and reproduced in action and speech," and through which (low-intensity) conflict is reconstituted (Fearon and Laitin 2000, 850, emphasis in original). In this vein, the chapter illustrates how the coercive forces of intersecting class, place, gendered, and age-specific identities function to reproduce local dynamics of conflict and facilitate leaders' ethnopolitical provocations. In doing so, the present analysis expands on observations from chapter one, illuminating how processes in the socio-political reproduction of conflict mentalities and practices are underscored, in part, by social and economic inequalities within, as much as between, historically divided ethnonational communities.

In the next two sections, geographical trends in sectarian violence are identified with reference to PSNI data,[2] to demonstrate dynamics in sectarian tensions between 2008 and 2014. Trends in the responses of leaders to contentious events identified through quantitative content analysis of newspapers is also identified.[3] The incidence and nature of these trends is then contextualized through in-depth interviews and qualitative content analysis of newspaper reports that implicate class inequities and the discourses of ethnopolitical elites in the social construction of sectarian tensions, with particular emphasis on the 2012–2013 flag and parade disputes. The data also reveal processes in the reproduction of ethnosocial fields which reconstitute the power of neo-paramilitary groups and other opportunistic actors at neighborhood levels, having serious implications on young people in segregated working-class communities, as well as on the influence of ethnopolitical elites themselves. How disconnects between the political priorities of socio-economically privileged and disadvantaged communities within and across the two main ethnoreligious blocs, coupled with ethnocultures of masculinity, facilitate such processes is also discussed.

TRENDS IN SECTARIAN VIOLENCE, 2008–2014

Perhaps the most significant achievement of the NI peace process has been the steady decline in lethal sectarian and political violence (Coakley 2008). Paramilitary-related killings and serious assaults causing injury continue post-Agreement, but have been overwhelmingly internecine in nature (Jarman 2004; Nolan 2014). There have been police officers, correction officers, and British soldiers killed or seriously maimed by dissident Republican terrorism in the post-accord period; however, such violence has been exceedingly rare. Periodic sectarian rioting and other street disorder, as well as clashes between mostly young males at interface locations, have been more persistent problems (Creary and Byrne 2014; Harland 2011). As results will show, fluctuations in such violence can be linked to contentious events and discourses pervading the socio-political environment.

In the period under examination (2008 through 2014) sectarian violence in general increased in some parts of Belfast, while declining in others. In the 2008/2009 reporting period (April 2008 through March 2009), 733 sectarian incidents were reported to the PSNI in West and North Belfast (district A), with 566 reported in North Belfast alone.[4] North Belfast contains the most interface locations and continues to experience demographic change as Catholics gradually increase in numbers relative to Protestants, contributing to the PUL community's sense of territorial insecurity. Frequencies of sectarian incidents in North Belfast then declined to 532 in 2009/2010 and 389 in 2010/2011 (see table 2.1). The number of incidents in the same area then declined again in the 2011/2012 reporting period to a low of 211. Sectarian incidents during the same time period also declined in West Belfast, from 124 in 2009/2010 to 99 in 2010/2011, and then 87 in 2011/2012 (see table 2.1).

Respondents indicated that a so-called "honeymoon period" in the immediate post-devolution period (2007–2010, approximately) contributed to a sense of goodwill among some influential grassroots actors, including some

Table 2.1: Incident Rates of Belfast Sectarian Violence by District, April 2009–March 2014

	W Belfast	N Belfast	S Belfast	E Belfast
2009/2010	124	532	74	67
2010/2011	99	389	74	101
2011/2012	87	211	90	172
2012/2013	103	288	106	131
2013/2014	74	246	102	152

paramilitary leaders who saw opportunities for themselves to contribute to peace by supporting cooperation at the state level (Shirlow 2012). For example, in 2010, the signing of the Hillsborough Agreement marked the devolution of policing powers for the first time since the imposition of British direct rule, introducing a Policing Commission co-chaired by representatives from both Unionist and Nationalist parties. The threat of dissident Republican paramilitary organizations, vehemently opposing any cooperation with the PSNI from the CNR community, was considered "severe" by the British security agency MI5 at this time. The most active armed dissident republican groups during this period were the Real IRA, the Continuity IRA, and Oglaigh na hEireann (ONH), led by former Provisional IRA members who interpret the Belfast Agreement as a betrayal by Sinn Fein leadership and an unjustifiable concession to an imperial Britain. These groups ramped up their bombing campaigns across the province in 2010; of the 26 official terrorist attacks recorded in the UK between April 2010 and March 2011, 25 of them occurred in NI (Nolan 2014, 37; see also, Horgan and Morison 2011). Many attacks targeted Catholic police officers, with the intent of intimidating other Catholics from joining the PSNI, and preventing the development of a fully integrated police service.

Despite the threat of dissident republican terrorism, responses of elected leaders reflected a joint effort to restrain the potential of such violence to escalate intercommunity hostilities. For example, there were exceptionally violent riots instigated by the same armed republican groups in 2010. About 200 rioters, including children as young as 10 were responsible for the violence, which included one officer suffering injuries from a shotgun blast, and a policewoman being knocked unconscious when a breeze block was dropped on her head from a rooftop (Belfast Telegraph 2010a). Political leaders from across communities generally responded in unison in condemning the Republican violence, including Gerry Adams—president of Sinn Fein and alleged former IRA commander—and DUP First Minister Peter Robinson. Deputy First Minister Martin McGuinness also condemned dissident republican violence later that summer after a private meeting held with Ulster Defense Association (UDA) leader Jackie McDonald (McKinney

2010). The fact that McGuinness, a former IRA leader, would be in private talks with a Loyalist paramilitary leader signified a deep commitment to the peace process at a crucial time. In another instance, after the home of a grandmother with a strong reputation for leadership in cross-community work in North Belfast was attacked with pipe-bombs, a huge rally took place, attended by hundreds from both sides of the community and politicians from both Unionist and Nationalist parties (Belfast Telegraph 2010b). Peter Robinson and Martin McGuinness jointly condemned UVF-initiated riots in East Belfast in June 2011, moreover. Although the parade violence in July of the same year did provoke some tensions among leaders, the extent of public fallout resulting from the disorder was relatively minimal. The public display of unity between Nationalist and Unionist leaders is reported relatively frequently throughout 2010 and 2011. The notable cooperation around policing at this time was particularly important given that it has historically been one of the most contentious ethnopolitical issues in NI (Mulcahy 2013).

There are self-serving explanations for such cooperation across ethnopolitical lines, of course. For Sinn Fein, condemnation of dissident republicanism was doubtless underscored in part by an interest in increasing the party's appeal to moderate (and largely middle-class) Catholics and those unaffiliated with Unionism or Nationalism (see Evans and Tonge 2009), as well as an interest to delegitimize potential political rivals in their core constituency areas—working-class republican communities—and keep the peace process on course. Thus, appearances of cooperation between Sinn Fein and Unionist parties could be largely coincidental. Nonetheless, from a symbolic standpoint, a single message sent by historically opposed ethnopolitical parties in a period of political uncertainty is notable. Such signs of cooperation seemed to splinter over the following two years during the spiraling of the flag and parade crises, however, having important implications for the long-term scope of socio-political relations in Belfast's more disadvantaged communities.

After rates of sectarian violence reached a low in 2011/2012, they would then increase somewhat in 2012/2013 in North Belfast and West Belfast to 288 and 103, respectively, up from 211 and 87 (see table 2.1). At the same time, even as sectarian incidents continued to decline between 2008 and 2012 in North and West Belfast, the number of incidents actually increased most years in the predominantly Unionist areas of East and South Belfast over the same period (though overall rates were highest in North Belfast). According to PSNI data, frequencies of sectarian violence increased each year in East Belfast from a low of 42 in 2008/2009 to a high of 172 in 2011/2012. The number of sectarian incidents would then decline only slightly to 131 in 2012/2013, and rose again in 2013/2014 to 152. Moreover, the number of retrieved newspaper reports about PUL attacks on police in East Belfast alone in 2013 was higher than in all previous years, comprising half of all incidents reported for that area. Retrieved reports about anti-police violence in East Belfast accounted for 37 percent of all such incident reports in 2013, up from 17 percent in 2012. The relatively high incident numbers for East Belfast between 2011 and 2014 in part reflect increases in Loyalist violence in response to Historical Enquires Team (HET) investigations in 2011,[5] and the ratcheting up of tensions over flags and parades the following years.

THE FLAG AND PARADE PROTESTS, 2012–2014

National flags hold much symbolic significance in NI. Throughout some PUL neighborhoods in Belfast, for example, Union Jack flags are literally everywhere and fly year-round, meant to claim territory and intimidate members of CNR communities. In rival Republican neighborhoods, tricolor flags fly (to a somewhat lesser extent, according to respondents and my own observations). Thus, when Sinn Fein brought the proposal to remove the Union flag to a vote, initially intending to remove it altogether, the risk of escalating tensions should have been clear. After deliberations with officials from the Alliance Party, Sinn Fein agreed to compromise by accepting that it fly on British holidays only, being the standard policy across the UK. Unionist politicians responded angrily, arguing that the vote was undemocratic and signified the escalation of the "culture war" being waged against Unionism. Alliance Party officials, blamed for selling out Unionist interests to the benefit of Sinn Fein, received much of the initial Loyalist backlash (Nolan et al. 2014). New state restrictions on Unionist ethnocultural symbols and parades are perceived by many in the Protestant community as symptomatic of a more general erosion of Unionist power, and another indication of a "slippery slope" toward a united Ireland (see also McCall 2003).

The hostile reaction to Belfast City Council's legislation to take the flag down from city hall for most of the year illustrates the fragile political identity of PUL communities and the constitutional and cultural insecurity they feel—an insecurity largely underscoring the discourses and legislative agendas of Unionist political elites. DUP representatives are most notorious in this respect, though the UUP has increased its appeal to Ulster Loyalist mentalities of cultural threat in competition with its main intra-ethnic party rival (the DUP) following its substantial losses in the 2003 elections (Evans and Tonge 2009; Tilley, Garry, and Matthews 2019). Although DUP and UUP party representatives did condemn the violence during the flag protests, it was hardly done in a consistent or genuine manner. As the flag dispute escalated, political rhetoric became increasingly divisive and contributed to escalations in intercommunal tensions. Content analysis of newspaper reports suggests that Sinn Fein and SDLP condemned Republican violence at higher rates than Unionist politicians condemned Loyalist violence. For example, the author retrieved an annual average of 22 newspaper reports for each year between 2010 and 2013 in which Sinn Fein condemned Republican violence and an annual average of only 6 such reports in which Unionists decisively condemned Loyalist violence.[6] In 2013, as violence was on the rise across Belfast, only 9 incidents of Loyalist violence led to Unionist condemnation, according to newspaper data retrieved by the author—some of which were ambiguous and haphazard, implying Nationalists were largely to blame.

During the initial days of Loyalist rioting in December 2012, most Unionist leaders accused Sinn Fein of intentionally invoking Loyalist hostility for political gain by "bulldozing" controversial legislation on culturally divisive issues (Morning Star 2013). Sinn Fein did not need to bring legislation to restrict the flying of the Union Jack, but chose to, according to critics, provoke Unionist backlash for their own political ends. Blame for violent PUL protests was largely deflected onto Sinn Fein and the Alliance Party by Unionist leaders, fomenting a particularly hostile political climate that would sustain throughout 2013 and 2014, when I visited Belfast. For example, after Belfast's Sinn Fein Mayor Mairtin O Muilleoir was attacked by a mob of 40 while attending the opening of a park in the Loyalist Woodvale estate in summer of 2013, a DUP representative refused to condemn the incident on radio (Irish Times 2013b). Moreover, DUP First Minister Robinson responded to early stages of the flag violence by saying that

> The decision to pursue the removal of the flag from City Hall and other council buildings, despite warnings of the likely consequential impact on community relations, was foolish and provocative. Those who talk most about building community relations have by their actions in the council substantially damaged relations across the city. (Belfast Telegraph 2012a)

Other Unionist leaders from the UUP and DUP made similar comments, condemning Loyalist violence while nonetheless implying that blame lies largely with the Nationalist parties and Alliance. In Mike Nesbitt's so-called condemnation of the Loyalist attack on the home of SDLP councillor Claire Hanna in January 2013, he insisted that Unionism "needs a strategy for moving forward and, in the first instance, that can only be arrived at by engagement between all members of the unionist community. Violence distracts from the real source of many of the problems, which are being created by parties such as Sinn Fein" (News Letter 2013a). Unionist criticisms of Loyalist violence takes place in a context wherein blame is still largely attributed to the Other, and in which ethnopolitical division is subtly reinscribed.

During a heated exchange over Twitter with critics immediately following the first flag riots in early December 2012, Peter Robinson defended the decision of his party to disseminate 40,000 leaflets around East Belfast encouraging people to contact Alliance Party legislators in protest of the decision to remove the Union flag from Belfast City Hall. DUP leaflets also provided contact information of elected Alliance representatives, who would later receive death threats and have their homes and offices attacked. Alliance Party leaders blamed the leafletting for inciting tensions that would predictably turn violent. Similar to other politicians (see, Smyth 2013), an elected official from East Belfast notes how the City Council vote to limit the number of days the Union Jack would fly resulted in

> all sorts of attacks. I don't think the Alliance Party appreciated the response to what that decision would be. On the other hand, you had the DUP basically ensure [that] that would be the reaction by releasing 40,000 leaflets around East Belfast letting everyone know that, according to them, the Alliance Party had torn down the flag from City Hall. (Interview with author, Stormont, May 2014)

A community worker in East Belfast makes a similar point, arguing that Loyalists are

> being fed by the DUP and the senior Unionists. When they need friction stirred up and their votes enhanced, they stir it up a bit. It was the Unionists who sent around letters when they asked for that flag to be taken down. They mixed it within those Loyalist communities. Billy Hutchinson, who is a [publicly visible] Loyalist within the PUP, accepted that the flag should only be flown on designated days. The Loyalists accepted it then. All of a sudden, these leaflets are going around saying "they've taken our culture." Then the Loyalists are going, "they've taken our culture, fucking Fenians!"[7] It's the old adage, "play the Orange card." (Interview with author, East Belfast, May 2014)

Others from the Protestant working-class community in Belfast were adamant in identifying the time sequence of events, indicating that political provocations preceded Loyalist disorder and violence. Of course, the actions of the DUP should not preclude recognition of the agency of grassroots actors in Belfast's PUL communities who took leading roles in the protests. Participation in elections has decreased in some working-class Protestant areas, due to residents' alienation from the dominant "middle-class parties" (Brewer 2013; Delargy 2017). However, the same communities are politically active in other ways (street protests, etc.) less common among the Protestant middle classes. A North Belfast activist corroborates a point made by Nolan et al. (2014), that grassroots "non-establishment" groups, without direction from any political party or paramilitary organization, were heavily involved in promoting the protests. From his experience, "the flag protest was led really on social media, and by individuals and small groups that weren't bedded to mainstream Unionism." Such groups, over the years since, "continue to develop their voice, to gain confidence, and, in a lot of ways, especially in North Belfast. . . . it's manifested itself in a very negative way at the street level" (interview with author, May 2021). Nonetheless, grass-roots protestors themselves acknowledged that "the DUP ramped everybody up" and "let the genie out of the bottle" when directing PUL attention to the flag decision (Nolan et al. 2014, 76–77). One interviewee, echoing a view espoused by several others, noted how "the DUP had difficulty condemn-ing . . . the flag dispute. They did after it started, but they already started it" (interview with author, West Belfast, May 2014). The DUP was criticized by many within PUL communities for not supporting the flag protests after the escalation of violence, and the party did not experience significant electoral gains in the subsequent 2014 elections (Nolan et al. 2014, 128). In a broader sense, however, the DUP (and UUP) helped reproduce the ethnosocial field of cultural Unionism in a way which maximized its insular nature. This phenom-enon would in turn illuminate the complex and often contradictory relations between middle-class Unionism and working-class Loyalism, and between Unionist political elites and Loyalist paramilitaries.

The limited connection of Unionist politicians with working-class Loyalist communities, and the former's reliance on Loyalist paramilitary elements to quell disorder was noticeable during the flag protests. DUP officials began to enlist the political influence of paramilitary leaders following the initial esca-lation of violence in December 2012. For example, Peter Robinson met in private meetings with UDA leaders Jackie McDonald and John Bunting and former UVF prisoner Billy Hutchinson in early December. At the same time, just prior to the meeting, the same men were seen at protests in which Irish tricolor flags were burned. Other known paramilitaries were seen watching masked youth burn cars. McDonald commented that protestors they purport to represent "would not be told what to do" and that "they hoped to give leadership about where we need to go next" (Rowan 2012). McDonald also "warned," according to the same source, that those involved in the protests must be part of any solution. Billy Hutchinson similarly commented that

"The focus must remain on Sinn Fein. Politics is about the art of compromise, not the art of surrender." Like McDonald, Hutchinson believes loyalists and not unionist political leaders are best placed to try to bring this crisis to an end. Asked what he would be saying to Mr. Robinson, he said: "Leadership needs to be given. He needs to support others out there trying to bring this to an end." (Rowan 2012)

While many former Loyalist paramilitaries do have the interests of their communities at heart, some nonetheless used the situation to advance their own influence and further embed themselves within the shadows of the political apparatus. DUP and UUP politicians, by promoting Loyalist anger at non-Unionist leaders, created a difficult situation in which they became increasingly dependent on Loyalists who resent compromise with Nationalist interests. Consequently, when some extent of compromise with Nationalists is needed to sustain government institutions, or Unionist political elites speak out against Loyalist disorder and violence, they risk losing some legitimacy in working-class Protestant communities. At the same time, the legitimacy of the same politicians in the eyes of more "moderate" constituents may be threatened when they do not have the capacity to quell intercommunal tensions that result (in part) from their own provocations. Still, by inciting grievance, political leaders can ensure that a large swath of their constituency remains focused on culturally divisive issues and that other parties with greater commitment to cross-community alliance become, or remain, relatively marginal. An example of Unionist exploitation of this tendency within PUL communities was observed in 2012–2013 when Unionist leaders who met with Loyalist paramilitary representatives over the flag protest conspired to discriminate against former politically motivated prisoners (including Loyalists) at the same time, under the guise of "victims' rights,"[8] by supporting the NI Special Advisers Act—legislation which bans ex-prisoners from serving as "special advisers" to elected officials (Belfast Telegraph 2013a). Nonetheless, despite discontent with elected Unionists among some paramilitary elements, many have nonetheless used their influence at the neighborhood level to support the dominant Unionist parties. One respondent explained that, in the lead up to the 2014 Assembly elections, the UDA was "spreading leaflets demanding people vote for DUP and UUP" (interview with author, West Belfast, May 2014).

The Parade Crisis, 2013

Twenty-five percent of all reports retrieved about violence in East Belfast between 2008 and 2013 was linked with flags and parades, and 66 percent of these were in 2012 and 2013. Rising tensions are also indicated by the sharp increase in the number of people intimidated out of their homes between the 2011/2012 and 2012/2013 reporting years, linked to the disputes over flags and parades (Nolan 2014, 11).

Sinn Fein politicians immediately blamed the Orange Order for attempting to cross the Ardoyne interface, in spite of the PC's ruling. DUP politician Nigel Dodds, in contrast, criticized the Commission itself for creating an inevitably dangerous situation with its ruling. The Assembly was subsequently "recalled to debate a DUP motion which said efforts to build a shared future had been harmed by the decision to ban Protestant Orangemen from marching on a contested stretch of road in north Belfast on July 12" (Belfast Telegraph 2013b). Later, Peter Robinson (DUP) and Mike Nesbitt (UUP) were criticized by Sinn Fein officials for exaggerating the role of Nationalist violence in East Belfast while refusing to acknowledge the violence undertaken by Loyalists (Young 2013). Immediately following the parade violence, a Loyalist protest camp was set up near the Ardoyne interface, costing the state more than seven million pounds to police by May 2014 (interview with public official, Belfast center, June 2014). At all hours, day and night, for nearly a year, there were people from Belfast's Loyalist community monitoring the protest site, observed during my 2014 visit. Elected Unionist's interests in centralizing contentious cultural issues in public political discourse was not restricted to the flag or parade disputes, however. More generally, "official recognition of and funding for Orange cultural themes and 'Ulster-Scots' . . . [were] at unprecedented levels" by 2014 (Nolan 2014, 12).

Unionists did receive some criticism for inciting sectarian division from within the Protestant community. There were also more general signs of resistance to sectarianism during this period, including a surge of donations to Alliance Party, an increase in its membership enrollment, and support for Protestant victims of sectarian attacks by their Catholic neighbors (Rutherford 2013). Nonetheless, signs of cooperation, though common enough to warrant mention, did not reflect a more systemic shift toward greater intercommunity dialogue which could gradually transform the dominant ethnonational trajectory of local politics. Rather, the capacity of discourses about the "culture war" being waged against Unionism to heighten intercommunal tensions and consolidate ethnopolitical identities over "bread and butter" issues was, somewhat paradoxically, jointly facilitated by deepening economic insecurity and ethnocultures of masculinity rooted in the legacy of the Troubles.

INOPPORTUNITY, RELATIVE DEPRIVATION, AND ETHNOMASCULINITY: CONTEXTS OF DISORDER AND VIOLENCE

The rise in violence and disorder linked to the flag and parade issues and provocations of ethnopolitical leadership should be considered within broader contexts of socio-economic insecurity, according to many of the community leaders I spoke with. Issues of marginalization and political neglect is unique to neither Loyalist nor Republican communities. However, the *relative decline* in perceived status is more apparent in the former and is unlikely coincidental to the public disorder witnessed in the 2012–2013 period. One UUP politician attempts to empathize with his working-class constituency, indicating awareness of the connection between socio-economic exclusion and PUL anger vis-à-vis the flag protest:

> In my constituency of East Belfast, I continue to witness at first hand the impact of economic recession on an already deprived section of our society. Wages are low, costs are rising, employment is at a premium and not a day goes past when good, honest people are not losing their jobs. This may sound bad enough, but when we consider the high suicide rates in east Belfast, combined with the pending impact of welfare reform, some people can be forgiven for seeking solace in our national identity, which is represented by the Union flag. (Belfast Telegraph 2012b)

Others have recognized that the flag "protests were ultimately the manifestation of the growing disconnect between those who have profited in the 'new' Belfast and those who have not" (Hearty 2018, 134; see also Mulvenna 2015, 162). Rhetoric about the flag and parade rulings, and corresponding fear of Unionist cultural loss helped channel simmering frustrations rooted largely in more general feelings of anomie and ennui. According to respondents, bleak socio-economic conditions contributed to an atmosphere of insecurity, becoming entwined with feelings of sectarian threat that "exploded" with the flag dispute. According to a former elected official in Belfast, "there's a political game that has gone on. When you cut somebody off here, all they feel is anger and resentment and what happens? An explosion; you have the [flag] protests" (interview with author, South Belfast, May 2014).

Certainly, the flag protests had a significant polarizing effect on young people. A Loyalist community worker explained in 2014 how "young people were stopping here to take part in the [youth-focused cross-community] project [she organized]. But after 18 months, they're not." Levels of participation in her project were high "before the riot situation . . . [N]ow it's not as successful as it was, after the flag situation" (interview with author, West Belfast, June 2014). A Belfast councillor commented that "the impact of the flag issue is still with us," revealing that the fallout over this incident has had detrimental long-standing implications on cross-community dialogue at the grassroots level. As he elaborates, "We've a lot of community tensions in North Belfast. . . . This year has taken a real dent. . . . Those tensions are still manifesting themselves nightly in some of the streets around North Belfast" (interview with author, May 2021).

When commenting on the strain in cross-community relations among young people resulting from the flag and parades disputes, one respondent refers to her preparation for a roundtable discussion with representatives from various stakeholder groups, including young people:

We brought in the usual suspects, but we also brought some of the groups that worked at the interface areas, to talk about the impact of the Troubles on children and young people. . . . It was looking at previous work that had been done, and questions that had been asked in the Life and Times survey here. And I think it was back in 2007, young people were optimistic and looking forward to the future. When we went back to them now, it was something totally different. Young people had become more pessimistic between 2007 and 2013.[9] You've had the flags protest, economic decline, all of that. No jobs for young people; young people talking about leaving. (Interview with author, South Belfast, May 2014)

Others imply how socio-economic "disaffection" has combined with cultural contentions to underscore rioting and other disorder among young Republicans as well. As a Republican respondent who works with at-risk youth observes,

Young people are disaffected. That's why they're up there throwing stones. They don't feel they have any future. They feel like they're being left behind in the education system. I'm meeting them and they have no GCSE's (which is the exam you do when you're finishing school and need to get a job). If you put on a chalkboard, one quarter plus a half, these kids couldn't answer that question. I did that when I was ten in primary school. (Interview with author, East Belfast, May 2014)

For those without strong educational credentials, job options are quite bleak, compounding feelings of ennui which potentially manifest in sectarian tensions. The late Joe Law—a well-respected leader in the labor and anti-sectarian movements in Belfast—asked rhetorically, "What jobs are they [young people] getting? Ten or twelve hour contracts at shops. There's some temporary jobs. . . . But [inaudible] sitting by the phone hoping you'll get a day's work. So that compounds it. Poverty obviously compounds it" (interview with author, West Belfast, May 2014). In fact, as of 2017, gross weekly private sector earnings in NI were 16 percent lower than the UK as a whole (Northern Ireland Statistics and Research Agency 2017, 11), not coincidental to the increased share of insecure work (one in three workers) defined as part-time, temporary, or self-employed (Wilson 2017). Law elaborates on how

Working class communities have suffered the most. . . . I don't really have any worry about the [well-off neighborhoods along the] Malone road. There's no buses burning up there or big barricades. Behind the wall here [along the Shankill road] they've got working-class communities who are the lowest [inaudible] of the communities, the poorest. So not only have people suffered here through the years of violence—family members killed, the separation of the two communities, which have become even more polarized—they are now suffering from economic downturn. That's a double whammy. (Interview with author, West Belfast, May 2014)

Law additionally pointed out how, for young men in poor areas of West and North Belfast, with poor educational records and few job prospects, "the only way that you can become a lad or somebody within the community is usually through a [paramilitary] group." Respondents who work predominantly in segregated, working-class areas of Belfast, in both Catholic and Protestant neighborhoods, describe how some young people in those communities feel robbed of their chances to gain recognition and status through participation in the conflict. For example, one interviewee suggests that

> The young people, they don't want to sit down and have a philosophical discussion about why it's a bad thing to join paramilitaries and why we've all moved on. Their first answer is, "Well, if it's good enough for you 30 years ago, then why not me?" I think in that also is a genuine desire to be involved, to do your bit, to contribute. . . . If you're a young republican, you want the republic in your lifetime, so you want to contribute to that. (Interview with author, June 2020)

In a similar vein, a Loyalist respondent active in peacebuilding work at interface areas explains, "Over here, we have young men mostly who weren't even born when the Good Friday Agreement was signed and they're more bitter and sectarian than the people who actually fought in that conflict. That's not right" (interview with author, June 2021). These observations are supported by polls indicating that "young people's attitudes tend to be less favorable to integration than adults, especially among Protestant youth" who witness a decline in the perceived status of their families and communities (Smithey 2011, 15; see also Byrne 2011, 11; McAuley and Tonge 2007, 43–47). Furthermore, highly-charged ethnopolitical rituals, such as parades, and the disorder that often accompanies them, provides opportunities for young people—especially those experiencing strained social mobility—to obtain a sense of power and solidarity within their ethnoreligious community. As one respondent told me, "go watch the tapes [of the July 12th parade violence in 2013]. One kid hits a cop with a rock, and everyone cheers. He's got his hands up in the air, you know, like he did something great. He was probably waiting all year for that" (interview with author, South Belfast, May 2014). The flag incident also revealed the role of street protests and riot events in reconstituting the meanings and identities connected with working-class loyalty to one's local ethnoreligious community. In portions of Belfast where ennui and poverty persist, sectarian incidents bring opportunities for young people to gain status in their communities, if only for a moment. These dynamics, as implied in the aforementioned quotes, take explicitly gendered forms. The romanticizing of the Troubles and the roles of paramilitary groups during the conflict contributes to the construction of male identities rooted in ethnocultures of hypermasculinity, crystalized in moments of ritualized aggression. Other respondents more explicitly implicate cultures of hypermasculinity, which are inextricably linked with constructs of (male) ethnopolitical belonging and identity. According to a public official in Belfast,

> A number of men that I've met said to their sons, "build a pair of shoulders." And I said, "What does that mean?" A couple of men said that it meant "stop doing that sissy stuff about handwriting and your brain." A pair of shoulders is about bricklaying and carrying metal. And so their parents are saying to them, in an outdated way, "go and become a manual worker." But there is no manual work. So they drop out of school. Then when they can't get a job, someone political says to them, "you can't get a job because the Nationalists have educated themselves and they're taking your jobs." (Interview with author, South Belfast, May 2014)

Social and economic exclusion marks the same young people as attractive recruits for paramilitary elements, who offer simple explanations as to why their communities are being left behind by the peace process. A pervasive sense of boredom, made more bothersome by socio-political resentment and alienation, "can highlight the need for alterity . . . [and] intensify the desire for change." Yet, while it can provide "an index of privation and malcontent . . . its inert demeanor offers no solutions" (Legg 2018, 18). Boredom is thus "a collective condition externally imposed" (Legg 2018, 3)—"an affective consequence of exclusion and disempowerment" (Mujamdar 2013, 15), or "objective desperation" (Adorno 1991, 166). The social change which is sought can follow from the innovations of young people themselves, or the various civic leaders in their communities who restlessly work to provide them with positive guidance. Yet "solutions" can also be offered by influential actors who know how to strategically frame young people's problems in sectarian or ethnopolitical terms, tapping into the heuristics that persist as a result of segregation and conflict, and signaling the potential for both excitement and collective purpose. Although many young people reject them, paramilitaries serve this function for others who are drawn to the romanticization of conflict, reversing the meaning withdrawal that comes with persistent boredom in contexts of marginalization throuch implicit promises of status. A community worker in a working-class Protestant estate explains how the attraction to paramilitaries is a serious and seemingly increasing obstacle to peacebuilding, underscored in part by mostly young males' rational responses to inopportunity and exclusion in "modern" Belfast. In her experience,

It's the young people. . . . I feel sorry for because there's absolutely no aspirations. . . . Suicide has gone up, drug taking. Who wants to go and get low-paid
jobs? There's nothing. . . . Well, [in the past] you could get, if there were 20
young people, you could maybe get 16 of them to go down the right road. Four
would join the paramilitaries or [go to] prison or whatever. You had a greater
number of young people who didn't go down that road. Now it's just, what's
the point? If you're young—it's mostly males—if you're a young man and no
prospect of a job or anything, you join a paramilitary. You get money, status,
flashy car. You're the new guy in town. All you have to do is stay away from the
police. . . . You'll take that risk. Why would you be doing any other role? It's too
difficult and nobody cares anyway. There's no one there to support you. That's
the way a lot of people figure here. A lot. (Interview with author, May 2021)

As even Belfast's former police constable commented, violence remains most
prevalent among "young people without enough to do," who lack access to
employment, and who reside in segregated areas or "estates historically con-
trolled by paramilitaries" (News Letter 2013b). One Republican respondent
reflects on dynamics within his own community when making a similar point:

It's great that there are not bombs going off in the streets and kids are starting
to mingle and go out in nightclubs and do different stuff. But if you haven't got
leadership bringing the working class with them, the working class is going to
be left behind and be apathetic. They'll be disaffected. So, what do young kids
do? They could go into drugs. Or other kids say, "It's the Brits' fault that you're
like this, do you want to do something about it? Well, join a [paramilitary] group
and we're going to get the Brits out of Ireland." (Interview with author, East
Belfast, May 2014)

Still another respondent notes how "people here are still poor and they live
in a scarcity mindset, and they believe that they still have to fight. They
can't cut this pie with any thinner slices. Politically, we have no vision of
politics beyond this. And so it's hard to imagine" (interview with author,
South Belfast, May 2014). The emotive ethnopolitical galvanization fueled
(in part) by such a mindset helps sustain paramilitary organizations, moreover. Indeed, recruitment by armed dissident groups continues in Belfast
and Derry's working-class Republican strongholds and the border counties,
having problematic implications on security. As one interviewee puts it, you
see "anti-social behavior [among marginalized young people] in Manchester
or Liverpool or Dublin. The difference here is that young people end up joining gangs that put bombs under people's cars." During the weekend prior to
our interview, "there were two attempts that the guards [An Garda Siochana]
stopped, with people bringing across bombs [from the Republic of Ireland].

So it brings with it a different level of threat" (interview with author, Belfast center, May 2014).

Working-class young people are disproportionately affected by the particular pressures of living in a community in which older adults tend to still construct social and political identities rooted in memories of the Troubles, with which younger generations have little-to-no experiential connection. Though some young people are attracted to the status that membership in paramilitary organizations can bring, others are resentful of paramilitaries and the undue control they continue to exert over particular working-class neighborhoods. As one community leader explains, "There's many young people I'd work with who would say, 'we absolutely hate the paramilitaries and it doesn't matter whether they're Republican or Loyalist.'" Many resent the street justice still meted out by paramilitaries in the form of "punishment attacks" on young people accused of "anti-social behavior."[10] During my time in Belfast, I saw graffiti in North Belfast which read "FAP" (i.e., "fuck all paramilitaries"). This message is apparently written by young people who do not find any meaning in the legacy of conflict and have no respect for paramilitaries.[11] Such graffiti disputes the control of "public space" by paramilitaries, and is a relatively rare phenomenon in working-class wards of Belfast because it challenges these groups' territorial control (Bush 2013, 12–15). For young people disaffected from paramilitarism and the conflict culture, forms of "anti-social behavior" devoid of ethnopolitical meaning are more likely responses to feelings of alienation. One respondent (like several others) indicated that "the problem with the peace process was that young men lost their identity and got involved in crime. There's almost a sense of loss" (interview with author, June 2020). Regardless of their relative connection to the legacy of the Troubles, young men in marginalized areas rely on expressing "toughness" and "resorting to violence to sort out issues that separate . . . them from their internal world of feelings and emotions" (Harland 2011, 417; Harland 2000). Many simultaneously hold a "ceasefire mentality . . . unclear as to whether their society [is] at peace or preparing for war" (Harland 2011, 421).

More generally, the integral role of ethnocultures in the reproduction of collective identity in Northern Ireland's urban working-class communities is also explained by interviewees as a product of what is absent; the fact that there is nothing else to feel or connect to "beyond those things" (parades, flags, etc.) which are inextricably linked with legacies of intercommunal conflict. A high-ranking PSNI officer conveys the perspective that the uneven development along class lines is lucid when traveling through the city, reflecting a fundamental problem with the peace process:

Throughout those years, from '98 to 2005, Belfast City Center boomed: hotels, nightlife. But when I drove up here in 2005, drove up the road to come back here [to work in north Belfast after being away for several years], it always struck me, when you looked around at the fabric of the place, [that] it hadn't changed that much. . . . When I came back . . . there were big parts of it that are just a scene that was [the same as] 30 years ago. Actually, the social deprivation, the lack of development, the lack of jobs, poor educational standards and stuff, all of that still pervades here and there's no question in my mind, it is a major part of the problem. Somebody said to me recently, "If we dealt with the parades, the past and the flags issues, would we have transformed here?" Personally, I'm not convinced that we would. I think there needs to be a whole-scale change in the fabric of this place. People need to see and feel something different beyond those things. (Interview with author, North Belfast, May 2014)

Boredom, coupled with a feeling that one's community "must fight" for resources, in contexts of ethnoreligious polarization and mistrust—and the sense of meaning that process can provide—establishes a fertile social atmosphere in which ethnopolitical leaders can work to reproduce the insular collective identities and concomitant constructions of threat which shore up their social and political relevance. While this dynamic occurs in Nationalist communities, the flag and parade crises and protests over "political policing" (see chapter 4) suggest it has greater centrality to Unionist politics. This is by no means the only Unionist politics that prevail in the North; rather, where, and the extent to which threat or grievance politics are utilized depends largely on local contexts of class and place. Feelings of fear and communal loss, and the conflict mentalities substantiated by such feelings in contexts of socio-economic exclusion, are hardly static; rather, they require activation (Brubaker and Laitin 1998). Poverty compounds feelings of insecurity while entrenching commitment and loyalty to the ethnic ingroup and a sense of purpose found therein, but only when regularly translated as a manifestation of ethnopolitical or sectarian threat.

Unionism, Loyalism, and the Protestant Class Divide

As indicated in chapter 1, parties such as Sinn Fein and DUP have worked to increase their appeal to middle-class voters within their respective ethnonational blocs through moderating their political narratives or, in the case of DUP, promising to deliver legislatively on agendas favored principally by their middle-class constituents. At the same time, constructions of threat or loss—whether cultural or physical, symbolic or material—remain paramount to Unionist parties' efforts to shore up support from their traditionally core working-class constituencies.

Overall, the PUL community shows keen awareness of Unionist political elites' neglect of broader working-class interests that transcend ethnoreligious difference. Even as some working-class Loyalists were galvanized to protest by DUP and UUP discourses about the flag decision, the same persons prove capable of critically interpreting the actions of their ethnopolitical representatives. As a former Loyalist paramilitary prisoner who now works in community-based restorative justice contends, referring to the DUP and UUP, "they'll go to the ordinary working person in the community, and they'll bang the drum around: 'If you don't vote for us, you run the risk of having a First Minister that's from the republican community' . . . But then they don't hear from them until the next" election season (interview with author, June 2020). Others suggest that the lack of positive outcomes resulting from investment of peace funds and a lack of political leadership has led them to acknowledge the problems of social and economic inequality that create common class-based subjectivities transcending religious and national binaries. For example, a Loyalist respondent envisages how divisive ethnopolitics from the top-down continues a function of dividing working-class communities along sectarian lines, while the need for greater investment in social development and community-based peacebuilding initiatives in the same communities is left unaddressed:

> The disengagement between people from the Protestant community and Catholic community, my own feeling is it's politically fueled. It's engineered in a way that I feel keeps us apart. The people that I work with from Catholic communities, I feel a lot of them have so many similarities . . . and they want so many things the same as me. They want better for their kids and their grandkids. . . . When it comes to voting time, they [political parties] bring out the flags and it's all working-class grassroots, socially deprived areas that they come to and say, "If you don't vote for us waving our union flag, you're going to get Sinn Féin." "If you don't vote for us, you're going to get the DUP." It's a scaremongering thing and it's always been that way. People want to vote. . . . In return, you get "fuck off." . . . We get absolutely nothing in return. When you go to these people for help, they palm you off. My own work, working with young people in this large housing estate, we don't even have a community center. I'm working with young kids, they're from desperate families. . . . There is social anxiety, the issues of depression with teenagers. A lot of that comes from their parents as well because their parents came through the Troubles as young parents. (Interview with author, June 2020)

Similar statements from other interviewees across the ethnopolitical divide reveal that, in some scenarios at least, mentalities of "losing" from the peace process fall along fault lines of class and place as much as ethnoreligious or ethnonational affiliation.[12] Thus, critical, "progressive" voices from within Republicanism *and* Loyalism recognize the manipulation wielded by ethnopolitical elites. Implied in the narratives of respondents is recognition of such manipulation as an "abuse of power, that is, *domination* . . . [or] the exercise of a form of *illegitimate* influence by means of discourse" (Van Dijk 2006, 360) by co-ethnic political leadership. Evidently, however, criticism of the mainstream Unionist and Nationalist parties within progressive Loyalism (i.e., UVF/PUP) and dissident republicanism does not necessarily correspond with a more general decline in sectarianism or the emergence of a cross-community working-class politics. A community worker from East Belfast explains a personal experience to that point:

> I went to a May Day parade a couple of years ago and [the] working class was carrying their banners for equal rights and all that. There was a small congregation from the PUP. . . . And we had an Éirigí[13] flag and the guys were standing with the PUP flag. And they took our banner down and walked out of the parade. I was thinking that we have more in common with those people than we do with the SDLP, who are a middle-class Catholic party. We've all got the same issues in our communities: we don't have jobs; our kids are being left behind by the education system. It's a sectarian mentality they have. Like Peter Robinson praising that pastor for making a racist comment about Muslims being the spawn of the Devil [in May 2014]. And these people are taking their lead from this guy? So my reasoning on this is [politicians say to themselves] "we want you to vote for us, but we don't give a shit about your kids, your poverty or your education." And this is the way we're going. It's now happening with the Nationalist community. (Interview with author, East Belfast, May 2014)[14]

Earlier in the peace process, Finlayson (1999, 49) warned against determining the sociological importance of class as having "an *immediate* or *singular* epistemological or political significance," and refers to Stuart Hall's (1988, 9) stipulation that ideology, and the identities and subjective realities it shapes and reflects, is not "merely the secondary or reflexive effects of some factor which is primary or more determining." The importance of class-specific social locations does not negate the influence of other coercive identities; rather, such identities coalesce into a complex, inexplicable nexus of meaning, which can be strategically manipulated by opportunistic political entrepreneurs. Because much of the cultural Unionism that forms a common political identity has been historically constituted by symbolizations of "Britishness" and evangelical Protestantism, even calls to reconnect middle-class Unionist politicians with grassroots, working-class Loyalism often implicitly subjugate discussion of class. The following critique of mainstream Unionist parties by Loyalist activist Jamie Bryson is one example. As he argues, there

> "needs to be a re-connection between the mainstream unionist parties and the working class. We don't feel we have adequate representation at Stormont.

We do not see a peace process but a piece-by-piece process to surrender our Britishness." Key issues for him have been the loss of the RUC and UDR [Ulster Defence Regiment], the conversion of the Crown Prosecution Service to the Public Prosecution Service, restrictions on flying the Union Flag and parades, and continuing attacks on places of worship and Orange Halls. (News Letter 2012)

Attempts to revive class consciousness in community-based political discourse have by no means rivaled the symbolic power of ethnopolitical identity constructs. In many instances, blame for the poverty and inopportunity in working-class communities is still framed with sectarian symbology, empowering paramilitary elements who offer simplistic solutions to complex problems. This is a socio-political dynamic seemingly more evident within the PUL community. As a prominent community leader explains, the ongoing control paramilitaries exert in working-class Loyalist neighborhoods partially "comes from the disconnect between political Unionism and Loyalism; the paramilitaries become the default to get things done, to make things happen in their community" (interview with author, East Belfast, May 2014). The "services" provided by paramilitaries are various, including extra-legal vigilante "policing." As a community worker from a Loyalist estate explains,

Just even on a community basis, if you look at any society where there are issues, people will turn to whoever will help them. Our problem here is that the police, the PSNI, they're losing funding all the time. They're also engaged in . . . [policing] protests. There's all sorts of things going on. When things happen locally, and communities need a response, they'll go to the paramilitaries because they'll get a response. There are still communities and certainly, the ones I work with, who feel that the paramilitaries . . . They'll need people who protect them. (Interview with author, June 2020)

While paramilitaries exert control over neighborhoods through intimidation, they couple this tactic with a strategy of self-legitimation (vigilante justice, providing services, etc.). As another respondent explains, the lack of state delivery on the substantive need within working-class PUL communities "has given paramilitary organizations an opportunity to pretend that they're social services, and gain that long term credibility and plausibility again." In contrast, grassroots actors in working-class Nationalist areas (including many ex-IRA prisoners) remain closely connected to Sinn Fein, putting the party in a better position to embody working-class interests and merge these with the interests from others (i.e., middle-class Catholics, and those affiliated with neither Nationalism nor Unionism). Several PUL respondents envisage how a collective feeling of isolation within Loyalism, underscored by a "class division" in broader Unionism, empowers paramilitary elements to take up "leadership" roles in working-class Protestant communities lacking effective political representation. As one interviewee describes,

> Just think of Martin McGuinness, Gerry Kelly. I could name a whole host of them. . . . Then you look at the Assembly on the Protestant side; there isn't one person in the Assembly [with a history of political violence], and that's because within the Unionist mindset, Loyalism is a pariah. . . . That same class division doesn't happen within Nationalism, Republicanism. There's very definitely a feeling within the working-class Loyalist community, that nobody likes us. The Unionists, the DUP, have no time for us either, so we are without voice and therefore we've got to do stuff for ourselves. They haven't delivered for education; they haven't delivered jobs or houses. You can see within that gap, where paramilitarism can come in. (Interview with author, June 2020)

Similarly, according to a different respondent from Protestant East Belfast, in comparison with Loyalism, Nationalist parties have more effective grassroots

> capacity building. . . . They're very strong in their [community organizing] capabilities whereas they're not as strong in Loyalist areas. Some of that also comes from the point that Nationalist and Republican politicians live in their areas. They live in working-class areas. In Unionism, there are very few councillors living in working areas. So there's a disconnect between them. The [PUL] community feels it's being left behind a bit. (Interview with author, Stormont, May 2014)

Another respondent similarly describes how "there's become a much more pronounced class divide" in recent years. "It's particularly evident in Unionist communities. . . . That's kind of hardened opinions. So 'Unionism as a whole' can't be said anymore" (interview with author, East Belfast, June 2014). The class fragmentation in Unionism remains a taboo topic which is rarely discussed. As another Unionist respondent says, "in Unionist communities, class politics is not discussed. There's very, very limited discussion about it. I think that reflects that there's a lack of political articulation about the issues of concern for working-class communities" (interview with author, North Belfast, June 2014). This element of the "leadership gap" described by several respondents further empowers the agency of paramilitary elements, some of whom are also "community leaders" in working-class PUL communities. There is a limit to which anti-establishment Loyalist leaders connected to paramilitary organizations can fill this "leadership gap," however. In most instances, when activists associated with the UDA or UVF run for local election, they barely receive any votes. Even the Protestant coalition that launched on the back wave of the flag protest failed to produce a successful political campaign. Thus, while working-class PUL communities are increasingly disconnected from the mainstream Unionist parties, they are also detached from the wider political process. Nonetheless, the "disconnect between Unionism and Loyalism" restricts the psychosocial channels mostly middle-class Unionist political elites can tap into to garner support across class boundaries without alienating certain sections of their constituency, making the manipulation of ethnocultural symbols a somewhat predictable political tactic.

DISCUSSION

The preceding analysis identified the following interacting conditions obstructing the development of more positive cross-community relations in NI: the cultural importance of readily available, ethnocultural symbols (flags, parades, etc.) to PUL socio-political identity; the economic marginalization of communities historically most susceptible to violence; the ongoing influence of shadow political factions unique to the society (i.e., paramilitaries) on local politics and community relations; and—as indicated in chapter 1—distinct political priorities of the middle classes and the poor and working-classes *within* the ethnopolitical "communities."

According to analysis of PSNI data used to identify fluctuations in intercommunal tensions, the frequency of sectarian incidents in North and West Belfast consistently declined each year between 2008 and 2012, while increasing in late 2012 and remaining relatively high throughout the following year across the city. In contrast, frequencies of sectarian violence increased exponentially in the predominantly Loyalist areas of East and South Belfast up to 2012, remaining relatively high in 2013 and early 2014, in comparison with the immediate post-devolution period. Intensive case study analysis of interviews with community leaders and newspaper reports suggests that sparks in sectarian tensions and violence in the 2012–2014 period corresponded with a shift toward increasingly provocative political discourse, blamed by many for inciting fear and amplifying a sense of loss among Loyalists. Moreover, it is far from apparent that dominant ethnopolitical parties become more moderate in their policy preferences (as suggested by Mitchell, Evans, and O'Leary 2009) or that a consolidation of power among traditional ethnocentric parties has led them to prioritize issues of "development" and downplay emphasis on cultural symbols in a gradual process of democratization (see McGrattan 2014).

The escalation of ethnosectarian discourses surrounding issues of parades and flags marked a departure from the more coordinated, less contentious politics of Nationalist and Unionist leaders prior to 2012. Although tensions have always existed between the two ethnopolitical blocs post-Agreement, there seemed a more coordinated commitment to cooperation in the 2008–2011 period, in support of the development of new, fragile state institutions, and policing in particular. At that time, cooperation was the most rational political choice, both for security purposes and for the political interests of elected leaders. The potential political consequences for Unionists specifically of failing to cooperate on major institutional reforms then underway likely outweighed any criticism they could receive for "surrendering" to Nationalism. DUP had already proven their commitment to Unionist interests through their hardline negotiating position in the lead up to the Agreement and during the first few years of its implementation (McGlynn, Tonge & McAuley 2014; Bruce 2007). Pressures to cooperate in the implementation of the Assembly in 2007, and in the subsequent creation of the cross-community Policing Commission in 2010, is seemingly reflected in the relatively low prevalence of contentious discourses identified in that time period. Such pressures seemed to dissipate following the successful implementation of the devolved institutions, however, and as discontent among working-class communities deepened in the years following the 2008 recession. In contrast, following burnout of the last phase of the "honeymoon period" (i.e., the Hillsborough Agreement) top-down instances of elite-sponsored provocation, combined with paramilitary influence and persistent economic marginalization of working-class communities explain at least in part the gradual increase in sectarian tensions across Belfast.

The resolve among disadvantaged boys and young men to protect their communities and, at times, enact revenge against "the Other" is hardened by their relative deprivation and immobility—problems which became increasingly apparent following the 2008 recession. With little else providing a vocation for many young people in deprived areas of Belfast, the corresponding sense that one's community is constantly under threat provides a trajectory by which mostly young males find meaning through "protecting their community," performed ritualistically through rioting and other (non-lethal) violence. In some interface neighborhoods, rioting is not always sectarian per se; at times, it involves mixed motives, or simply a bit of ritual "fun" among boys and young men.[15] Yet these young people live in communities where they are subject to recruitment by paramilitary organizations, who offer simple explanations for their problems and a path to social status. The ongoing role of paramilitaries within both Northern Ireland's political apparatus and smaller, informal community networks has had an important impact on the peace process, paradoxically, for both better and worse. It has enabled cooperation while constraining its transformative potential and providing a channel through which Unionist leaders can promote backlash and escalate tension (a paradox explored further in chapter 3). The ratcheting-up of the flag and parade crises in 2012–2013 reveal how traditional, ethnocentric fears remain integral to the political calculations of some leaders. The inefficacy of those leaders on "quality of life" issues, at the same time, reconstitutes the power of paramilitaries in the informal goings-on of social life in some poor and working-class communities (especially Loyalist communities). The very re-entrenchment of paramilitary influence in this way nonetheless provides an asset for leaders who opt to provoke tensions for self-serving political purposes. It is unlikely that DUP leaders were unaware that the leaflets they disseminated in East Belfast about removal of the Union flag would incite aggression from elements of the UVF and UDA.

It is possible, too, that as post-conflict stability is taken for granted and peace process reforms remain in place, leaders underestimate the extent to which tensions they promote may rise or overwhelm the capacity of the state to deter violence when opting for provocation. For example, the consequences of DUP leafleting and other provocative actions spiraled out of their control as street violence escalated, putting them in a difficult position politically and garnering some significant intracommunity debate over the legitimacy of their leadership. (As we will see in chapter 5, a similar, and perhaps more consequential, criticism unfolded during the Brexit negotiations as well.) Nonetheless, the flag and parade disputes contributed significantly to long-lasting intercommunity fallout and a recentering of communal discourses around culturally contentious issues which reconstitute the relevance of dominant ethnopolitical parties. On the other hand, Nationalist officials are not completely innocent with respect to the flag dispute, either. Respondents acknowledge that few people were even aware that the Union flag was flying over City Hall before the measure to remove it was introduced by Sein Fein councillors. Nationalists did not need to bring attention to the issue, but chose to, with the likely expectation of Unionist backlash.

Ethnopolitical and sectarian provocations are nothing new in NI—especially in Unionism—and contributed significantly to the escalation of the Troubles (Bew, Gibbon, and Patterson 2002). DUP founder Ian Paisley was the most notorious of such figures, whose fiery rhetoric about the impending unification of Ireland and the threat of "Papism" incited Loyalist violence (Rowthorn 1981; Bruce 1986). In contrast to Republican violence, which was partly motivated by a socialist ideology and equality agenda, Loyalist violence was more purely reactionary, geared primarily toward combating Republicanism and maintaining Northern Ireland's constitutional status quo, and having little association with economic grievances or civil rights. Not coincidentally, today, there is relatively little connection between Unionist and Loyalist politics and class identity—though class contexts shape the distinct ways in which such politics manifest. Historically and contemporaneously, the lack of *secure* cultural identity beyond evangelical Protestantism (Bruce 1986) and distinct political identity which transcends narratives about being *against* potential change—namely, a change to the constitutional status of the North and rising Irish influence within NI—compounds the likelihood that Unionist "defeatism" remains or even deepens (see Finlay 2001), and is not coincidental to the particular importance given to ethnocultural symbols and rituals, such as flags and parades. Generally, ritual forms of Unionist cultural expression are indistinguishable from forms of political expression, a phenomenon largely transcending class difference. As explained by Unionist politician Jeffrey Donaldson, "Ulster British culture" tends "to be expressed much more in an affinity with the Crown and the symbols of the British state" than in "language" or politically neutral cultural symbols (quoted in McCall 2003, 99). Bryan's (2000) and Jarman's (1997) work from early in the peace process reveal how "Orange parades, as deeply emotional events, enable the class and denominational diversity of Ulster Protestants to be subsumed to a commemorative focus on a common ethnic origin" (McCormack 2017, 54). The ongoing centralization of identity politics through disputes over ethnopolitical symbols and rituals continues to obstruct any emergence of a cross-community working-class politics two decades after the Agreement. Undermining Sinn Fein, a "left-wing" party led by former IRA militants takes top priority for many working-class Protestants. More generally, as internal criticism of the main Unionist and Nationalist parties by some community and (former) paramilitary leaders from their respective working-class communities occurs, it has not given way to the development of a supraethnic politics of class.

NOTES

1. Parts of this chapter were originally published in: Holland, Curtis, and Gordana Rabrenovic. 2017. "Social Immobility, Ethno-politics, and Sectarian Violence: Obstacles to Post-conflict Reconstruction in Northern Ireland." *International Journal of Politics, Culture and Society* 30 (3): 219–244.

2. The annual PSNI incident-reporting period starts in April and ends in March of the following year. Such data are based on police reports and subcategorized according to police district, allowing for comparisons between each of the four parts of Belfast: North and West (police district A) and South and East (district B). The PSNI data is also subcategorized by incident type (sectarian, racist, homophobic, etc.). However, like any police data, the frequencies recorded by the PSNI are underestimations, as many incidents are simply not reported. Moreover, the PSNI data on hate crimes do not include "public order incidents"; thus, most cases of intergroup clashes at interfaces, and rioting and disorder associated with the parade and flag disputes, are not included. For this reason, data retrieved from newspaper reports were especially useful in the analysis of dynamics of political violence. At the same time, the police data help supplement the newspaper analysis by revealing how tensions over flags and parades correspond with fluctuations in other forms of violence as well (attacks

against individuals, homes, businesses, etc.). Further, it is important to recognize a history of bias in policing that may underscore skepticism about the validity of the data among some from within the province. Among Republicans specifically, the police continue to be commonly perceived as predominantly serving Unionist and British interests. Notwithstanding the potential limitations, PSNI data contain the best quantitative estimates available, especially with respect to serious incidents involving firearms and explosives, as they are almost always made known to police. If anything, the trends reported here, including increases in violence within predominantly Loyalist locations, were likely *more* prevalent than the data suggest.

3. Information from all reports discussing sectarian incidents were coded as variables and entered into a SPSS data file. Numerous variables were included, but most importantly this dimension of the research sought to identify responses to a particular event by politicians, community-based leaders, and other influential actors cited in newspaper reports. There are limitations to this method, of course. First, different newspapers may report differently about a given incident. For example, *The Irish News* is read predominantly by Catholics, and may be perceived as biased by some Protestants. Similarly, the *Belfast News Letter* is read mostly by Protestants. Thus, to provide a comprehensive and balanced analysis, I decided to include all newspapers in the UK and Ireland in the LexisNexis search, to obtain as much relevant information as possible from different sources and perspectives on each event.

4. Although these numbers might not seem especially striking at first glance, it is important to consider that Belfast is a relatively small city, holding approximately 300,000 people.

5. Historical Enquiries Team was a specially designated unit of the PSNI charged with investigating killings during the Troubles.

6. This is partly due to the fact that Republican violence is reported at higher rates. Dissident bombings and attacks on police officers, for example, typically receive media coverage and united condemnation is expected. Thus, it is partly the nature of dissident Republican violence that explains this difference. Still, "less severe" violence by Republican groups, such as vigilante beatings and shootings, is, according to the newspaper reports retrieved by the author, reported at higher rates than similar violence by Loyalist groups, and it is unclear whether this reflects disproportionate activity by armed Republican groups or is a matter of reporting bias. The author's conversations with community leaders in Belfast suggest that Loyalist paramilitaries are involved in a range of criminality, "punishment attacks," and sectarian violence, but the author found far fewer newspaper reports about the latter such incidents in comparison with similar events involving dissident Republican groups (see also Knox [2002] and Jarman [2004]). In 2009, when the number of newspaper reports on paramilitary violence greatly increased from previous years, only 9 implicated Loyalists while 46 implicated Republicans; and with respect to newspaper reports from 2010, 9 implicated Loyalists and 51 implicated Republicans. Numbers stayed relatively consistent in the following years, except when there was a noticeable increase in Loyalist attacks in December 2012, during the initial flag disorder (24 reports). But even for that year, Republican violence was reported at higher rates (33 reports). In 2013, reports on Loyalist violence were relatively low given that tensions were extremely

high over flags and parades, as they were implicated in only 12 attacks, compared with Republicans, who were implicated in 42.

7. "Fenian" used to be a prideful term for Catholic warriors used within the Catholic community, but is now a derogatory term used toward Catholics by Protestants.

8. For a thoughtful analysis of how the SPAD Act moved "political disagreement over the issues of victimhood and wrongdoing in Northern Ireland onto a formal legislative footing," see Hearty (2015, 333).

9. *The Life and Times Survey* is an annual survey asking a range of questions on attitudes about NI society and the peace process, intended to mark important changes and continuities over time, starting in 1998. See https://www.ark.ac.uk/nilt/.

10. Such attacks are also used to intimidate and extort various members of local, mostly working-class and poor communities (not just drug dealers and other criminals) and consolidate paramilitary control over neighborhoods—phenomena discussed further in chapter 4.

11. For more detail on the attitudes of young men toward paramilitary influence, see Harland (2011, 423–424).

12. Hearty (2018, 139) identified a similar dynamic occurring in the context of "political policing" in Northern Ireland. He refers to comments by one influential loyalist, Jamie Bryson, who criticized state prosecutors "for failing to charge those aligned with Sinn Fein while at the same time bringing 'very convenient prosecutions against not only Protestants but also against anyone within the republican community who speaks out against the Sinn Fein peace strategy'" (Hearty 2018, 139).

13. Eirigi is a socialist republican political party founded by former Sinn Fein members who became critical of the party leadership following the peace agreement.

14. Chapters 4 and 5 will examine with more depth specific instances where Nationalist political elites utilized divisive posturing over policing and Brexit to galvanize ingroup support.

15. The line between recreational and sectarian rioting is often opaque and malleable. In some instances, usually in the wake of a public political or sectarian dispute, what at first appears to be "recreational" rioting is manipulated by older, more sinister elements. One PUL respondent described how his son, who "had friends from the Catholic community," and who "never followed the [Loyalist] marching bands," was arrested for rioting. He went on to explain how "I discovered he was on his Xbox, [and a message] came up on the screen: 'Come on up to the Awnings road.' It was a social thing. . . . In the wrong place at the wrong time while all the big men, paramilitaries, they stood back and encouraged the young ones to go and throw the stones." See also Harland (2011, 420).

Chapter 3

Post-conflict Masculinities, Exclusion, and Contradictions in Ex-combatant Community-based Peacebuilding

The role of ex-paramilitary prisoners in sustaining relative peace in the post-Agreement era has been the subject of significant scholarly debate (McEvoy and Shirlow 2009; Shirlow et al. 2005; McAuley, Tonge, and Shirlow 2010; Gormally 2001; Edwards and McGrattan 2011; Edwards and McGrattan 2013; Ashe 2009; Rolston 2007).[1] Emphasis on ex-prisoner leadership in peacebuilding in NI complements a broader scholarly discussion about the imperatives of disarmament, demobilization, and reintegration (DDR) campaigns and the benefits and challenges of incorporating ex-combatants at the center of post-conflict reconstruction schemes (Nilsson 2005; Ginifer 2003). Since the Agreement, both Republican and Loyalist ex-paramilitary prisoners have become central players in grassroots peacekeeping, peacebuilding, and transitional justice initiatives. The NI Association for the Care and Resettlement of Offenders has been the most active voluntary organization involved in the promotion of offender-based cross-community restorative justice, facilitating the development of Coiste an n-Irarchimi and Ex-Prisoners Interpretative Center (EPIC), Irish Republican and Loyalist ex-prisoner coalitions, respectively. These organizations engage together in a variety of work, including cross-community peacekeeping and peace-building, while also providing employment for ex-prisoners in the tourism industry and guidance on issues commonly faced by ex-combatants, such as unemployment and struggles with family reunification (McAuley, Tonge, and Shirlow 2010; Rolston 2007).

Some suggest that supporting such organizations is necessary in preventing ex-combatant disaffection by helping them feel included in the emerging society, mitigating the potential of remobilization. Proponents even suggest that ex-combatants "can represent a major force for the reconstruction and rehabilitation of war-torn societies" as a result of their previous participation in conflict (Klingebiel et al. 1995, 6). Liberation armies in particular "produce individuals who are committed, disciplined, and politically astute," evidenced by the rebel forces of South Africa, Eritrea, and NI (among others) (Rolston 2007, 263). Skeptics argue, however, that prioritizing approaches to peacebuilding that promote ex-combatant leadership in the community sector ultimately privileges the interests of perpetrators over those of victims, perpetuating the "terroristic narratives" and ideologies that underpinned the escalation of mass violence in the first place, and thus minimizing the transformational potential of "peace" (Edwards and McGrattan 2011). It is argued that such measures undermine the scope of social transformation by legitimizing the power of those who remain committed to "ideological continuities with the past" (Edwards and McGrattan 2011, 363) as well as ethnocultures of (semi) militarized masculinities (Ashe 2009). Academic critics of offender-focused transitional justice suggest that prioritizing the needs of ex-combatants stymies the voices of victims and other stakeholders whose concerns should take precedence over those of "terrorists." Ex-terrorists tend to hold the same ideological goals pursued during the Troubles; thus, centering this group within NGO peacebuilding coalitions "militates against the stated goals of the British government and the community sector [of] encouraging some form of a shared future for Northern Ireland" (Edwards and McGrattan 2011, 363). Indeed, even proponents of ex-combatant participation in community-based organizations acknowledge that most in this milieu continue to hold traditional ethnonational ideologies and goals, and that cooperation rarely transfers to a *political* form (McAuley, Tonge, and Shirlow 2010).

A disproportionate amount of research on ex-combatant agencies more generally focuses on ideological dynamics of disengagement and "de-radicalization," or processes of community-based restorative justice (CBRJ). In NI in particular, paramilitary acquiescence to the peace process was bought, so to speak. As conditional to the successful implementation of the Agreement, political prisoners convicted of violent offenses were released from prison early,[2] without any mechanism for dealing with the past. Indeed, evidence of positive ex-combatant contributions to local peacebuilding efforts does not necessitate political "de-radicalization." "Often there can be physical disengagement from terrorist activity, but no concomitant change or reduction in ideological support" for the historical objectives of the terrorist organization (Horgan 2008, 5). More empirical attention is needed to illuminate the systemic cultural tenets and political dynamics which have unique impacts on former combatants and may minimize processes of de-radicalization.

At the same time, relatively little empirical attention has been attributed to how intersectional gendered and class identities underscore or (re)shape ex-combatant ethnonational mindsets, and facilitate or undermine the scope of peacebuilding and conflict transformation. Given the exponential growth in attention to masculinities in social research more broadly, it is surprising that emphasis on the subject has been relatively sparse in studies of conflict and peacebuilding—especially when considering the inextricable link between masculinities and nationalisms (Nagel 1998; Yuval-Davis 1997). Nonetheless, in the peacebuilding literature specifically, what O'Brien (1981) originally termed "malestream" research remains dominant. Generally speaking, it is "all about men and severely neglectful of talking explicitly about them" *as* men (Hearn 1997, 48). Ashe (2009, 302) illuminates how the promotion of ex-combatant CBRJ among academic proponents conspicuously excludes attention to issues of "gender equality and power," thus having important "gendering effects." She goes on to point out how a "kind of in-depth positive evaluation of ex-paramilitaries reflects a 'realistic approach' that accepts the importance of demilitarization and reintegration" without proper consideration of the counterproductive implications otherwise evident with explicit recognition of the gendered contexts of masculinity and patriarchy (Ashe 2009, 304; see also Zuckerman and Greenberg 2004).

Building on previous work which implicates cultures of masculinities in inhibiting conflict transformation and reconciliation (Ashe 2019; Bairner 1999; Harland 2011; Harland and McCready 2015), this chapter critically examines how masculinities and intersecting ethnonational and social class identities underscore the social and political agencies of ex-combatants in the context of community-based peacebuilding. More specifically, the chapter identifies how such intersecting identities, in parallel with state-led practices of exclusion interact in restricting prospects of ex-combatant agencies in the community sector. Findings show how the social exclusion of ex-combatants by elected officials, and the former's more general "limits of legitimacy" (Mitchell 2008) help sustain ex-combatants' political disaffection and underscore the importance of ethnomasculinist cultures of paramilitarism in their efforts to maintain power and control on neighborhood levels. Results also take account of the structural forces which constitute ex-combatant alienation and shape their social agencies of "resistance"—agencies that are underscored at the same time by desires for autonomy and recognition, and channeled through ethnocultural, gendered scripts rooted in both violent and "non-violent reconstituted masculinities" (Ashe 2009, 306).

Moreover, in order to not "assist [in] the forgetting of women and the gendered power relations between men and women" when analyzing the behavior of this group of men (Hearn 1997, 50), the implications of the aforementioned dynamics in the (re)silencing and socio-political (re)displacement of women in working-class communities in particular are integral to the subsequent analysis. In contrast to most work on the prospects and limitations of male ex-combatant peacebuilding, this chapter puts the voices of women involved in peacebuilding at the center of analysis and, by doing so, offers important insight into concomitant gendered and class dimensions of power which operate on both the state and grassroots levels to undermine the transformative potential of community-based peacebuilding.

THE STATE AND COMMUNITY SECTOR IN EX-COMBATANT PEACEBUILDING

Significant differences in the aforementioned arguments regarding ex-combatant participation in social reconstruction are due largely to authors' disparate political and cultural interpretations of conflict and the limits of particular analytical approaches. Both proponents and critics tend to focus *either* on state-led *or* grassroots-led approaches to peacebuilding and restorative justice, inadvertently restricting adequate attention to dynamics through which practices of state and extra-state or non-state actors (i.e., ex-combatants) are inextricably linked in shaping peace process outcomes. Moreover, the research tends to examine either positive contributions of ex-combatant-led peacebuilding, *or* the practices and beliefs of former militants which obstruct the peace process.

Some critics of offender-based participation in peacebuilding charge that those rationalizing ex-combatant reintegration, based on "the lack of a comprehensive [state] mechanism for dealing with the past," precariously posit the state in "Weberian terms" as a "malevolent," external force, exaggerating the disconnect between state and civil society (Edwards and McGrattan 2011, 363). Such theoretical critiques tend to downplay or overlook policies of the state which detrimentally impact former combatants and, more generally, the local communities in which they are embedded. Authors favoring the latter perspective tend to implicitly reject claims that former combatants or terrorists are often victims as well as perpetrators, restricting theoretical and empirical focus on potential practices of political exploitation and manipulation of these actors, in both past and present. As research in critical criminology suggests, acknowledgement of state responsibility in shaping criminal violence or terrorism necessarily signals a reconceptualization of victimhood (McEvoy and Gormally 1997; McGarry 2015), including recognition of the problems in distinguishing victims from perpetrators (Moser 2007).

Research by Mitchell (2008) suggests that degrees of legitimacy attributed to the state and ex-combatants in (post) conflict societies generally differ according to the historical identities and experiences of opposing groups, reflected, for example, in deficits in the state's moral monopoly on the use of force (see also, Rolston 2006). Utilizing a type of quasi-Weberian approach in analysis of post-conflict relations between state and non-state actors (such as ex-combatants) is appropriate, insofar as conflicting notions of legitimacy have historically underscored dynamics of conflict. For example, while middle-class Unionism has typically posited the state as the sole legitimate user of force, Loyalists perceived Britain's unwillingness to properly protect their communities from Republican violence as legitimating their extra-state violence. Militant Republicans, on the contrary, perceived the presence of British troops, the sectarian nature of policing by the RUC, and instances of these actors' complicity with Loyalist paramilitary violence as evidence of state illegitimacy and justification for their terrorist insurgency. The persistence of such contradictory perceptions of legitimacy along ethnic lines continues to underscore the agencies of competing groups following the establishment of peace. The deficits in legitimacy in this sense do not persist in a primordial, historical vacuum, but are (re)shaped or (re)constructed by contemporary political and social practices and structures within a given (post) conflict society (Smithey 2011; Brubaker and Laitin 1998; Finlayson 1999). In societies in which the political disputes underscoring conflict are unresolved, and there is no clear victor—as in Northern Ireland—perceptions of ethnopolitical threat, promoted by collective actors in either the state or civil society sectors, might compound or exacerbate other social, economic, and psychological insecurities rooted in the unique experiences of former combatants and thereby increase the likelihood that such individuals take preeminent actions to thwart that threat. Ex-combatants might experience disaffection while still maintaining enough power on local levels to take preeminent actions in countering perceived external and internecine threats to themselves and communities.

In NI, somewhat paradoxically, the strong participation of Republican and Loyalist ex-combatants in social reconstruction efforts has occurred *despite* weak investment by Unionist political elites and the British government.[3]

In fact, it was the capacity of one local NGO—the Community Foundation of Northern Ireland—to secure funding from the EU in support of ex-prisoner peacebuilding initiatives that facilitated their participation in the first place. Elected officials, and Unionists in particular have played minimal roles overall in supporting DDR, and established a variety of social and legal restrictions on ex-prisoners (Rolston 2007, 272). The British government, at the same time, has generally neglected such issues (CAJ 2016). For example, ex-prisoners cannot claim compensation for injuries under the Criminal Injuries legislation; they are typically denied loans for small businesses and mortgages; they are denied visas to travel abroad; and they are unable to adopt children (Ritchie 2002; Shirlow 2012). The NI Special Advisers Act

(SPAD), passed by the NI Assembly in 2013, functions as an additional piece of legislation targeting former prisoners convicted of politically motivated acts of violence, barring such persons from employment as high-paid "special advisers" to elected officials (Belfast Telegraph 2013). The bill received strong support across the Unionist parties (absent the PUP), who sought to remove former IRA prisoners from such posts under Sinn Fein. (Not surprisingly, Sinn Fein opposed the bill, and SDLP—a middle class Nationalist party with less sympathy toward the ex-prisoner community—abstained.) Such exclusionary practices remain common and underscore ex-paramilitary prisoners' sense of insecurity and the "limits of legitimacy" available to them, especially Loyalists (Mitchell 2008), who were also negatively impacted by SPAD. Indeed, even while Republican ex-prisoners are barred from such advisory positions, and from international travel and various social entitlements, they have comprised a significant number of Sinn Fein candidates since the first Assembly elections. (The pool of the ex-IRA prisoners running for elected office in NI is decreasing, however, as they get older, retire, or pass away.) Unlike Loyalist ex-prisoners, who are generally seen as "pariahs" within broader political Unionism, and remain active primarily in the community sector, Republican ex-prisoners have been active in *both* the community and political sectors, indicating the greater level of support received by the latter from within their ethnonational community. As the subsequent pages will show, the "limits of legitimacy" for Loyalist ex-combatants disproportionately are rooted (in part) in the political strategies of those intent on capitalizing on broader societal resentment toward the ex-prisoner population. In addition, neo-paramilitary cultures of hypermasculinity and concomitant avenues toward social status provide an important motivation for *some* ex-combatants' continued engagement in hostile street politics. The effects of exclusionary practices of the state do not continue independent of socio-structural gendered and class conditions, but are necessarily underscored by, and in turn reconstitute, such conditions.

EX-PRISONER PEACEBUILDING AND IDEOLOGICAL CONTINUITIES WITH THE PAST

Although respondents emphasize the problems of ex-combatant or ex-terrorist roles in the community sector disproportionately, as well as the persistence of hypermasculinist cultures, most nonetheless acknowledge that ex-paramilitary prisoners continue to make significant contributions to the peace process. In line with previous research, some point out that many in the Loyalist ex-prisoner community remain more willing to engage in cross-community work with Republicans—including ex-IRA militants—than agents of middle-class, "law and order" Unionism. According to a senior participant in the NGO peacebuilding sector,

> That's totally normalized in a way in which it wouldn't be for members of the Orange Order for example. They will be community leaders as well very often and have considerable respect in their communities, the ex-prisoners. What I'm trying to get at is quite a few of the Orange Order make a big deal about, "we wouldn't sit down with a residents group because there might be terrorists involved," whereas people who were actually out killing Catholics are quite happy to sit down with IRA men now. Its routine, it's normal. (Interview with author, Belfast center, June 2014)

Another respondent similarly indicated that ex-prisoner involvement in cross-community relation-building work surpasses that of politicians in many respects. He suggests that EPIC and Charter—UVF- and UDA-oriented ex-prisoner community organizations, respectively—are "producing material for schools and all kinds of things. That is an area where people who were armed and active are cooperating in a way that you don't find at a political level" (interview with author, North Belfast, June 2014). In an especially insightful account, a Republican community leader in Belfast discussed a variety of projects he has worked on in cooperation with Loyalist ex-prisoners. Such projects include cooperation with a local housing association to transform a derelict mill into an apartment complex housing both Protestant and Catholic families. The project was meant to meet housing needs of vulnerable members of both ethnoreligious communities in a non-exclusionary manner:

> The housing association built this property on the basis that myself and others did work within the area to make sure that that [absence of sectarian tension] was the case. So you have an area that, on Christmas day, had a riot, completely, utterly transformed over a few years, because of relationship building and because of breaking down barriers, and strong willpowers of [Republican and Loyalist] people who are working together. (Interview with author, North Belfast, May 2014)

The same respondent explained how he, in cooperation with Loyalists from Tigers Bay—a working-class Protestant estate—moved a sectarian bonfire away from a volatile interface, reducing the likelihood of sectarian violence. Although many respondents conveyed criticism of ex-paramilitary community leaders in a variety of respects, many also felt obligated to admit that the work undertaken by some of them at volatile interfaces has been integral to the peace process. The response of one woman from a North Belfast Protestant community is a case in point:

I'm involved in funding what is basically peace and reconciliation. But when things get really difficult, I'm at home watching TV like everyone else. The people who are out on the street at the interface, trying to stop the kids getting into rioting or situations are the ex-combatants, the ones that have already been to prison. They have a voice that can be heard. They've definitely played a role in that. Some parts of the community aren't recognized for it. There's also the thing about, why is the burden still on them? (Interview with author, June 2020)

Some respondents suggest that ex-prisoners are driven by co-ethnics into fundamental community roles for which they receive inadequate recognition, resulting from broader community norms associating leadership qualities with ethnomasculinist identities. A similar view is conveyed by a Loyalist, who indicates how

many communities still feel some kind of . . . I don't want to say affection for them, but they still feel there's a need for them to protect them. They are given some security in their communities. There is that tension that exists at the moment. There's sometimes an overadulation of former combatants, but that says more about the community from which they come. (Interview with author, June 2020)

A Nationalist ex-combatant similarly contends that, because "people are still determined by what they did before rather than what they do in the moment now, in the present," their reputation, linked to political violence during the Troubles, actually puts pressure on ex-combatants to fill voids in community-based peacekeeping roles when tensions rise (interview with author, May 2021).

Others admit that some residents in working-class communities, where paramilitary vigilantism continues, have a difficult time fully transitioning to a more "democratic" form of criminal justice that they perceive as procedurally too slow and ineffective. Historically, paramilitaries in both Republican and Loyalist communities became *default* informal police forces, exercising vigilante justice on behalf of complainants who lived in the same neighborhoods. During the Troubles, the RUC was invested primarily in conflict mitigation, and had little-to-no legitimacy in Nationalist communities. Several respondents note that fear and intimidation by paramilitaries explains their ongoing influence, though most nonetheless suggest that a degree of voluntary support from "the community" still remains. As a Nationalist respondent working in reconciliation work comments, paramilitaries currently

get some [support] but it wouldn't be substantial. But the difficulty is, when there's somebody in your street and you've got young children around, dealing drugs and you want it stopped and the police want evidence to arrest the person, that takes time and by the time they get the person through the criminal justice system, your kid could be on drugs. You remember a time where you can go to a person up the street, and say, "can you deal with this guy who's dealing my kid drugs?" and it's dealt with there and then. You can understand why a community might not want to go back where we were but still might want some justice as it was before. And justice through policing doesn't seem as effective. I can fully understand why. If I was a parent of a teenage child, I'd want somebody to do something about that guy. (Interview with author, west Belfast, May 2014)

Others explain how ex-combatants are maintaining "leadership" roles despite some decline in state and international funding for the community sector and their ongoing exclusion from various state entitlements and employment opportunities. For example, a Sinn Fein councillor describes how

over the last few years, it's been much more difficult for ex-prisoners, as a sector, to do a lot because their funding has been removed and they're still fighting . . . a fight around issues about insurance, issues about getting a job, issues about their family members maybe [being prevented from] joining the police. All that's just ridiculous at this point in a peace process. But . . . in terms of playing leadership, in terms of ensuring that there's a sensible head . . . they are people who can be looked up to in many ways. No matter if anyone thinks that's right or wrong, it's the truth. (Interview with author, May 2020)

Even those Republican respondents who openly resent Loyalist ex-prisoners and paramilitaries admit that some have played integral roles in sustaining relative peace. Such positive agencies, however, are exercised within contexts in which traditional, ethnocentric identities and ideologies are simultaneously celebrated and reified with reference to histories of ethnopolitical violence in the broader Republican and Loyalist communities. For example, one respondent explains how "some individuals [with histories of paramilitarism] have had a positive influence. . . . The one thing they can do is speak to more hardline individuals who would be less likely to negotiate. They would respect them in driving change" (interview with author, East Belfast, May 2014). The normative, masculinist ethnocultures of former *male* paramilitary prisoners integrally involved in the community-based peacebuilding sector are implicitly legitimized via reference to their histories of political violence and the respect such histories elicit from "hardline individuals" (among others) in the broader communities.

Moreover, echoing a point made by other respondents, one Republican community leader involved in a variety of peacebuilding ventures emphasizes that cross-community work intended to transform political ideologies is rare and, for most, undesirable. Rather, such ideologies are linked affectively with loyalty to comrades who fought and were killed in the conflict:

Even though the constitutional question here, and your ethnicity, and whether your allegiance is to Britain or to an all-Ireland—even though that has been the basis that has driven us to conflict over the years—they're still genuine aspirations. So I don't think any of us would want to work to an end goal where we water down our own aspirations. . . . At the end of the day, many people here fought, killed, went to jail for, died for, those beliefs. So why would you want to get rid of them? (Interview with author, North Belfast, May 2014)

Ingroup loyalty contributes to the reconstitution of ethnopolitical binaries, the sublimation of alternative political priorities and alliances, and concomitantly, the reproduction of normative "post-conflict" masculinities. More generally, respondents from both Republican and Loyalist backgrounds suggest that the ultimate political goals of both Loyalist and Republican ex-combatant communities generally remain mutually exclusive and that—as one Nationalist respondent put it—"putting aside the constitutional question is not something" they are willing to do (interview with author, North Belfast, May 2014). Loyalty to dead comrades underscores much of the resistance to a transition to more political forms of cross-community cooperation. Another respondent comments on how "this notion of betrayal of former comrades or whatever . . . brings with it guilt. If you're going to engage with another person who was formerly the enemy, there's a guilt associated with that. . . . But we can't talk about that" (interview with author, West Belfast, June 2014). According to a senior community leader, the narrow political agenda of ex-combatants involved in peacebuilding generally reflects a broader trend, in which "these groups [are] doing this [peacebuilding and restorative justice work] through the lens of a single identity" (interview with author, Co Antrim, May 2014). While former paramilitaries have contributed significantly to the peace process in a variety of capacities, the transformation of traditional ethnopolitical objectives, in most cases, is not one of them. Cooperation between (former) members of Loyalist and Republican groups does not generally translate into goals of transforming ethnocentric, political ideologies or building cross-community *political* alliances with the Other.

At the same time, the reproduction of mutually exclusive politics and ethnoreligious segregation on local levels is largely a result of underlying cultural, gendered motivations, reflecting the marginalization of female influence following the initial establishment of "peace." According to one female community leader, ex-paramilitary prisoner groups

have good leaders. [But] they've been preceded by an army of female leaders who were moved out of positions of influence as the ceasefires happened gradually, when jobs [in the community sector] became available. And that was obvious when we were organizing community meetings, that it was women [leading]. After the ceasefires started . . . some of that was about people feeling safe and some of that was about people taking a step back and other people deciding that they needed to take more [control]. [Consequently] there's a whole history of [women] organizing and building work on common issues and soldiering along through difficult times that is therefore lost and not held by the new people. . . . Fifteen years on, why is "ex combatant" the key determinant feature of why someone is seen as a leader in an area? That seems to be a very skewed form of analysis of political or civil leadership. (Interview with author, West Belfast, May 2014)

Similarly, according to another female respondent, "in terms of the peace process, there's certainly a theory out there that a lot of the work was initiated by women and women's organizations. And then men followed through and took over what was happening. . . . The movement doesn't [exist] in the same way . . . I wouldn't see the women still very much part of making things happen" (interview with author, Belfast city center, May 2014). Although some disagreed with this perspective, many female respondents emphasize how the grassroots peacemaking efforts led in many ways by women would subsequently transition to a peacebuilding phase coopted by men, including ex-paramilitaries uneasy about their future roles in the society. While they filled central roles in public life during the height of conflict, peace brings a potential loss in status for such individuals who also tend to face bleak employment prospects as a result of their criminalized status. The takeover of community roles marked a *partial* turn away from militarized masculinities and transition to peacebuilding masculinities. Although ex-prisoners have made important contributions to the peace process, the marginalization of women in community leadership positions restricts the transformative potential of the peace process. In this sense, the transition from "conflict" to "post-conflict" masculinities is incomplete and has, at least in certain respects, entered a liminal stage.

EX-COMBATANT COMMUNITY CONTROL AND THE PATRIARCHY OF PEACE IN WORKING-CLASS BELFAST

Respondents' in-depth descriptions of their experiences working with and observing the ex-prisoner community implicates masculinist cultural prerogatives of power and control as partially underscoring both the violent and nonviolent activities of some (former) male paramilitaries involved in peacebuilding and CBRJ. One female community leader, for example, explains how limited development in the innovation of peacebuilding projects has much to do with "leadership within the communities. . . . A lot of it is men, and a lot of it is people who were at war ten years ago and they're still in learning curves." She elaborates on how "just because you happen to be a former paramilitary doesn't make you good at this stuff. They still have a crude measurement of their politics and their ethnicity and all of those issues" (interview with author, West Belfast, May 2014).

At the same time, some paramilitary elements maintain a quite hostile political presence in ways that are counterproductive to the creation of cross-community integration or the transformation of identity politics. In 2010, in response to the murder of a dissident Loyalist by the UVF, Dawn Purvis, the only elected official of the PUP serving in the NI Assembly at the time, resigned. She cited the obstruction the UVF poses to the PUP's ability to serve its constituency effectively as one reason for her resignation. Jeanette Cunningham, the widow of the former head of the PUP, David Ervine, added that Purvis "suffered from a macho culture where some Loyalists might not have listened to the female politician" (Irish Times 2010).

The same culture of paramilitarism provides means through which former leaders in the conflict can retain power and status amid their criminalization and stigmatization. Not coincidentally, female respondents offer most detail on this point. One such respondent commented on ongoing "punishment attacks" or violent vigilantism as one example:

> Remember, these [ex-paramilitaries] were the somebodies of yesterday who are the nobodies of today in the peace process . . . [T]hey weren't a part of the political process, and they were used to having this power base, and being able to keep control. . . . And we still have communities where there is huge paramilitary existence. And those people really haven't seen peace because there is still that threat and fear. . . . I had huge concerns around Community Restorative Justice. I've seen that meted out in totally inappropriate ways in my community. People pretending to be around Community Restorative Justice, you know, turning up where there was a group of young people standing, and then taking the baseball bats out and [with] the balaclavas on and just, you know, beating them nearly into submission. (Interview with author, South Belfast, June 2014)

Several respondents emphasize the issue of ex-paramilitary prisoner desire for control and power as driving the participation of some members in peace process initiatives, ultimately restricting its scope. According to one respondent, ex-prisoner participation in community-based restorative justice schemes is "still about this control within a community. So 'we control the purse strings,' so 'we say what service goes in and what service doesn't.' It goes back to that rather than what is actually in need in the community" (interview with author, Belfast city center, May 2014). Another respondent, also highlighting the issue of control, described how a young person who wanted to initiate an educational community project for underprivileged youth ultimately gave up due to resistance by a local paramilitary "community leader" who was unhappy that the young person did not go to him first for permission:

> when they went back to their old community [for approval], the head boy from the paramilitary then put the form together that said, "we exclude these people, we don't deal with them. They went above our heads, and they went to government, and they were . . . " And that was it. And the young person who had no skills, who was trying to help support the young people in the area, all of a sudden didn't bother any more. So that has to tell you something. (Interview with author, South Belfast, June 2014)

In another example, a respondent describes what she considers "the worst of community restorative justice [she had] ever seen":

> A pensioner's house was broken into and the young person was identified, and [representatives from] the Community Restorative Justice, and the elderly person, went to the father, who was connected to paramilitaries. And the next thing was CRJ was putting a petition around the area to get the elderly woman out of her home. So the community, for once, was up in arms and saying "this is not happening. It's not appropriate." And the best part about it was the paramilitary person rang the police and said he was being harassed by these people. (Interview with author, South Belfast, June 2014)

The issue of ex-paramilitary "community leaders'" control on neighborhood levels is also exemplified by one respondent's account of the organization of schools in a working-class Protestant community in South Belfast. Not only are schools generally segregated by religion, but there is a noticeable extent of fragmentation between the different subgroups within the working-class Protestant community, each corresponding to the influence of distinct paramilitary factions (Loyalist Volunteer Force [LVF], UVF, and UDA):

> You have a Protestant community, but there's [*sic*] three communities in the one community—Sandy Row area and the Village. You've got the LVF, UVF, and UDA and they're all there. . . . You have three separate schools. You have 400 children; 155 of them have special needs. And what better way to break that cycle than bringing those children together and educating them, because the schools aren't fit. . . . They can't agree on a site. There's room on one of the schools to build a big enough school for everybody, but the other two lots have to agree. (Interview with author, Belfast city center, May 2014)

Elaborating on problems of funding community-based organizations led by the same groups, the same respondent explains how they're competing now because the plots are getting smaller and smaller. Government should have said, "look, here's what is needed in this area. If you can come together collectively, and work in partnership to make sure it's delivered, then the money can be mainstreamed through government." But it never happened. Because if you do away with three organizations into one, then who's going to head the one? (Interview with author, Belfast city center, May 2014)

Such competition over local leadership roles in community-based organizations reflects the imperative of maintaining a sense of social status through masculinist practices (competition) and goals (power and control). The aforementioned dynamics underscored by ethnocultures of masculinity restrict the scope of change participants will pursue, and silence the voices of potentially innovative contributors to social and political transformation. As the previous quote suggests, moreover, this process helps reproduce structures of ethnoreligious segregation and fragmentation which more generally act as long-term impediments to intergroup interdependency and trust. Several respondents suggest that the creation of an "industry" in "peace consultancy" made the peace process overly dependent, paradoxically, on the perpetuation of paramilitaries historically opposed to political compromise with the Other. As one woman and prominent community leader explains:

I've been involved in the women's sector and rights for women. And the peace monies—they're spending something like £6.25 on children and £3.20 on women and £120 on ex-prisoners. You know, so they're creating an industry for ex-prisoners. . . . But also, if the paramilitaries have gone away, how can we still have this ongoing industry of ex-prisoners, you know? (Interview with author, South Belfast, May 2014)

Like other post-conflict societies in transition (Potter 2008) reforms intended to promote greater inclusion of women in conflict transformation initiatives do not take priority in NI. While there are grassroots organizations working to empower women, they receive relatively little financial support in comparison with other organizations. Another respondent, who also works to empower women in working-class PUL communities, explains how "a massive investment" in paramilitary-led "community groups" continues to disincentivize transition away from paramilitary identifications: "That investment is still there. When do you stop it? I've had this conversation with paramilitaries. When do you stop being a paramilitary? It seems now you don't. . . . It's not a few people running around. It's quite a lot of people using the cover" of paramilitary membership to exploit peace funds (interview with author, May 2020). The marginalization of women and children reflected in the allocation of peace monies is hardly coincidental to the reconsolidation of men's power in community roles and the concomitant masculinization of "community leadership." Paradoxically, ex-paramilitary prisoners have retained "community leader" status in peacebuilding largely *because* of their (former) paramilitary ties, while such a process has, in turn, helped to reconstitute the legitimacy of paramilitary organizations and, accordingly, the imperative of sustaining them. While such practices have provided an avenue for men with histories of violence to obtain employment and exert influence in working-class communities, some of the women in the same communities have consequently become re-marginalized and re-silenced. The importance of membership in paramilitary and community organizations is also underscored by ex-combatants' exclusion from full citizenship and the social entitlements it entails as well as the marginalization of the broader working-class communities in which they tend to reside and exert the most influence.

EX-PRISONER ALIENATION AND THE CONTINGENCIES OF PEACE

The formal labeling of political ex-prisoners convicted of violent offenses cuts them off from alternative channels of social mobility while displacing their sense of political agency. Although they gain income and influence within community-based NGOs the opportunities available through such organizations are limited and, given impending budget cuts, increasingly uncertain (see chapter 6). Indeed, interview data do not indicate that ex-combatants feel particularly empowered by their agencies in the voluntary sector. The structural restrictions on social entitlements and perceived contempt from political elites are fostering alienation and resentment toward mainstream Unionism among Loyalist ex-paramilitaries in particular. Such trends risk influencing the latter to opt out of important grassroots peacekeeping and peacebuilding work or even exploit positions in the community sector for their personal interests. (Although seemingly less widespread, such trends are also indicated by respondents to be ongoing problems in Republican communities.) Loyalist respondents cited here demonstrate a strong understanding of the political dynamics underscoring their social exclusion and sense of socio-political abandonment. When commenting on ex-prisoner disenfranchisement, a Loyalist suggests that the aforementioned state practices are spearheaded by, and in the political interests of, the two largest Unionist parties, DUP and UUP. According to him, "they see that as coming down strongly against the IRA. But they do it with a nod and a wink to their own [ex-prisoner] community: 'Don't think we mean you. It may affect you, but we don't really mean you.' Basically they don't care" (Interview with author, West Belfast, June 2014). During the Troubles, elected Unionist politicians incited paramilitary violence indirectly through coded speeches (Bruce 1986; Bruce 2007) and directly in private interactions with Loyalist paramilitary leaders (Rowthorn 1981, 27). Most of the same politicians, predominantly from privileged middle-class backgrounds, have publicly oversimplified Republican *and* Loyalist terrorism as "driven by a small number of 'men of violence' with criminal and psychopathic tendencies, rather than in response to any wider structural or ideological contexts" (Shirlow 2012, 3). Ultimately, the exploitation and criminalization of ex-combatants by elected Unionist officials continues to undermine the latter's faith in the political process, especially Loyalists'. According to one ex-prisoner, "the only thing that's going to sort that out is when they [ex-prisoners] all die off" (interview with author, West Belfast, June 2014). Another Loyalist explains how while former paramilitary prisoners may receive "a pat on the back from the Justice Minister" for leading in restorative justice programs, there is a perception of exploitation, since "that's the same people who can't go to America with their families; who can't get house insurance; who can't adopt a child—all because of their political background" (interview with author, West Belfast, June 2014).

However, others suggest that some ex-prisoners' personal interests in the continuation of peace funding, made especially integral in the context of their political, social, and economic marginalization, often takes a greater priority than actually effecting conflict transformation. Respondents from the community and public sectors concur that the results of ex-combatant reintegration and peacebuilding in particular have consequently been quite ambiguous. According to a woman from a Nationalist community in Belfast, ex-prisoners are essentially given the message not to

> join the political process, but . . . apply for a bit of funding and you can start this community organization, so you've got a job and an income. . . . When we look at the thousands and thousands of pounds that have been pumped into West Belfast, and we're no better off . . . So what was that money doing all those years? If we still have young people doing racist attacks and sectarian attacks, then what was it achieving? (Interview with author, West Belfast, June 2014)

A woman from a Protestant community in South Belfast recalls a conversation she had with a former combatant that similarly implicates ex-combatant manipulation of community-based peace funding. As she observes, from a security perspective,

> It's just been a process where it started out almost as, "Here's our way of paying you." I remember asking an ex-combatant one time, "What do you do with this money?" They say, "Well, it keeps us from the night in the streets and causing trouble." I said, "They're actually paying you not to do the activities that you're doing?" In a sense, I think that that's what it is. They [the state and international donors] never got a grip. (Interview with author, May 2020)

The overreliance of former paramilitary prisoners on the voluntary sector for employment and social status is, in important respects, counterproductive. Apparently, money from the International Fund of Ireland (IFI) and EU Peace Funds "deliberately targeted communities who historically have suffered from deprivation," but have also "provided a bedrock of support for the various paramilitary factions" (Byrne 2011, 11). Respondents, including Loyalist ex-prisoners involved in peacebuilding, describe a situation in which peace monies are regularly extorted by hardline elements that use the threat of violence to sustain a stream of revenue. Respondents simultaneously convey criticism of the government's lack of vision in how it allocates funding, and its failure to promote projects which could truly resolve issues in ways which eventually eliminate the need for ex-paramilitary-led peacekeeping projects in the future. Given the dynamics of provocation promoted by ethnopolitical entrepreneurs (as discussed in the preceding and subsequent chapters) the restrictive nature of state-sponsored, top-down peace funding is not surprising. Moreover, eliminating the need for such work might threaten the social and economic interests of various actors within the broader "peace industry," including the ex-prisoner community. As a senior leader in the community peacebuilding sector explains,

> it's not always about throwing money at a problem, which is what we did. The government here uses the stick and plaster approach. Every time a crisis appears, throw money at it, stick a stick of plaster on it, and go away for a while, instead of getting to the bottom of what's going on and why communities feel the way they do and what we need to be able to do to help them out of that. How do you turn all that negative energy into something positive, so that they have a community that they're proud of, that they want to regenerate, that they want to be part of, to be proper leaders in, rather than a dictatorship for want of a better word? And in some instances that has kind of happened, and it's still about this control. (Interview with author, South Belfast, May 2014)

Indeed, some evidence suggests that neo-paramilitary elements effectively manipulate this "stick and plaster" approach to funding community-based initiatives. Apparently, it is assumed by such actors that if authorities witness bouts of violence and disorder, the threat remains real and thus the services of ex-paramilitary prisoners in peacekeeping remain warranted. As one Loyalist ex-prisoner maintains, "If other ones are seeing that violence is being rewarded, what incentive does that give them to stop the violence" (interview with author, West Belfast, June 2014). A community worker from the Short Strand area of East Belfast offers his own allegation of Loyalist paramilitary extortion of peace monies:

I see some of them who are very positive, without a doubt. But I see others, who are called "community leaders" who are agitators. . . . If the UVF tell them to send kids down to smash cars up, they will do it. In fact, I was talking with them one time, and said "since you're saying kids are causing trouble because there's sectarian squabbling and you're getting no money into your community, why don't we make a joint effort to get money into our communities in general?" When it comes to it, they don't go through with it. They think that by causing trouble at the interfaces, the British Government will pour more money into their communities. They will get a community worker and a paid job. (Interview with author, East Belfast, June 2014)

Incidentally, the preceding statement reflects a dynamic that is seemingly taken for granted but nonetheless important: the very fact that a self-proclaimed hardline Republican would be conversing with former Loyalist paramilitaries, who might have killed him twenty years prior, reflects evidence of the impressive depth of conflict transformation that has occurred. At the same time, the marginal social locations occupied by ex-prisoners outside cross-community-projects, restricting access to alternative agencies, help shape counterproductive, self-interested practices and motivations to maintain status within the shadows of the political apparatus—especially given the increasing uncertainty of funding amid the UK's neoliberal and isolationist agenda. One respondent, who works at a youth-focused, cross-community organization, similarly suggests that an ex-prisoner community leader in North Belfast organized attacks on a Protestant estate to escalate talks over peace money. Ironically, one Loyalist he implicated was the same identified by another, Nationalist respondent as an important person in grassroots, cross-community peacebuilding networks. (The same Loyalist ex-prisoner he referred to was attacked by rival UDA members shortly before the interview, following his alleged complicity in a nonfatal shooting of a "dissident loyalist") (Black 2014). This interviewee referred to Loyalist ex-prisoners' tenuous promise to monitor the behavior of Loyalist crowds in order to obtain funding and state permission for annual sectarian bonfires. He asserts that "the Loyalists want violence. People will throw money at them to stop it" (interview with author, West Belfast, May 2014). Some also identify the ongoing financial support for former paramilitaries through community-based peace funding as symptomatic of the lack of government vision on how to finally dismantle paramilitary structures and the cycles of conflict they facilitate. A different respondent claims that a similar dynamic takes place within Republican communities, in which "some guys keep dissident groups going to keep their [British] informant positions" (interview with author, North Belfast, June 2014).

When asked if those former paramilitaries involved in community peace-building are disconnected from disruptive paramilitary activities, another interviewee answered that

> They would like you to think that. . . . What the UVF and the UDA seem to have deteriorated into is a lot of gangsters and criminals. I understand them saying this isn't the old UDA, this isn't the old UVF [that is involved in crime and street disorder]. I have to tell you, those organizations haven't gone away. The extent to which criminality still happens and people fall into debt and are kneecapped, and the threats in both communities, is still there. (Interview with author, May 2020)

Many suggest that there is significant overlap in the membership of ex-combatants in community-based peacebuilding and restorative justice organizations, and paramilitary groups. The boundary separating "legitimate" and "illegitimate" community activists in this respect is quite opaque. A PUL respondent who works to reintegrate ex-combatants explains how

> A lot of people hide behind that [paramilitary title] or conveniently put people into the little pigeonholes because of the whole Troubles thing, without the understanding that a criminal would have been a criminal, with or without the political Troubles behind that. We don't even separate that either. The failure to do it at the moment and look at paramilitaries as opposed to organized crime is hampering people leaving the whole Troubles behind. . . . In Northern Ireland, it becomes gray and fluffy, because we can't tell the difference between a para-military and a criminal. (Interview with author, May 2021)

While "criminals" have effectively adopted paramilitary titles and used them "as a comfort blanket" to evade arrest and prosecution, former paramilitary militants *not* involved in illicit activities have become seen increasingly as criminal, compounding their sense of stigmatization. Others, who traverse the boundary between roles of pseudo-paramilitary actor and "community leader" contribute to the problematic conflation of political paramilitarism and criminal gangsterism. A Loyalist respondent explains how

> there is a gray area within Northern Ireland that doesn't exist in other parts of the United Kingdom or in the Republic of Ireland. I personally feel our govern-ments aren't mature enough to even begin to deal with those issues. To say, "Right guys, it's over. From now on, you've had a chance to transform, to go back to your communities, to do whatever you need to do. From tomorrow if you're caught, you're a criminal and will be dealt with as a criminal," which would take a lot of the political shenanigans that we face here out of the whole system when people do things. People want this comfort blanket around them

that if things go wrong, they've got their little private army jumping up and down going, "We'll fix it for you." (Interview with author, June 2020)

As a Nationalist respondent similarly commented,

If, when we signed the Good Friday Agreement, it was about a seismic shift in the way we did things and people agreed to that, then there shouldn't be any paramilitaries and they certainly shouldn't be recruiting, no, because they're still deemed by the government as being on a prescribed list of illegal organizations. Of course they still exist, but the government has to take that step and say, "It's finished. No, you're an organized crime gang. That's all you are," but they won't do that either. (Interview with author, May 2021)

Adding to the complicated nature of this problem is the apparent fact, "certainly, in terms of Republican paramilitaries, that there's a very faint line between politics and the workings of those organizations" (interview with author, May 2020).

Without rationalizing aggressive behavior and criminality, however, it is important to acknowledge that ex-combatant and paramilitary influence occurs within broader contexts of exclusion over which neither they nor "their" broader working-class communities have much control. Such contexts include not only state policies targeting former combatants specifically, but the broader persistence of poverty and inopportunity in the communities in which they reside, and which have historically experienced disproportionate levels of sectarian and political violence. Respondents emphasize how poor conditions in working-class communities substantially impact the political mentalities and practices of (former) paramilitaries. Some Loyalists, for example, while elaborating on the deprivation experienced within their neighborhoods, espouse a belief that the main Unionist parties exploit them to maintain order while ignoring the underlying social and economic problems which compound intercommunity tensions and episodic (low-intensity) violence. As one ex-UVF prisoner commented, "The DUP doesn't care about the working-class community. They only care about us when it comes to getting the votes. They need to be coming in [to our communities]. They can ring us and say 'there's trouble at the interface.' Fine, we go. But if trouble goes on, [they'll say] 'it was your fault' or 'you didn't help it'" (interview with author, West Belfast, June 2014). According to another ex-UVF prisoner, "people know that politicians aren't interested in fixing things. . . . They're more interested in bickering about things that doesn't really matter . . . [like] the education of our children" (interview with author, West Belfast, June 2014).

According to respondents within and outside Loyalist networks, the deficit in services and opportunities for working-class Protestants actually sustains a bedrock for neo-paramilitary power. According to one respondent, because of the neglect of the issues of concern in working-class communities by Unionist and British politicians in particular, there is "a level of community support or at least acquiescence that allows [paramilitary elements] . . . to be in that place" of community influence (interview with author, May 2020). Loyalist respondents also referred to the more negative treatment they receive from broader Unionism compared with what Republican ex-prisoners experience from within Nationalism, when explaining why some of their colleagues continue to engage in illicit activities. As one former UVF prisoner explains,

> going back to the Good Friday Agreement and what happened there and the cease-fires, after that was done, Tony Blair come out and says he would look after Republicans and the chief constable come out and says he would look after the Loyalists. At that very beginning, they were grouped into that category. They [Loyalists] were involved in criminality, where Republicans are all going to go wearing suits and ties and go in the [unintelligible 00:45:23] and being treated differently. No, we're not naïve. Those with the suits and ties had guns in their hands at one time. You know what I mean? We know that. They were treated differently and they were allowed to be treated differently and that got up the nose of some Loyalists, which then in turn made it easier for them to get involved in the criminality type things, because they could say, "I'm sure that we're going to get it blamed on us anyway, so we might as well do it." They were treated differently. (Interview with author, June 2020)

Loyalist ex-combatants acknowledge their exploitation by Unionist political elites, who rely on them to maintain order in marginalized communities but also contribute legislatively to their stigmatization to avoid being seen by middle-class Unionism as sympathetic to "terrorists."[4] As one Loyalist ex-paramilitary prisoner and DDR activist explains, Republicans are "more benevolent to seeking ways of engagement with each other than necessarily some of our own Unionist politicians are internally within our own communities with groups like ours" (interview with author, June 2020). As established in previous chapters, Unionism's historical ideology that the pro-British Unionist state holds sole monopoly on the legitimate use of violence puts it in conflict with the interests of extra-state Loyalist groups with histories of political violence. To balance their political interest in displaying such "law and order" Unionism with the interest of sustaining cooperation from Loyalist paramilitary elements, who maintain political influence in some working-class communities, a dual, contradictory strategy of Loyalist exclusion and affirmation is exercised by Unionist politicians—a strategy identified by PUL respondents as one cause of their broader "disillusionment" with the state. In the words of one Loyalist ex-paramilitary prisoner,

When it comes to ex-prisoners and ex-combatants, there's a lot of disillusionment. Recently there was a fella elected in Coleraine. I read the headlines: "a Loyalist elected: ex long-term UVF prisoner elected in Coleraine." They know who Martin McGuinness is. They know who Gerry Kelly is. They are all ex-IRA prisoners. But that's not what they're seen as. They're seen as the peacemakers. But when a Loyalist steps forward and comes out, even DUP shuns them out. When it suits them they help them out, and when it doesn't suit you, you shun them. (Interview with author, West Belfast, June 2014)

Some Loyalists implicate broader concerns regarding class power as underscoring the "shafting" of progressive Loyalist ex-paramilitary prisoners following the Agreement. As noted by one,

former political prisoners coming back into their communities do not have the route of politicization that Republican former combatants do by easily segueing into the machine of Sinn Féin. In PUL communities, the same luxury does not exist. There is no defined route for former political activists during the conflict, particularly those that took up arms . . . because nobody wants us. The early successes following the Good Friday Agreement of the Progressive Unionist Party was cemented in that feel-good factor after the cease-fires and after the profiles being risen of people like David Ervine and Billy Hutchinson, who were elected to that first legislative assembly. . . . Unfortunately, they were [later] shafted within their own community by their so-called own. Mainstream Unionism saw this threat from working-class Loyalism and quickly sought to deter it. That's what they did. As they did in the past, they began to bad-mouth those political activists like Ervine and Hutchinson and others because of their past and were able in some way to build this momentum that demonized people like them because of what they had done in the past. (Interview with author, June 2020)

The "progressive" UVF/PUP wing of Loyalism certainly engaged in violence against Catholic communities but later stood down rival Loyalist elements (such as, the LVF) which sought to derail peace negotiations in the 1990s and early 2000s. In fact, there is a long history of progressive Loyalism dating back to the early 1970s, when UVF leaders Gusty Spence and David Ervine, after engaging with IRA militants during their incarceration in Long Kesh prison, developed a critical class consciousness and opposition to sectarian Unionist politics which had traditionally fractured the broader working-class along ethnoreligious lines (see Novosel 2013; Cassidy 2008). Early in the peace process, the PUP openly challenged the DUP's self-defined role as the party of working-class Protestant Loyalism, and criticized DUP leaders for refusing to consider negotiating with Nationalists on a way toward peace after the 1994 ceasefires (McAuley 1997). Indeed, "peace" would not have occurred as it did if not for those former Loyalist combatants involved in the Agreement's design, who understood the need to accept that concessions to

Irish Republicans would be necessary to achieve any long-term cessation of violence. Thus, in some ways, those Loyalists involved in peacebuilding were "more visionary than most Unionists, and aware of the need to undermine the perniciousness of conflict on behalf of civic society through taking political risks" (Shirlow 2012, 13). It was this very willingness to "take political risks" that presented a significant threat to middle-class Unionism. Referring to mainstream Unionist politicians, another Loyalist describes how

> they can't seek to engage actively [with former paramilitary prisoners] because they run the risk of sounding like they're condoning what I did in the past. They can't ride two horses, so to speak, by criticizing Republicanism for their muck-ing outside the law and not doing the same with Unionism or with Loyalism, so what they do is they tar us with the one brush. . . . Jim Allister, who's been quite high profile within mainstream Unionism—he brought a bill to the floor to stop anyone with a criminal record of holding a position of Special Advisor to the Ministerial Portfolio within the Executive. The irony of that is you could have spent 20 years in prison as a political prisoner, be released, get elected to the Assembly, hold a Ministerial Portfolio—for example, education—and you can implement the policies to the rest of your tenure. But if you're not elected, you cannot hold a position of a Special Advisor to that elected person. It's almost a contradiction. He has implemented that, preventing . . . people like me, tak-ing up any special advisory role irrespective of how experienced or qualified I may be. These are policies being implemented that further discriminate against people with the background like myself. (Interview with author, June 2020)

Clearly, Loyalists are not oblivious to processes of their exploitation by Unionist political elites, contributing to the ambiguity of mainstream Unionist parties' legitimacy in PUL communities. This contrasts with the experience of many Republican ex-prisoners, who are more accepted within the Nationalist community than Loyalists are within broader Unionism. While Sinn Fein has presented itself more convincingly than other NI parties as a "progressive" party working in the interest of economically marginalized persons, dissent among dissident Republicans, including former IRA mili-tants now disenchanted with the peace process, has presented some internal conflict over the political direction of Nationalism. Top Sinn Fein leaders come from working-class Catholic communities and maintain intimate con-nections to these communities. On the one hand this connection contributes to Sinn Fein's legitimacy among the Catholic working classes; but it also makes them vulnerable to criticisms from anti-Agreement Republicans of betrayal for their cooperation with neoliberal Unionist and British elites. Although most Republicans remain loyal to Sinn Fein at the polls, many also sympa-thize with some of the dissidents' complaints. As one Republican explains, some former IRA prisoners, now serving as elected Sinn Fein officials, and once referred to in his community as "blanket men, when they went on the dirty protests," are now referred to by some Republicans as "banquet men, as all they seem to do is go to banquets." He goes on to explain how his "comrades that live [in West Belfast] . . . agree that the working class is being left behind by the so-called peace process," and that Sinn Fein leaders are accommodating British interests in advancement of their political careers. As he explains further,

> I don't agree with the Sinn Fein political leadership. I think they have taken Republicanism down a road that no one ever envisioned they would go down. Meeting the British Queen for example, when there are 5,000 British troops in my country. I don't want them in my country. I will do anything possible to get rid of them. I would disagree with Sinn Fein. Maybe they would say they don't want them either but they're facilitating them now. I think they've gone from a working-class socialist to a catch-all party. Now they have career politicians and are trying to get rid of their baggage. (Interview with author, East Belfast, June 2014)

The same respondent identified Sinn Fein's joint effort with Unionists to reduce the corporate tax rate, and their openness to Westminster's austerity reform plans as examples of Sinn Fein's betrayal of Irish Republican ideology (see Coulter 2018). The move to the "center" by Sinn Fein is perceived by dissident critics as a move toward accommodating not only British rule in Ireland, but neoliberalism and austerity as well. Another Republican interviewee indicates that he

> would agree with street protests to highlight working-class inadequacies and how they've been left behind in the [peace] process. . . . I know people who can't send kids to school because they can't pay for their lunch and this is in my [East Belfast] community. In West Belfast, child poverty is the second highest in the UK. . . . West Belfast has an MP, they have countless numbers of assembly members, and they have hundreds of councilors. And yet, that area is statistically second [in the UK] for child poverty levels. So all this is very alien to me because I'm a socialist Republican and I don't know what Stormont is supposed to be doing. (Interview with author, North Belfast, June 2014)

Coupled with widespread experiences of "political policing" among dissident Republicans by a police force endorsed by Sinn Fein (Hearty 2018) these observations underscore the alienation from the peace process of some within the Republican ex-combatant community, including individuals involved in the community-based peace sector.

More generally, the marginalization of working-class communities, while helping maintain some extent of neo-paramilitary influence in one sense, also more broadly compounds the economic and social dislocation of former paramilitary prisoners who are simultaneously targeted by policies intended to permanently criminalize and disenfranchise them. The fact that there "has been no peace dividend" in terms of economic and social development for the working classes (as put by several respondents from both ethnoreligious communities), combined with ex-paramilitary prisoners' perceived unfair treatment by the state, helps intensify the latter's resolve to maintain power and control on neighborhood levels independent, or, in spite, of the state.

CONCLUSION

This chapter sought to trace the reconfigurations and reproductions of former combatants' ethnomasculinities in a society emerging from conflict and link such phenomena to broader political and social conditions. Findings illustrate how ex-paramilitary prisoners serve both productive and disruptive functions to Northern Ireland's peace process. In certain respects, findings mirror those from previous studies (McAuley, Tonge, and Shirlow 2010; Rolston 2007; Shirlow et al. 2005) which indicate how some ex-paramilitary prisoners consistently show genuine effort in facilitating cross-community cooperation, albeit on "nonpolitical" or "practical" matters. At the same time, the extent of the "transformative role of former prisoners in community-based reintegration" identified by Dwyer (2012, 274) is actually quite limited. To some degree, the contention that funding community organizations run by former combatants "replicates societal divisions" and reflects "ethnosocial power structures of paramilitarism" (Edwards and McGrattan 2013, 353) is, in certain respects, supported by the findings. Yet motivations to maintain such power structures are ultimately rooted in concomitant cultures of semi-militarized masculinities, state practices of exclusion, and social immobility in the working-class communities in which (former) paramilitaries live and work. Male ex-combatants' reassertion of power on neighborhood levels is rooted not only in mentalities of political threat, but also by cultural or masculinist motivations (power, control, etc.) that pervade the broader society, including political elites. Even among those former male paramilitaries who contribute positively to local peacebuilding initiatives, normative masculinities rooted in histories of violence largely underscore the "legitimacy" of their social power.

Former paramilitaries tend to rely on the voluntary sector for income and social status, a dynamic that is largely a result of their formal exclusion from employment, social entitlements, and travel. In one study, approximately 55 percent of ex-prisoner respondents in NI acknowledged being denied employment due to their history of imprisonment; and 81 percent of Loyalists from the same study stated that they experience economic problems (Jamieson, Shirlow, and Grounds 2010, 28–32). Rather than being passive in processes of their marginalization, neo-paramilitary networks, including ex-prisoners simultaneously involved in productive, community-based organizations, attempt to reclaim autonomy and status through ethnomasculinist practices of community control. In this respect, findings illustrate how post-conflict institutions which fail to address issues of gender and class inequities and promote a more generally inclusive society undermine positive reconfigurations or transitions in the cultures of masculinity. In this case, such dynamics compound the mutual mistrust and resentment between Republicans and Loyalists rooted in the lack of any comprehensive, state-based mechanism for reconciliation and dealing with the past (see also Rolston 2006; CAJ 2016). Partial memories of conflict which exclude the crimes of ingroup members and celebrate the sacrifices of fallen comrades remain integral to reconstituting the ethnopolitical solidarity and mutual exclusiveness of PUL and CNR identities.

Moreover, ethnopolitical elites, by their unwillingness or inability to promote social inclusion and reconciliation on the one hand, and exclusion of ex-prisoners from legitimate institutions, on the other, ensure not only the reliance of the latter on grassroots peacebuilding positions for income and social status but also sustain the very paramilitary networks to which they are variably linked and thus their capacity, somewhat paradoxically, to disrupt broader peacebuilding processes. Former paramilitary prisoners remain both "inside" and "outside" the political apparatus, deprived of formal channels of social mobility yet active in processes of informal (and sometimes violent) social control. Due in part to perceptions of the reformed judicial process as too slow and generally ineffective, there is some (albeit limited) support for violent vigilantism, which is used by paramilitary elements as much to reassert control over local communities, settle personal disputes, or provide cover for criminal activities as to exercise traditional modes of "justice" (Knox 2002; Jarman 2004; Ashe and Harland 2014). In some instances, young people charged with "antisocial behavior" are beaten or shot in the knees and ankles; and many have also been forced to leave the country or face the prospect of being killed.

More generally, the social and political status of ex-prisoners remains contingent on sustaining paramilitary networks and, concomitantly, their strategic place in the "peace consultancy industry." As several respondents acknowledge, being a former paramilitary prisoner has become in itself a qualifying rationale for participation in community-based initiatives. Yet their overdependency on the voluntary sector raises the incentive for some ex-paramilitary prisoners to sustain the very need for their "peace work," which may be effectively communicated to state authorities and external funders through extortion and violence. Hence, the overreliance on employment in the community sector, combined with their entrenchment within semi-militarized cultures of masculinity and sustained commitment to traditional, ethnopolitical objectives restricts the maturation of the peace process. At the same time, paramilitary control on neighborhood levels is facilitated by politicians' social and economic neglect of the broader working-class communities most impacted by legacies of violence, opening a power vacuum filled by neo-paramilitary elements. As a respondent quoted in chapter 2 indicated, the ongoing control paramilitaries exert in working-class Loyalist neighborhoods in particular "comes from the disconnect between [middle-class] political Unionism and [working-class] Loyalism; the paramilitaries become the default to get things done, to make things happen in their community."

At the same time, the exclusion of women from grassroots, "community-based" organizations, corresponding to the re-entrenchment of the power of former male paramilitaries is especially worrisome when considering that women had led in grassroots peace work prior to the Agreement (Ashe and Harland 2014, 754; on the central role of women in peacemaking more generally, see Levin and Rabrenovic 2004, 187–94). Such women could thus offer potentially valuable perspectives on important challenges to cross-community peacebuilding efforts while bringing the concerns of women to the forefront of political discourse. Women's experiences can shed pivotal insight into the role of unequal power relations in fueling ethnopolitical conflict (Guhathakurta 2008, 190). Women are especially capable of articulating the limitations in how "conflict resolution is currently devised and conducted," with particular insight into related problems connecting the private and public spheres (Gilmartin 2015, 72). An increasing prevalence of domestic violence and alcohol abuse, for example, is highlighted by Nationalist women ex-combatants in Gilmartin's study as indicative of the limitations of the peace process and the internal community struggles which pose negative implications for social and political transformation. Thus, their marginalization and silencing on both state and grassroots levels undermines "a more transformative and inclusive approach towards conflict resolution" (ibid., 72). While Sinn Fein has put more emphasis on gender equality than the Unionist parties, moreover, feminist politics has not gained significant traction even among this relatively "progressive" Nationalist party. As findings here suggest, the class-specific locations and identities of former combatants, and personal perceptions of, and relations with, the state, ultimately influence their relative (and often fluctuating) commitment to peacebuilding, while being inextricably linked to particular gendered norms and traditions (i.e., ethnomasculinities). At the onset of the Troubles and increase in sectarian violence, male paramilitaries' mobilization and self-ascribed roles as "defenders of the community" overshadowed the integral community roles of women, having long-term implications in shaping dominant discourses and memories of the conflict. Women "became framed as representing the vulnerability of the community that required male protection from the 'enemy,'" displacing their political voice within the respective ethnoreligious communities (Ashe and Harland 2014, 752; see also Peterson 1999). In societies emerging from conflict more generally, "ethnicity appears in part to be created, maintained and socialized through male control of gender identities," while "women's fundamental human rights and dignity are often caught up in male power struggles" (Handrahan 2004, 429). In NI, like other (post) conflict societies, "ethnic dividends" (Cockburn 2004, 35), or the advantages that might accrue to individuals due to their membership in a particular ethnic or nationalist group, have also been mostly "patriarchal dividends." Apparently, advantages *still* seem to accrue mostly to men, "as individuals and as a collectivity, from a gender order in which men and [semi-militarized] masculinity are dominant" (Cockburn 2004, 34).

At the same time, evidence of state hostility toward the ex-prisoner community reflects a broader trend of domination politics spearheaded by ethnopolitical opportunists. Because ex-combatants are the "most visible concentration of everything that people feel about the conflict," including resentment and blame, political discourse surrounding "prisoner release and reintegration is one that tends to highlight and exacerbate the differences between the dominant ideologies" of opposing ethnonational groups and is symptomatic of a key obstacle in the "struggle to resolve these differences in a common vision of the future" (Gormally 2001, 6). For example, according to Loyalist ex-prisoner interviewees, Unionist politicians support exclusionary policies in order to "target the IRA" (as put by one respondent) while accepting that Loyalist ex-prisoners are also impacted in similar, detrimental ways. Such a trend is not coincidental to the ideological and historical differences between the mainstream Unionist parties and Sinn Fein: while the former have historically kept arm's-length from armed combatants and are overwhelmingly middle class, Sinn Fein is composed largely of former IRA insurgents. Correspondingly, the criminalization of ex-prisoners is intended to serve one set of ethnopolitical parties (Unionists) over the other (Nationalists). The disenfranchisement of ex-prisoners is an example of an attempt to institutionalize the power of one ethnopolitical bloc and give it "moral grounding" (Mitchell 2008, 2) over against claims of legitimacy by the Other. In general, problems posed by the ongoing influence of ex-combatants at neighborhood levels are not unrelated to the hypermasculine political strategies of domination by those intent on capitalizing on broader societal resentment and blame of the ex-prisoner population, which is unfairly seen as solely representative of the violence of the past (Gormally 2001). In this sense, ex-prisoners have served as pawns in a zero-sum political game, and they are aware of it. It is the very lack of state action on reconciliation and the past (discussed in the following chapter) as well as poverty and cultures of hypermasculinity that sustain the power and control of former and active male paramilitaries.

Nonetheless, it would be misleading to downplay the vital work women continue to undertake in the community sector, and risks "lump[ing] women together as 'victims' or an undifferentiated category without agency" (Mac Ginty and Williams 2009, 84). In many ways, women continue to make positive impacts on community development outside the public gaze, even if it does not eclipse the power of paramilitaries or former male combatants. For example, the head of a women's empowerment organization describes her work in which participants—women from Belfast's working-class PUL communities—learn skills that help them support their families and help educate others in their communities. In her words,

it's not about tackling paramilitaries as individuals, it's about tackling the issues that they have created through their paramilitarism or criminality. It's how can we empower—particularly for us in [organization name redacted]—young women, [with] the skills to be able to become leaders within their own communities in order to make that change without having to challenge somebody. (Interview with author, May 2020)

A different respondent from the same organization similarly explains how

women on their own can't eradicate paramilitarism; it won't happen. They'll be shot. . . . We're providing a service that people really genuinely need, that will help them. To eradicate paramilitarism or work towards that is a noble goal but realistically, what woman's going to stand up to man? You give them all the tools. If you lift them out of economic depression, if you start to give them ideas, they get to get a job, they don't need to live in that kind of atmosphere; then you strengthen them in other ways. (Interview with author, June 2020)

As the same respondent observes in the context of women's community volunteer work during the early stage of the Covid-19 pandemic, "they're doing things to address some of the gaps within their community that is not impacting on what some of those ex-combatants are doing. It's not a challenge to them. . . . Actually, the men in the community are seeing the good because it has a ripple effect across the whole community."

These statements suggest that the male ex-prisoner takeover of community leadership roles is far from total. There is substantial recognition of the positive work undertaken by women within Belfast's working-class communities. The degree to which such work can gradually undermine the coercive power of (former) paramilitary elements, however, is contingent upon future efforts by the state and broader public to address issues of gender inequity and construct more creative approaches to dealing with the problem of paramilitarism and the legacies of the Troubles. While perhaps an important step in the conflict transformation process, terminating policies which stigmatize and criminalize former paramilitary prisoners by itself will unlikely result in the decentering of ethnocultures of hypermasculinity and a reversal in the corresponding marginalization of women. Broader investment in working-class communities' social and economic infrastructure, systematic efforts to change the normativity of hypermasculinist cultures and empower the political voices of women, and cooperation between political elites from both ethnonational communities on dealing with the past will all be essential in transforming NI to a truly post-conflict state.

NOTES

1. Parts of this chapter were originally published in: Holland, Curtis, and Gordana Rabrenovic. 2018. "Masculinities in Transition? Exclusion, Ethnosocial Power, and Contradictions in Excombatant Community-based Peacebuilding in Northern Ireland." *Men and Masculinities* 21 (5): 729–755.

2. Politically motivated prisoners were released early on license under the Agreement. The license contained various terms of early release, the violation of which would have them returned to custody.

3. Several respondents, along with the NI Committee on the Administration of Justice, claims that the British government has failed to properly follow through with various procedures meant to improve peace process outcomes, including the transition to "human rights based policing." Ultimately, many feel that the British government is not prioritizing investment in conflict transformation in NI as much as was promised during the lead-up to the Agreement. See CAJ (2016) as well as chapter 4 for more detail on this point.

4. Due largely to laws protecting employers from accusations of discrimination against them by those with convictions for political violence, former paramilitary prisoners have unprecedented rates of unemployment. See Shirlow (2012).

Chapter 4

Identity, the Politics of Policing, and Limits to Legitimacy

Ensuring that distinct groups with conflicting understandings of state legitimacy, justice, and nationhood endorse a peace process requires the restructuring of organizations that once served as instruments of domination by one ethnic or national group over another.[1] The reform of the police is especially pivotal in this respect, since "they are the primary institution that establishes the presence and authority of the state in people's everyday lives" (Powell 2014, 166). "The police" serve this socio-political function not only through organizational policing practices, but also through its symbolic power. As Loader and Mulcahy (2003) indicate, images of policing communicate meaning about the social and political order of things; how they are and how they ought to be. Because the police—or, *representations* of the police—constitute, reflect, or undermine the relative degree to which imagined national or ethnic communities feel politically and culturally secure, the development of coercive *and symbolic* police powers inclusive of the historically polarized groups is integral to the promotion of a legitimate post-conflict state.

While prominent authors on the issue recognize that police reform in divided societies has significant political implications, their primary analytical foci have remained centered on problems with policing "on the ground." Due to its empirical depth, the dominance of the procedural justice literature in academic discourses on police legitimacy is part and parcel of this trend. This literature suggests that police organizations will increase their capacity to gain legitimacy when citizens feel that their grievances will be taken seriously, that they are treated with dignity, and that policing procedures are applied neutrally and consistently (Tyler 2006; Sunshine and Tyler 2003). Considering that the trajectory of police reform in NI was geared largely toward realizing these objectives, it is understandable why the rich academic work on police legitimacy in the post-conflict era has mostly followed procedural justice frameworks. More often than not, the main analytical emphasis

119

is on changes to bureaucratic procedures, police symbols, and accountability mechanisms (Murphy 2013; Mulcahy 2013; Marijan and Guzina 2014; Starmer 2007; Hays 2013; Ellison and Smyth 2000), including the potential, and limitations of "community policing" in increasing trust and legitimacy (Topping 2008a; 2008b; Jarman 2006a), and police responses to "anti-social activity" and rioting among young people experiencing social and economic exclusion (Byrne and Jarman 2011). As Powell (2014, 166) indicates the procedural justice literature is largely rooted in the US social and political context; thus, its lessons are not fully applicable to the contexts of more fragile, divided transitional societies where policing has historically been a central site of conflict between mutually-exclusive ethnonational ideologies, and in which a dominant, inclusive civic nationalism[2] is yet to develop. Rather than influencing a greater focus on the role of broader, multi-institutional socio-political processes and discourses in shaping disputes over policing, the general recognition of the inextricable link between policing and politics has more so led to an implicit agreement, among practitioners and analysts, "that if policing can somehow be 'got right' many of the other pieces of the [political] jigsaw will slot into place" (O'Rawe and Moore 2001, 181).

It is important to emphasize, though, that the symbolic power of the police is not exclusively a police power. Rather, such symbolic power is subject to appropriation by political and cultural actors external to the police, having important implications on intercommunal relations and police legitimacy post-conflict. In this vein, I argue here that the strongly affective nature of the symbolic power of the police in Northern Ireland's conflict history is inextricably linked to contemporaneous ethnopolitical projects of conflict reproduction. The key question guiding the analysis in this chapter is how the symbolic power of the police in the post-accord period is politically and culturally appropriated (or weaponized) at both the state and grassroots levels and the implications of this process on the reproduction of ethnopolitical identity and legitimacy, particularly in working-class communities most affected by legacies of conflict.

THREAT, SYMBOLIC POWER, POLICING, AND THE REMAKING OF ETHNOPOLITICAL BOUNDARIES

Loader (1997) was the first to apply a Bourdieusian framework to illustrate the symbolic power of the police by connecting the cultural salience of popular images of policing to dominant forms of English national identity. Given the limited capacity of police reform by itself to improve crime control, Loader (1997, 3) explains how the ongoing demand for stronger policing is more so linked to prevailing "structures of feeling" within which "the police figure is central to the production and reproduction of order and security." Such dominant "structures of feeling," inculcated by police symbols, further legitimate the police's power of "pronouncement: a power to diagnose, classify, authorize, and represent both individuals and the world, and to have this power of 'legitimate naming' not just taken seriously, but taken-for-granted" (Loader 1997, 3). The framework developed by Loader provides a strategic point of departure through which to understand the quite different nature of the symbolic power of policing in divided societies like NI. While popular attachment to policing has always been strongly affective in NI, it has taken two divergent forms: one Protestant/Unionist/Loyalist, one Catholic/Nationalist/Republican.

Before the onset of post-conflict police reform, the Protestant/Unionist-affiliated RUC pronounced the *ethnopolitical* order of things, which to the minority Nationalist population meant state-sponsored exclusion and victimization. In contrast, to most Unionists, the RUC represented (and still represents in many cases) agents of a benevolent state that defended their community from Irish Republican terrorists throughout the Troubles. The power of the police was thus never taken-for-granted through dominant cultural images and narratives but rather has historically been an ideological site of explicit intercommunal conflict demonstrated through public political discourse and violence—so much so that "implicitly, bargaining about policing became meta-bargaining as to the nature of the conflict" (Campbell, Aolain, and Harvey 2003, 342).

The uncertainty of the Northern Irish state and the ontological insecurity it brings, I argue, continue to manifest through images of policing because such images still pronounce dynamics of ethnopolitical power. Yet this is not necessarily inevitable, especially considering the lengths public and grassroots organizations have gone to facilitate cooperation between communities and the police post-conflict (see Hays 2013; Jarman 2006a; Jarman 2006b). The perceived stability of reformed institutions, including the police, may well be taken-for-granted by political leaders and other, shadow political actors intent on exploiting their symbolic importance to "groupness" and concomitant reconstructions of threat. Here I refer to Brubaker's (2002, 167) plea to think of "groupness as a contextually fluctuating conceptual variable," as a process identifiable in "cultural idioms, cognitive schemas, discursive frames, organizational routines, institutional forms, political projects and contingent events." In a similar vein, Finlayson (1999, 52) stipulates how "what appears as the identity of a people is only a temporary crystallisation of various processes and conflicts, of struggles to identify and define the people in question." Byrne (2011, 4) explains how "The constructed nature of psychocultural stories can . . . facilitate successful conflict transformation through the inclusion of more inclusive stories, ritual expressions, and identities" (see also Ross 2007). Yet the deep roots of the conflict, including chosen memories of ingroup victimization and simultaneous exclusion of accounts of outgroup persecution, can be manipulated to re-escalate tensions (Darby 2001). In this way, threat, whether exogenous or indigenous, tangible or symbolic, "is intrinsic to the possibility of recognizing and defining an identity. . . . Identity is discovered to be in question or under threat and the purpose of political action is to re-establish or defend it" (Finlayson 1999, 55). As previous chapters have established, the operation of threat is contingent upon the multiple social hierarchies through which identities ultimately emerge.

The integral role of *policing* in such processes, however, has been ill examined in Northern Ireland (and divided transitional societies generally) even as evidence reveals an increase in PUL frustration about policing and the persistence of anti-police attitudes in working-class Republican strongholds (Hearty 2018; Byrne and Jarman 2011). Following Christopher Patten's recommendations in the Independent Commission on Policing in Northern Ireland, the Protestant-affiliated Royal Ulster Constabulary (RUC) was transformed to the Police Service of Northern Ireland (PSNI) in 2001, accompanied by significant human rights and accountability reforms. Police oversight procedures regarding the use of force and due process in NI have been hailed as among the strongest in the world. For example, officers must file a report whenever they take out their batons, even if they are not used. Numerous independent regulatory bodies were created, and changes in uniforms, badges, and other symbolic markers of neutrality occurred (Mulcahy 2013). By 2008, 140 of the 175 recommendations from Patten had been implemented (Bayley 2008, 237), leading some to question whether NI is a model for democratic policing "anywhere in the world" (Ellison 2007, 243). The 2010 Hillsborough Agreement marked the devolution and democratization of policing powers, establishing the Policing Commission in which elected Unionist and Nationalist leaders share decision-making authority on policing policy. As of 2014, moreover, the proportion of officers that were Catholic rose to about 30 percent, with the numbers of female officers also growing (Nolan 2014).

Yet, not all have accepted these reforms as evidence of a successful peace process. Some events, such as Sinn Fein leaders' attendance of a PSNI recruitment rally in 2020, suggest that the party has become increasingly supportive of the PSNI;[3] however, many of Sinn Fein's strongest supporters remain skeptical about the extent to which policing has reformed since Agreement. Working-class Republican communities still feel that they are "politically policed" (Hearty 2018). At the same time, Mitchell, Evans, and O'Leary's (2009, 416) study found that a large portion of DUP supporters believe that police reform "has gone too far" (see also, Hayes, McAllister, and Dowds 2005).

A critical examination of the ethnopolitical appropriation of symbolic representations of policing can help build a more comprehensive understanding of the disconnect between official narratives of progress in police reform and ongoing resentment toward the police among Republican *and* Loyalist communities. In divided societies in which the very logic of the state has been contested along national or ethnic lines, representations of policing extend into broader representations of ethnopolitical distributions of power, making images of policing particularly instrumental to the construction of threat and concomitant (re)productions of identity. The implications of such representations, and how they interact with lived experience to shape socio-political mentalities of threat and loss is illuminated in the following pages. The analysis further illustrates how connections between identity construction and (de) legitimation is facilitated through such processes and are ultimately situated within contexts of social class.

A CONSOLIDATION OF POST-CONFLICT POLICE LEGITIMACY?

Data reveal that respondents' attitudes about the police are complex and at times ambiguous. Respondents from across the main ethnonational blocs and from working-class and middle-class communities acknowledge improvements in "everyday" policing, such as the time and quality of response to calls and participation in community-based peacebuilding initiatives. Some respondents, including those critical of the PSNI's adherence to principles of human rights policing noted improvements in police accountability mechanisms. A Nationalist respondent who works on such issues admits that "We've got probably the most powerful complaints and oversights procedures in the world" (interview with author, North Belfast, May 2014). A Protestant respondent similarly claims that "in general, we've got the place accountable, with policing boards. But we also have the MI5 and the black ops people operating everywhere" (interview with author, West Belfast, May 2014). Some emphasize how the police have shown genuine effort in working with cross-community peacebuilding and restorative justice projects, even as "political policing" and British secret agents remain active. For example, a Nationalist involved in such projects explains how "Policing . . . on the ground in North Belfast, is absolutely on the right course. There's no doubt about it. We're doing excellent in terms of community policing work. . . . But that's completely different from high-end, politically-based policing" (interview with author, North Belfast, June 2014).

Both CNR and PUL respondents differentiate evaluations of "ordinary policemen" on the street and their views about "political policing" at higher levels. Even some former IRA militants acknowledge improvements in everyday policing tactics. The experiences of former paramilitary prisoners in restorative justice and peacekeeping initiatives are identified by respondents as having helped foster greater acceptance of the PSNI, at least in certain respects. At the same time, respondents from working-class Protestant and Catholic communities express anger toward policing command structures. Issues or events involving the PSNI that are particularly sensitive to political manipulation emerge from opaque institutional processes and include emotive collective behaviors (protests, marches, etc.) which entrench collective imaginations in ethnopolitically, mutually-exclusive ways. Accusations of political policing are particularly powerful within such contexts, as narratives signaling ingroup persecution can resonate without empirical falsifiability. In some contexts, interpretations of lived experience are mediated by heuristics constructed through ethnopolitical discourses, illuminated in the aftermath of protests over emerging restrictions on Unionist symbols of hegemony (i.e., flags and parades).

Policing, Loyalist Alienation, and the Parade and Flag Disputes

Recall from chapter 2 that annual parades celebrating milestones of the centuries-old conflict important to one side or the other have long been central sites of both physical and symbolic conflict over the right to the state in NI (see also, Jarman 1997). Loyalists were particularly angry over the mass arrests of young PUL protestors in 2012–2013 related to the flag and parade protests. One respondent explained how the Loyalist population is "disaffected at the moment. . . . [P]eople are now coming before the courts and getting serious sentences for rioting. It's like 'what's happening to us?'" (interview with author, East Belfast, May 2014). In 2014, a Loyalist expressed frustration over how

> In the past year we've had at least a couple hundred grown men go through the courts, and most of them now find themselves in jail. Mostly from the parade issues . . . and the flag issues. We're watching republicans go through the courts, who were found with guns. They get a suspended sentence, fines, community service. Nobody can tell me that we're imagining this great big conspiracy against us. People pick up on it. (Interview with author, West Belfast, June 2014)

Rolston (2006) indicated earlier in the post-accord period that Loyalists viewed the transition of the RUC to the PSNI and the early release of Republican political prisoners convicted of violent offenses as a "betrayal" by British leadership, and symptomatic of an impending consolidation of the "Republican agenda." More than a decade on, such attitudes persist, most acutely in working-class Loyalist areas. However, they are now underscored substantially by the perceived injustice of police responses to Loyalist protest over state restrictions on Unionist parades and flags, and perceptions of disproportionality in the punitive judicial treatment of young Loyalists convicted of rioting and other public order offenses.

Moreover, Unionist and Loyalist respondents convey narratives that reflect the public discourses of Unionist political leadership at the time of data collection. Leading Unionists claimed that "republican violence is rewarded with concessions" from government and the police to appease Sinn Fein/IRA elements intent on using the threat of violence to coopt post-accord institutions. Unionist politicians have asserted this narrative to "insist that institutions are stacked against them" (Walsh 2013). Paralleling this narrative, a PUL respondent described how the quality of relations between Loyalists and Nationalists was

> decreasing, because of the blatant attacks on our culture and identity, which is continuing, as it was proved this morning, when the Parades Commission refused the return of the parade from last year. And it's because they're threatened with Republican violence every time they meet with them. They're getting the opinion that there will be violence at this parade. There's been violence at this parade each year for 10 years caused by Republicans. And now they got their way, and got the parade gone. So, relations, in my eyes, in my opinion, is at an all-time low. (Interview with author, West Belfast, June 2014)

During the period of data collection, public discourses suggested that the parades crisis was being manipulated by politicians to promote fears of the "culture war" allegedly waged by Nationalists. For example, a UUP leader "spoke of fears of a political design that will see every trace, vestige of Britishness . . . removed, bit by bit." Another DUP representative, McCausland, was quoted saying "that 'after 150 years the Parades Commission has de facto banned' unionists from marching. 'Previous commissions were bad, but this is the worst ever,' he said, describing the ruling as an attack on Protestants" (Walsh 2013). McCausland also criticized the police handling of the violence surrounding the parades dispute (Irish Times 2013).

With respect to public protests over both parade and flag restrictions, the main target of Loyalist violence in 2012–2013 was the police. In July and August of 2013 alone, more than 680 (or one in ten) police officers were injured as a result of public disorder (Nolan 2014, 13). For many Loyalists, the heavy police presence in response to these protests signified a turn by the state against the PUL community, marking the PSNI as legitimate targets. One young person argued that "The main point about the [flag] violence is the police and the way so many of them come to the protests, as if they want trouble. If the police come in those numbers then they are provoking it. It's a disgrace what is going on" (McDonald 2013).

As Hearty (2018, 138) points out, "When 'high policing' subjects 'us' to 'anti-terror' provisions but not 'them' [in the case of dissident Republicans] or, conversely, when 'low policing' aggressively batons 'us' but not 'them' [as per Loyalist claims during the flag protests], political policing is seen to operate along biased lines." Respondents' perceptions of biased policing compounds a more general sentiment among working-class PUL communities of state betrayal. For example, a Loyalist who serves in a community-policing partnership, explains how

> the relationship with the police has deteriorated rapidly, from last July to the present day on how they're treating the Protestant people. Last July we had some Sinn Feiner [a Nationalist Sinn Fein politician] coming around saying [the police] didn't use their baton rounds quite enough. Having been on the ground— we were on the ground last 12 of July—they opened up in say fifteen or twenty minutes. Republicans have fired live rounds at them [in previous years], dropped breeze blocks on them, and they didn't open up with baton rounds.[4] So, you have Sinn Fein ordering more baton rounds. . . . The Protestant people have no faith whatsoever in this police leadership. (Interview with author, West Belfast, June 2014)

Since policing "is about who has the power to define for society as a whole what use of force is acceptable under the law, and what is unacceptable" (Powell 2014, 166), perceptions of hostile policing tactics in response to Loyalist public disorder signify powerfully to PUL communities a transition in the trajectory of the state toward Nationalism—a belief mirroring cultural Unionist public political discourse.

It is important to acknowledge that public order policing has improved overall since the establishment of the PSNI, at least according to official data. The frequency of complaints about "oppressive behavior" by the police has declined steadily, from about 2,000 in 2010/11 to just under 1,000 in 2017/18; and complaints about police "incivility" have declined by almost half (Gray et al. 2018, 124). Overall confidence in the police, according to the NI Crime Survey, increased from about 60 percent in 2007/08 to 71 percent in 2016/17 (Department of Justice 2018). Although Protestants remain more favorable of the PSNI, confidence in the police has increased among Catholics since the Agreement (Nolan 2014, 59; Gray et al. 2018, 119–125).

However, among other weaknesses,[5] most surveys on attitudes about policing supported by public bodies do not make comparisons *across class*. The one poll that did consider class—a September 2013 *Belfast Telegraph* poll—found, not surprisingly, that dissatisfaction with the police is highest in working-class communities. Other studies have found that problems of police-community relations are most acute in those same communities (Bryne & Jarman 2011; Hearty 2018).

Hearty (2014, 157) identified the flag protests "as an avenue for disaffected PUL communities to assert a new counter-memory that challenges not only the 'other' but also those within the leadership of political Unionism who are said to have used PUL communities during the conflict only to abandon them in the post-conflict transition." Young Loyalists conveyed criticisms of mainstream Unionist politicians from the DUP and UUP in response to their silence following clashes between police and Loyalist crowds. One young person claimed that the DUP "are letting things like this happen in Belfast and are not giving real representation to people like me" (McDonald 2013). Some comments by Loyalist respondents reflect a similar phenomenon in the context of emerging restrictions on Unionist parades, in contradistinction from the alleged lax policing of Republican parades. For example, one contends that "with a Republican parade, you won't see a policeman. They seem to be able to do and say whatever they want, when they want, and there's not a word, even from our own politicians, the DUP and UUP" (interview with author, West Belfast, June 2014).

Recall from chapter 2, that the impact of class-specific social locations does not negate the influence of other coercive identities; rather, such identities coalesce into a complex, inexplicable nexus of meaning which can be strategically manipulated by opportunistic ethnopolitical entrepreneurs. Similar to the manipulation of other ethnocultural symbols, representations of the police are particularly strategic in this respect. Several respondents from the Protestant community indicate that mistrust of the police is rife in working-class Protestant *and* Catholic communities. However, due partly to prevailing ingroup discourses, this trend compounds rather than obviates ethnopolitical and sectarian allegiances and intercommunal hostilities. Joe Law indicated how protests over parades and flags has led "some people in the Protestant community [to] want the RUC back. They think the PSNI doesn't work, they want the RUC. You have other one's [Republicans] saying the PSNI not welcome. So, the reaction from the working-class areas to the police will still be very suspicious, and very untrusting" (interview with author, West Belfast, May 2014).

The double-bind of policing in this respect is as much a consequence of socio-political discourse as lived experience. The RUC, symbolizing a past in which the pro-Unionist state consisted with the trajectory of Loyalist collective action and violence, serves as a symbolic medium through which anger based on experiences specific to one's class location is translated in classless, ethnopolitical terms. The power in images of policing, coupled with other cultural symbols (flags, parades, etc.) signify the changing trajectory of the state in ways which reify historical Nationalist threats and concomitantly subjugate critical or structuralist narratives about dynamics of working-class marginalization in progressive Loyalism. As the combined Unionist responses to the flag and parade protests, and to the police reactions to those protests illustrate, cultural materials "have an inner logic or connectedness that makes them at least moderately refractory to willful manipulation" (Brubaker & Laitin 1998, 442). The disconnect between dimensions of Loyalist loss is transmuted by cultural Unionism's threat politics, particularly narratives connecting PUL working-class alienation to "political policing." Cultural Unionism has maintained a type of convoluted cooperation between Loyalism and the Unionist political establishment because the cultural materials most symbolic of ingroup membership are inherently ethnopolitical and largely transcend class difference.[6]

Although methodologically the direction of causation cannot be definitively determined, it is not coincidental that some of the exact language used by Loyalist or Nationalist respondents in rationalizing their arguments were also identified in statements made by politicians from the respective ethnonational communities quoted in newspaper reports and heard on the radio during my stay in Belfast, during which an ontological plane connecting distinct sections of Unionism and Loyalism vis-à-vis the supposed "political policing" of PUL communities became evident. At the least, PUL complaints about police responses to their protests are noted and incorporated into politicians' and grassroots leaders' public rhetoric. Equally (or more) likely, such rhetoric is constructed by politicians and subsequently adopted by constituents when rationalizing their perspectives on dynamics of political policing. For example, at a 2013 rally in the aftermath of Loyalist rioting over Belfast City Council's decision to reduce the number of days the Union flag will fly at City Hall, DUP politician Ruth Patterson exaggerated the PSNI reaction as an example of "political policing and persecution of the Protestant people"—the same exact phrase used by one Loyalist respondent—and went on to say how she was "ashamed of the PSNI at the minute. . . . They beat our women and our children off the streets, they throw our pensioners into jail. They jail our young kids for waving the Union Flag of the country provocatively. That in my book is wrong and they must be held accountable for that" (quoted in Nolan 2014, 58). Phrases used by Patterson here were repeated imprecisely by PUL respondents. For example, as one Loyalist ex-prisoner implored,

> you can take my word for it. They'll [PSNI] beat pensioners, they'll beat women, they'll beat children. . . . Unfortunately, we don't have the CTV footage to prove it, but it's happening in North Belfast on a regular basis, and it's about time these people were held to account for what they were doing. At the moment, they're still getting away with it. . . . The Protestant people have no

faith whatsoever in this police leadership. (Interview with author, West Belfast, June 2014)

Similar narratives were offered by influential Loyalists with public personas, such as Jamie Bryson (see Nolan et al. 2014, 109). Protestors acknowledged that "the DUP ramped everybody up" and "let the genie out of the bottle" when directing PUL attention to the flag decision (Nolan et al. 2014, 76–77). The anger with the state which the DUP's actions helped provoke was heightened when a heavy police presence in response to subsequent protests materialized, reaffirming to Loyalists the transition of police powers to the benefit of Nationalists. Subsequent Unionist elites' claims of "political policing" of Unionist parades then further entrenched anti-police attitudes among PUL communities.

POLICING THE PAST, POLICING POLITICS

Understandings of the past persist in relation with the needs and objectives of the present (Mead 1959). Attention to how the past is reconstructed is thus useful to analyses which intend to identify dynamics of power and domination inherent in discursive processes. Olick and Levy (1997) illustrate how politicians use the past to pursue their interests, but are also constrained by the cultural and moral imperatives signified in dominant socio-political reconstructions of the past. Ethnopolitical leaders in divided societies are unlikely to engage wholeheartedly with new interpretations of the past which challenge the fundamental bases of their party's long-standing claims to political and moral superiority. The "political opportunity structures" which encase "cultural access points" (Ferree et al. 2002, 62) are especially contracted in polarized societies, in which the discursive field has been historically split along ethnopolitical lines. Especially in contexts of "ethnic frontier" societies in transition, "historical accounts are significant and contentious precisely because of their relationship to the legitimacy of power in the present, and because of their contribution to disputes about it" (Beetham 2013, 103). Discursive frames which reconstitute mutually exclusive ethnopolitical meanings and identities through reconstructions of the past are instrumental to broader divisive political projects because of the restrictive nature of the cultural access points available in connecting leaders and their ingroup constituents.

The socio-political fallout over the arrest and subsequent release-without-charge of Sinn Fein President Gerry Adams provides a lucid representation of how ethnopolitical disputes and framing of the past are appropriated by influential actors to reconstruct ethnopolitical identity. In the spring of 2014,

Gerry Adams—then President of Sinn Fein and presumed former Provisional IRA leader—was taken into custody by the PSNI in response to new allegations that he had ordered the 1972 murder of Jean McConville. The mother of ten was alleged to have been a British informant by the IRA before she disappeared the same year. Adams's arrest came after the PSNI had successfully subpoenaed Boston College in 2013 to hand over confidential tapes of interviews with former IRA combatants implicating Adams as having ordered McConville's execution (Clarke 2014).

Sinn Fein representatives portrayed Adams's arrest as evidence that those in command at the highest levels of criminal justice and security remain committed to defeating Irish Nationalism and exercising revenge against the IRA. Sinn Fein representative Martina Anderson describes how her constituency saw Adams's arrest as politically motivated, "an attack on democracy and an attack on the peace process" (Irish News 2014). Adams himself characterized his arrest as part of "a sustained, malicious, untruthful and sinister campaign going back many years," geared toward charging him with "membership of the IRA . . . [to] link . . . [him] to the McConville case" (Adams 2014). Most Nationalists who voiced their views in the local news media agreed that Adams's arrest "was a sham," because the PSNI waited months after receiving the tapes until the election season was underway before making the arrest (see Gibney 2014). The same views were consistently conveyed by Nationalist interview respondents. Data indicate substantial evidence of connection between the discursive frames of politicians and media personalities, and responses of interviewees, up to the specific language used to characterize events connected to the arrest. Two Nationalist respondents, for example, argued that the research from Boston College used to justify Adams's arrest was part of "a get Adams project," the same phrase used during the period of data collection in Republican media (see O'Dowd 2014). Some CNR respondents directly referenced the narratives of Sinn Fein leaders in rationalizing their own views about Adams's arrest and the broader problem of "political policing." One Nationalist, for example, indicated that he "believe[s] absolutely what Martin McGuinness was saying about that arrest. Because I do believe that there had to be some sort of political thought going into the timing of that arrest" (interview with author, North Belfast, May 2014). The respondent is referring here to remarks made by then Sinn Fein Deputy First Minister Martin McGuinness, who claimed "that a 'dark side' of the PSNI was behind [Adams's] detention" (McHugh 2014). Another Nationalist pointed to the "many examples of where policing is moving forward in a good way. But I actually think that [that] arrest shows that there's still a remnant [of the old RUC] there that is fighting an old fight" (interview with author, West Belfast, May 2014). Again, everyday policing "on the ground" is positively evaluated; "high" policing is posited as inherently political and corrupt.

Following his release, Adams acknowledged that his arrest had "galva-nized the Sinn Fein party and the broader republican family. . . . Now they are focused, there is an alertness that the process here cannot be taken for granted and people are looking to the work that . . . our other representatives have done around raising peace process issues" (Adams 2014). The fact that "the process cannot be taken for granted" was made particularly evident by the subtle threats from prominent Nationalist politicians to withdraw from the Policing Board if Adams was not released (Whitehead 2014). To Loyalists, the apparent success of such a tactic reaffirmed their suspicion that policing decisions reflect the gradual Nationalist takeover of the state, facilitated by British political elites and even Unionists to some extent. The dual adages of Republican threat and state betrayal historically reli-able in galvanizing Loyalist protest were facilitated indirectly by the Adams incident. Several Loyalist respondents, echoing the discourses of Unionist leadership (see Telegraph 2014), noted how Sinn Fein and "IRA" elements had responded to Adams's arrest by essentially extorting the criminal justice system, threatening to withdraw Nationalist support for the PSNI (and, thus, the peace process) if Adams was not released without charge. According to one Loyalist ex-paramilitary, when Adams was being questioned "on the murder of Jean McConville, they [Republicans] put the mural [of Adams] on the [peace] wall [in West Belfast]. And it just so happens that that mural overlooked the area where that woman was taken from. Now that wasn't done by accident" (interview with author, West Belfast, June 2014). The mural of Gerry Adams,[7] erected during his detainment, signified to Loyalists a return to Republican "bullyboy tactics" that had allegedly helped bring them to power and which reflect their illegitimate role in government—an allegation conveyed by Unionist politicians as well, down to the language used (BBC 2014). A different Loyalist elaborated on how

> Sinn Fein, the IRA, has power over the police. It's all based on the idea that, if we don't get our own way, we'll walk out [of power-sharing institutions]. You see on the banners, when they had the protest by the mural of Gerry Adams on the Falls road, that if they don't let him out the peace process would be in big trouble. One of the head men of the IRA, [name redacted], stood up and turned around and said "We still haven't gone away, you know." So, what does that tell people within my community? They're still there. (Interview with author, West Belfast, June 2014)

Other incidents surrounding Adams's arrest and detention provided additional anecdotal evidence for Loyalists convinced of their victimization via "high" *and* "low" political policing. One Loyalist points to the fact that "Gerry Kelly, as a member of the Policing Board, was allowed to visit [Adams during his detainment]. Now what other country in the world would let somebody who has been charged with a murder go in to see one of his colleagues and find out why he's still in police custody" (interview with author, West Belfast, June 2014)?

Respondents across the ethnonational divide consistently described how politicians from both ethnoreligious communities exploit the fragility of law enforcement and judicial bodies and manipulate their power over policing decisions to capitalize politically. A senior leader in the peacebuilding community indicates how "what we've seen now with Sinn Fein . . . we've [also] seen last year at the flags protest. . . . [T]he DUP and Unionism also threatened to withdraw its support for policing" (interview with author, Co Antrim, May 2014). A young Nationalist activist similarly points to

> how quickly people will jump off the bandwagon if the police do something that doesn't suit them. And even Martin McGuinness threatened, you know, that Sinn Fein would drop the policing board. So, no, I mean that was a litmus test that clearly shows [that] there is not unconditional support of police. It is very conditional. And you could argue that it is conditional on them [the police] to not dig up things that, you know, could hurt [the peace process]. (Interview with author, South Belfast, June 2014)

This young man was not the only respondent to imply some degree of acceptance of the police as partly responsible for maintaining political stability. There is little hope among most I spoke with that the political climate would become increasingly inclusive or integrated: because the status quo of nonviolent conflict is implied as the best possible situation due to the nature of the country's ethnopolitics, "neutral" institutions are deemed responsible for political mediation. The contradictory responsibility of balancing basic principles of justice with concerns over political stability essentially rests with the police, who are ultimately required to police politics even as they are used as political pawns. The lack of transparency in this respect helps to validate and deepen mistrust of the police among the socially and economically vulnerable segments of both ethnonational communities, which can then be more effectively appropriated by leaders in the interests of themselves and their parties, and at the expense of police and state legitimacy.

Also facilitating the ethnopolitical entrepreneurism of elected Unionist *and* Nationalist leaders is the ambiguity of the British government's and PSNI's approaches to dealing with the past in Northern Ireland. Article Two of the European Convention on Human Rights—essentially, the right to life—has theoretically been incorporated into UK law and is an integral component of the Agreement. The European Court has imposed investigative obligations on states to review suspicious deaths in independent, prompt, and efficient ways. Yet, even before Brexit, the UK government was slow to implement mechanisms which fully adhere to Article 2. A respondent who investigates such matters explains how "there are huge intelligence stashes, but all that is classified and top secret and the PSNI has control over it but the actual people [controlling it] are ex-special branch RUC personnel. They have to go through every document and take names out and it's a nightmare" (interview with author, South Belfast, June 2014). Because of the PSNI's lack of transparency and consistency in its approach toward dealing with the past, and the responsibility for security issues still resting largely with secretive British intelligence agencies, both PUL and CNR communities have opportunities to draw speculations which validate claims of ethnopolitical policing. Again, accusations from both ethnonational blocs that the police are catering to the whims of the Other emerge, this time with respect to Historical Enquiries Team (HET) investigations and "supergrass" trials.[8] Disparities between the relatively low numbers of military and police killings reviewed in comparison to Republican and Loyalist cases led Nationalist leaders to accuse the HET of being "too soft on state violence" (Nolan 2014, 56–57). In fact, Nationalist complaints about PSNI bias against non-state actors in their investigations of Article 2 complaints have been vindicated through the ruling in the case of Jean Smyth-Campbell, who was shot and killed in June 1972 in West Belfast. The British Army's Military Reaction Force unit has long been suspected of involvement. In 2019, The Court of Appeal in London found that "the PSNI Chief Constable had not shown that a legacy unit within his force had the practical independence for a new probe into the killing" (Simpson 2021, 1). In 2013, Her Majesty's Inspectorate of Constabulary (HMIC) report concluded more generally that the HET—later named the Legacy Investigation Branch (LIB)—was treating cases of state violence with "less rigour" than cases of violence by non-state militants (BBC 2013a), consistent with criticisms from human rights groups such as CAJ and the European Council. There is now sufficient evidence to conclude that "the PSNI has obstructed and frustrated truth recovery by delaying the disclosure of necessary information, being overly sensitive with redactions" (Lawther and Hearty 2021, 11; see also CAJ 2019, 4). The PSNI also attempted to "curtail grassroots truth recovery by seizing materials from investigative journalists making a documentary on collusion" (Lawther and Hearty 2021, 11).

Moreover, in February 2021, Mark Sykes, a survivor of the 1992 Ormeau Road Bookmakers' massacre—where five were killed and many others injured by two UFF gunmen—was arrested during a wreath-laying ceremony at the site of the killings under the auspices of COVID-19 public health restrictions (Duffy 2021). It is widely suspected among Nationalists that the massacre was facilitated by RUC collusion with the UFF, leading many to question whether Sykes's arrest was part of a larger politically-motivated campaign by the PSNI to intimidate victims who continue pressing for ongoing investigations into RUC crimes during the Troubles, and causing yet another "nationalist crisis of confidence in policing." Shortly after Nationalist outcry over the incident, the PSNI Chief Constable apologized and suspended the officer who made the arrest, leading to accusations from DUP members of the Policing Board that the PSNI were acting in pursuit of a pro-Nationalist "political agenda" (Young 2021).

At the same time (and somewhat paradoxically) the lack of transparency and consistency in decisions to charge those suspected of crimes during the Troubles are cited by PUL interviewees as underscoring their increasing suspicion of a supposed police-state-Nationalist nexus, making them distrustful of the police and resistant to any official state mechanism to deal with the past. According to one Loyalist ex-paramilitary prisoner, for example:

> There was a failed supergrass system within this country. Once again, I find there's a supergrass system being used, mainly against Loyalists, during this period of time. . . . Do you see it in the Republican side? I don't see it. I see dead people who were significant Republicans [such as] [inaudible] Hughes, who came out and made a statement against Gerry Adams. What did Gerry Adams say? "Liar." He led a bunch of thugs who murdered and bombed this place to smithereens for years, but he won't admit it. So why deal with the past or even [inaudible]? No chance. (Interview with the author, East Belfast, June 2014)

Similar comments were made by other grassroots leaders from Belfast's PUL community I interviewed. By shifting discourses to questions about the past in contexts of policing, the moral dimension of membership in the ethnopolitical group is reconstructed through emphases on outgroup hypocrisy, state betrayal, and past ingroup persecution, re-centering identity in opposition to the historical Other and subjugating structuralist class discourses and identities revealed in other interview phases.

To offer additional evidence of purported pro-Nationalist political policing by the PSNI, another Loyalist refers to the "letters of immunity" received by almost 190 ex-patriot Republicans giving "assurances they were not being sought by the British authorities." Evidence of one such letter led to the collapse of the trial of a former IRA man accused in the notorious Hyde Park bombing which killed four British soldiers in 1982. In response to the controversy over the incident, and threat of resignation by then DUP First Minister Peter Robinson, British authorities asserted that the so-called "amnesty letters" did not "have any value anymore," implying that anyone is subject to investigation if additional evidence on their alleged past crimes surfaces (Sweeney 2014). Yet formal efforts to locate and detain those Republican suspects were not subsequently undertaken. For many Loyalists, this was yet another incident validating their suspicion of the police and broader criminal justice apparatus, while reflecting an example of the general ambiguity of the British approach toward addressing crimes of the past. The following statement of a Loyalist ex-paramilitary prisoner reflects this perspective:

> You see that program they did a month or so ago about the fella who was [inaudible]? That guy can't be arrested, who had a real part in that [IRA bombing]. Should we just forget about that part of the past? How are we ever going to deal with that, when them [Republican] people are receiving letters of immunity for their parts? (Interview with author, West Belfast, June 2014)

The distrust linked to inconsistencies in the application of the law contributes to skepticism about the intentions of multistate post-accord governance bodies among the former Loyalist paramilitary community especially. Such events, paired with claims of PSNI crackdowns on Loyalist protestors at the supposed whim of Republican leaders, work to underscore the PUL community's distrust of the state. This distrust facilitates political and grassroots leaders' reconstructions of ethnopolitical threat vis-à-vis the police. Like the symbolic power of emblems (i.e., flags), rituals (i.e., parades), and imagery of public order policing, disputes over the policing of the past serve to realign Loyalism with the ethnopolitical trajectory of reactionary cultural Unionism.

CONCLUSION

This chapter draws connections between the lived experiences of key stakeholders in the NI peace process and dominant socio-political discourses and practices of leaders to identify (de)legitimation processes and the concomitant reproduction of ethnopolitical identities. Findings reveal ontological planes animated by narratives about the so-called political policing of public disorder and disputes over the past which align the identities of otherwise quite different and often opposing constituencies within the two ethnonational blocs. When conditions emerge which have the potential to provoke feelings of betrayal and threat in marginalized communities suffering most from the legacy of the conflict and persistent socio-economic disadvantage, discourses which implicate the police are especially likely to activate collective mentalities of ethnopolitical victimhood and resistance. Findings respond to criticisms of literature on ethnopolitical entrepreneurialism and culturalist approaches to ethnic and national conflict, namely, that there is little evidence that the belief systems and mentalities of fear promoted by opportunists are internalized by constituents (Brubaker and Laitin 1998, 443), and that researchers have generally failed to "ascertain empirically what the beliefs of those subject to authority may be, and how consistent they are with the legitimacy claims of the powerful" (Beetham 2013, 256). On the contrary— the analysis demonstrates how policing is perpetually re-politicized through framing contests, and draws connections (and disconnects) between dominant public discourses spearheaded by political and cultural elites, the discourses of respondents, and behaviors of grassroots actors and the police.

Improved though imperfect policing outcomes, including greater neutrality and accountability in "everyday policing" (in some respects) suggest that police reform has effectively moved forward. On the other hand, due to the very logic of its foundation, and the basic nature of policing responsibilities, the PSNI provides opportunities for manipulation by ethnopolitical opportunists. The police are typically inextricable to public *ethnicized events,* that is, emotive situations which energize ethnically homogenous crowds, prime collective mentalities of threat, and thereby reproduce insular identities within relatively deprived working-class communities most powerfully. Ethnicized events involving the police (riots, political parades, investigations of the past, etc.) connect contemporaneous subjective experiences of state oppression with interpretations of the past in ways which activate the ingroup cultural repertory, solidify "groupness," and moralize ethnopolitical identity. In this way, "official" representations of the reformed police which pose challenges to ritual reproductions of "groupness" are moderated and manipulated by ethnopolitical actors to restore the imagined community and their positions of power which are justified by it.

The PSNI is charged not only with enforcing the law but also with *officially representing* the image of the new, so-called shared society, presenting an ever-constant challenge to projects of ethnopolitical and ethnosocial ingroup reproduction. It is because policing—or *images of policing*—is so central to unmaking ethnopolitical boundaries in this respect that it is so integral to their *remaking*: it presents a core symbolic site of ideological contestation. Policing processes which become disputed, due to their historically central role in constituting and reflecting the contested logic of the state provide events or social and organizational fields in which opportunistic actors can effectively reconstitute ethnopolitical boundaries, in ways which provide both rational (for political and organizational leaders) outcomes and inexplicable phenomenological or cultural ends of "groupness."

Hearty (2018, 140) argues that "where ethno-nationalism was once the most obvious policing fault line in the six counties, today it appears to be one falling along whether communities have 'moved on' with post-conflict transition or been 'left behind' by the process" socio-economically. Dissident Republicans and alienated PUL communities express similar criticism of the post-accord state and its supposed use of the police to silence their dissent. Interviewees also suggest that a strategy of "containment" is also used to control at-risk youth in areas of concentrated deprivation. As one respondent, from a North Belfast PUL community, explains

> There's a lot of young people who won't go outside their own area, and certainly won't go with people from another religious background. For a lot of young people here, life's really good. If you're in a middle-class area, and your parents have good jobs, and you've got a nice house, and you don't live in a bad area, yes, life is really still pretty good in Northern Ireland. When you live in these [under-resourced and highly segregated] areas, it's not. More and more, the state are dealing with areas like this on both sides of the community by sending the police, by doing the raids, by confiscating. (Interview with author, May 2020)

However, despite a degree of cross-communal class consciousness with regard to the functions of policing, discursive constructions of ingroup persecution linked to processes of alleged *ethnopolitical* policing inform recollections of personal experience with the police in ways which are manipulatable by political opportunists. The multifaceted and often contradictory relationship between Unionism and working-class Loyalism is illuminated through discourses about political policing. Yet such discourses also have material effects. Because Ulster Unionist culture has been historically constructed in part to subjugate political discourses about class inequality, and thereby maintain PUL communities' sense of collective unity with broader Unionism, manipulation of socio-political symbols (especially the police) ultimately compromises the power of class-based discourses to transform the nature of Loyalism. Loyalist protests over new restrictions on Unionist flags and parades channeled this community's sense of loss, compounding the insecurity rooted also in persistent poverty and inopportunity. The subsequent experience of aggressive public order policing by the PSNI reifies notions of persecution by the (supposedly) increasingly Nationalist-controlled state, allowing political elites and "community-based leaders" to reproduce ideologies which reconstitute incentives for ethnic outbidding. Experiences of political policing "on the ground" has primarily affected the working-class segments of the PUL community but, coupled with public discourses of ethnopolitical opportunists, has served, somewhat paradoxically, to realign this community with distinct elements of Unionism in response to the perceived threat from Irish Nationalist ascendancy within the Northern Irish state.

For both Republicans and Loyalists, public disputes over how to resolve crimes from the past reaffirm the moral dimension of their ethnopolitical identity while highlighting inconsistencies in "high" policing, particularly with respect to how paramilitary and state crimes are investigated. Such inconsistencies validate claims of state bias against one's own ethnopolitical group, while facilitating claims of abuses of power by the Other. Although a dissident Republican community opposed to Sinn Fein's peace strategy has gained a voice (Hearty 2018), investigations into alleged past crimes of the party's leadership, and ongoing influence of former RUC personnel helps reproduce images of Sinn Fein as a populist Republican resistance party for many in the heart of working-class Catholic communities.[9]

Although limited in time and place, findings suggest that socio-political constructions of threat implicating the police are integral to the reproduction of ethnopolitical identities. Such identity reproductions simultaneously undermine the legitimacy of both the police and the post-accord NI state more broadly. The politicization of the policing of parades and issues of the past by the DUP and Sinn Fein in particular, and the ontological planes animated by this process, connecting otherwise fragmented constituencies, has continued since the period of data collection, and is not isolated to the case studies analyzed above. Other notable events and public discourses suggest that it is unlikely PUL perceptions of the Nationalist takeover of the police and justice systems will substantially shift in the near future (see McClements 2019; Bryson 2019; Farrell 2015; McClements 2019a; Bell 2018). At the time of writing, the decision of the PSNI not to charge Sinn Fein leaders for violating COVID-19-related restrictions on social gatherings resulted in calls from the DUP that both Sinn Fein president Mary Lou McDonald, as well as PSNI Chief Constable Simon Byrne, resign. About 2,000 people gathered in attendance of former head IRA man Bobby Storey's funeral, including 24 Sinn Fein representatives. Unionist leaders' accusations of pro-Nationalist political policing in response to that incident continued for months after (Hutton 2021; Young and Black 2020). The framing of the issue by DUP leaders, that the PSNI appears guilty of pro-Nationalist "two-tier" policing, was echoed by interviewees. A Loyalist community worker in the DDR sector, for example, used some of the same terminology. In her words, the Storey funeral incident is another example of

> two-tier policing. The police had arrested and handed out COVID fines to people who attended Loyalist funerals, to people who attended the Black Lives Matter protests in Belfast. . . . There is a huge sort of thing about, "It's one law for them and one law for us." That's going to be hard to overcome. . . . Bobby Storey wasn't the only Republican funeral that there were crowds and crowds and crowds of people out [at]. (Interview with the author, May 2021)

The fallout over the policing of Storey's funeral has had detrimental consequences on local peacebuilding initiatives as well. As the same respondent explains, "because of this thing over the funeral, the LCC[10] have said, 'Now there's two-tier policing.' . . . Just as my projects were coming to an end, we were being told that they weren't working with the police anymore because of it. . . . Things like that really do have a huge impact" (interview with author, May 2021).

NOTES

1. Parts of this chapter were originally published in: Holland, Curtis. 2021. "Identity, the Politics of Policing, and Limits to Legitimacy in Northern Ireland." *Innovation: The European Journal of Social Science Research* 34 (1): 44–68. Copyright © Interdisciplinary Centre for Comparative Research in the Social Sciences and ICCR Foundation reprinted by permission of Taylor & Francis Ltd, http://www.tandfonline .com on behalf of Interdisciplinary Centre for Comparative Research in the Social Sciences and ICCR Foundation.

2. Civic nationalism is typically distinguished from ethnic nationalism by the degree to which it is "liberal, voluntarist, universalist, and inclusive." On the contrary, ethnic nationalism is typically "glossed as illiberal, ascriptive, particularist, and exclusive" (Brubaker 1999, 56). As Brubaker points out, though, in practice, the differences between the types of nationalism are more nuanced, and may contain more overlapping qualities than these definitions suggest.

3. Sinn Fein leadership attended a PSNI recruitment campaign launch for the first time ever in February 2020. In an effort to reverse the trend of falling Catholic recruitment in the preceding years, the 2020 campaign sought to enroll 50 percent of the new recruits from Catholic communities—the first time the "50/50" policy was enacted since 2011 (O'Neill 2020). Interestingly, although DUP First Minister Arlene Foster criticized the proposed 50–50 recruitment plan as a "return to [anti-Protestant] discrimination" (McClements 2019a) she nonetheless attended the recruitment launch (O'Neill 2020).

4. For more information on the incident described here, see Belfast Telegraph (2010a).

5. It is important to note that survey data on public attitudes about the police and official data on citizen complaints in NI have always been hotly contested politically, and should be interpreted with caution. Some would argue, for example, that declines in the number of complaints about "oppressive" police behavior are not indicative of an actual decline in such behavior but the result of people not reporting because they have no confidence in oversight bodies. Others I spoke with suggest that surveys such as the NI Life and Times survey do not adequately represent community-police relations and public attitudes toward the police, since most of the respondents probably rarely, if ever, interact with the police.

6. This point is explained more fully in chapter 2.

7. This mural of Gerry Adams, created by artist Danny Devaney, was erected while the Sinn Fein leader was in police custody. It was taken down shortly thereafter, at Adams's request. The mural was located on the Falls Road, not far from the home of Jean McConville, the mother of ten who was killed by the IRA in 1972. See Belfast Telegraph (2014).

8. "Supergrass trials" refer to trials based on the testimony of informers from within the organization under investigation.

9. My conversations with young people in Nationalist parts of West and North Belfast suggest that there is some sympathy with dissident views, but most still display loyalty to Sinn Fein.

10. The LCC is the Loyalist Communities Council, an organization that represents the main Loyalist paramilitary groups (UVF, Red Hand Commando, and UDA).

Chapter 5

Brexit

A Constitutional Moment in Unionism?

A key provision of the 1998 Good Friday Agreement was cementing partnership between the UK and Irish governments in the implementation and maintenance of power-sharing institutions within NI. Facilitated by European Union (EU) integration, this "east-west" cooperation would occur in addition to a "north-south" partnership between the NI Executive and Irish government (Hayward 2020a, 274). The terms of EU membership could do what neither Britain nor Ireland could on their own, to normalize and legitimize the disconnect between territory and sovereignty in NI. The conflict between Nationalism and Unionism over the constitutional status of NI was symbolized most sharply at the border, "where British-Irish tensions could be made manifest and visible" (Hayward 2020a, 274), and a large portion of Irish Republican anti-state terrorism occurred. McCall (2011, 201) suggests that the opening of the Irish border region facilitates the production of "a cultural space in which Irish nationalist and Ulster unionist ethnonational communities can explore cultural differences and commonalities . . . " More generally, a central goal of the Agreement—to allow incompatible ethnonationalisms to co-exist in NI—would not have been realized to the extent that it has without EU integration and the concomitant "creation and maintenance of an *open border*" (Teague 2019, 691).

It has also been argued that, despite the numerous dysfunctions of post-accord political institutions in NI, the aforementioned components of the Agreement contributed to a "higher function, namely embedding the principle of consent in the political culture" (Gormley-Heenan and Aughey 2017, 9). The principle of consent, to put simply, is essentially the recognition among Unionists and Nationalists alike that, realistically, to have peace, the political interests of the outgroup—including its constitutional preference—requires substantial political accommodation.[1] Because of Brexit, however, experts warn that "Both Nationalism and Unionism are dangerously close once again to the politics of 'compellence,' where the impulse is to seek victory over the other side" (Teague 2019, 708). In this vein, it is argued that Brexit has regenerated "the border of the mind" in Unionist and Nationalist communities, thereby threatening to undermine the principle of consent (Gormley-Heenan and Aughey 2017, 14; see also, Cochrane 2020; Connolly and Doyle 2019). Thus, important questions emerging from Brexit, such as whether NI residents can continue to choose Irish or British citizenship (or both) is about more than restrictions on travel, trade, or citizenship; such questions are also about whether the psychosocial power of shared or de-territorialized sovereignty heretofore facilitated by EU membership is sustainable post Brexit. It is feared that the creation of a new border down the Irish sea between NI and other UK countries, and a corresponding strengthening of north-south economic interdependency (due to the entire island following a singular EU customs agreement) will seriously damage the mutuality between Nationalism and Unionism previously established by the Agreement in the context of joint EU membership of the UK and Ireland.

Though still a new and rapidly changing situation at the time of writing, scholarly attention to issues connecting Brexit and the NI peace process has mostly taken the form of theoretical speculation on the implications of Brexit on regional British-Irish relations and the cascading effects of such relations on the local politics of NI (Guelke 2017; Connolly and Doyle 2019; Teague 2019; Hayward 2020a; Braniff and Whiting 2017). Of course, there are good reasons for such a focus, as intimated above. Less explored, though, are the impacts of Brexit on the political discourses *within* the ethnopolitical blocs. How an exogenous shock such as Brexit shapes intercommunal politics is necessarily mediated or shaped by the *intra*communal discourses surrounding the event. As Todd (2017, 2) explains, identity change does not typically occur through change in the categories of national identity, but through shifts in the "meanings of the national categories and in relations with others." Such "relational practice" does not only occur in interaction with outgroup members, but is also "endogenous, within the diverse clusters of the group itself where collective identity is challenged and sometimes changed from within" (Todd 2017, 2).

This chapter draws on 18 semi-structured interviews in 2020–2021 with actors in community-based organizations and government bodies, and qualitative content analysis of newspaper reports on the politics of Brexit in NI to identify common themes in the social construction of post-Brexit Unionist identity. Findings indicate signs of an inflection point in sections of Unionism, underscored by a criticism of the threat politics of the DUP, a desire for more tempered and effective leadership, and a discursive reification of the consent principle in spite of increased Nationalist rhetoric promoting a referendum on Irish unification. The analysis unfolds with caution to Unionism's historically reactionary nature, though, identifying a parallel development of increased anger in PUL communities over Northern Ireland's treatment in the Withdrawal deal between the UK and EU. It also recognizes that many in poor and working-class communities feel like they have less to lose from EU withdrawal than others who have received more material benefits from EU integration and thus have greater attachment to a European identity.

IDENTITY AND UNIONIST POLITICS

Todd (1986, 1) identifies two ideological traditions in Unionism. The first, "Ulster Loyalism," holds "primary allegiance to an imagined community of Northern Protestants, and a secondary and conditional loyalty to the British state." It is similar to the idea of the "sovereign people" (see Aughey 1997),[2] ritually reproduced by "dominatory" street parades and marches, and supportive of democratic principles only insofar as they uphold Northern Ireland's political and cultural separation from the Irish Republic. Todd's second typology of Unionist ideology, the "Ulster British," holds primary allegiance to the "imagined community of Great Britain and its secondary regional patriotism for Northern Ireland" (Todd 1986, 1). The latter ideology is more open to regional definitions of sovereignty (including a "new Ireland") and is similar to Aughey's (1997, 22) idea of the "constitutional people"—a collective identity defined by "the procedures and the forms of its established constitution." Throughout the Troubles, the "Ulster Loyalist" position dominated Unionist responses to attempts by the British and Irish governments to arrange a cooperative conclusion to the constitutional conflict, precluding a transformative moment for cross-communal politics within NI.[3] By the ceasefire period (1994), however, segments of the working-class PUL community, including some Loyalist paramilitaries, challenged Unionist political leadership's "no surrender" position, pushing for greater compromise with Nationalists in the interest of peace (McAuley 1997; Shirlow 2012). And although the Ulster Loyalist position has remained powerful in the post-Agreement era, DUP and UUP acquiescence to police reform and power sharing (among other official peace process reforms) speaks to the power of moderating forces within broader Unionism. Unionist and Loyalist communities have always been heterogeneous communities, despite stereotypical depictions to the contrary that have for decades pervaded the accounts of journalists, academics, and political leaders (Shirlow and McGovern 1997, 1–7; Shirlow 2012, 1–10).

Considering scholarly recognition of the heterogenous nature of Unionism, it is surprising that recent debates have not fully explored the range of positions on Brexit *within* Unionism. Important new work has analyzed the party politics of Unionism in the wake of Brexit (Murphy and Evershed 2019) but not the cultural and political fissures within the broader PUL community that Brexit is potentially fostering, or may at least reveal. As Finlayson (1997, 76) reminds us, "The so-called two communities in Northern Ireland are products of different imaginings of community, and these imaginings are the products of discursively constructed categories of belonging." As such, collective Unionist and Loyalist identities (as most identities) are plastic, and subject to the conjoined influence of competing discourses and the felt experience of one's position in the society. Within a collective, individuals are not solely conditioned subconsciously by discursive processes and ingroup pressures toward conformity (though these pressures are powerful) (Tajifel and Turner 1986; Coymak and O'Dwyer 2020); individuals can also creatively construct alternative political imaginations through conscious reflection on lived experience, exercising agency and contributing to "bottom-up" re-articulations of identity which transgress historically imposed boundaries. Following Bourdieu, Smithey (2011, 27) conceptualizes social boundaries as fluctuating entities which are established and change "within an inherently conflicted field of rules that define the parameters of what is possible and yet, provide space for innovation." In periods of peacebuilding, the very parameters of what is possible widen as "rules," or socially acceptable behaviors reinforced via everyday interaction, change.

Moreover, the nature of a perceived threat and the cultural, economic, and political contexts in which it unfolds will ultimately shape how individuals and organizations react, and those reactions will never be singular. It is even possible that exogenous shocks such as Brexit can result in a "constitutional moment," a period "where popular and political discussion create a new frame for future politics" and new forms of collective identity (Todd 2017, 5). Jennifer Todd reminds us of Hannah Arendt's (1963) initial framing of such a moment as "paradigmatic of civic freedom, where norms rather than interests frame the future" of a nation and state (Todd 2017, 5). Constitutional moments "require a public openness to change in values, expectations and practices: a public not itself constrained by identities and interests, but open to political creativity, to a new beginning" (ibid., 5).

Guided by these ideas, the current chapter addresses the following questions: What discursive frames are emerging within broader Unionism in the wake of Brexit? How do they indicate a departure from conventional Unionist political ideology? And how (if at all) do such frames reveal the relative strength of post-Agreement norms of mutuality, such as the principle of consent? More generally, to what extent do the answers to these questions reveal a "constitutional moment" for Unionism and, by extension, Unionist-Nationalist relations? And what are the limitations of this "moment" politically and culturally?

THE POLITICS OF BREXIT IN NORTHERN IRELAND

Findings identify several important themes emerging from within the Unionist community regarding the impacts of Brexit on political discourse and identity construction. Not surprisingly, respondents indicate that Brexit has indeed brought to the surface that type of insecurity over the Irish threat and British betrayal which has historically constituted "Ulster Loyalism." One Unionist respondent explained how Nationalist calls for a border poll following the Brexit vote "created a Protestant backlash from Loyalism and I think it's still toxic" (interview with author, May 2020). Subsequently, the final proposed Brexit deal for NI was coined "the Betrayal Act" by many prominent Unionists and Loyalists. In November 2019, shortly after plans for withdrawal—including a customs check in the Irish Sea—were finalized, meetings held by Loyalists included discussions about "whether threats of violence would be needed to change the U.K. government's approach" (Reevell 2020).

Earlier dynamics also suggest that the hardline Ulster Loyalist position on the Protocol has resonance within elite circles of Unionism. Prominent Unionist Leave supporters consistently argued against a hard border between the Irish Republic and NI as a condition of Brexit (Gormley-Heenan and Aughey 2017, 2), but they also rejected alternatives proposed by the EU (Teague 2019). It appears that the DUP campaign for Leave was guided primarily by interests of "political expediency and electoral opportunism" rather than a genuine ideological commitment. In the lead-up to the 2016 Brexit vote, most DUP representatives assumed that Remain would win and were not particularly worried about it. More of concern to them was showing uncompromised commitment to the Union. Then DUP First Minister Arlene Foster adopted a pro-Leave position "to placate and tap into these Eurosceptic urges while seemingly posing little by way of real risk to the 'modernising' project of the DUP's more economistic, generally younger and more (neo) liberal wing" (Murphy and Evershed 2019, 12).

After the referendum, the DUP dug in its heels and took hold of an opportunity to wield greater power in British Parliament. The DUP found itself with substantial influence in Westminster after forming a Confidence and Supply Agreement with then Prime Minister Theresa May's Conservative Party in 2017 (Tonge 2017). For some time, DUP opposition to all proposed solutions on how to maintain an open border between NI and the Republic of Ireland resulted in logjams in EU-UK negotiations over the terms of withdrawal. However, the DUP eventually lost favor with the Tories, who became increasingly divided over how to move negotiations forward. Following May's resignation, and replacement by Boris Johnson, the final trade agreement, effective January 2021, maintained an open land border, but imposed the customs border down the Irish Sea (i.e., the NI Protocol). In effect, NI is now in a unique situation in comparison with the other UK countries: it will have access to the EU single market of goods coming from south of the border while trade relations with other UK countries are subject to new regulations and customs checks. Confusion over trade laws between NI and other UK countries occurred through 2021 after the Protocol went into effect, causing serious disruptions to trade (Drewett 2021; Kelso 2021).

Earlier in the post Brexit period, some Unionists and Loyalists were driven to defend their historical constitutional position (as were Nationalists) as the negotiations between the UK and EU over the terms of British withdrawal became increasingly uncertain and contentious. One respondent noted that, "under Brexit, actually there was this sense that the people were being driven back into community positions." As he elaborates,

> What it's done is polarized that sense of [ethnonational] identity. . . . Of course, the whole island of Ireland reacted. The Irish began immediately on a narrative that's all about, "Will you be better trading as one island?" . . . Of course, that then works itself all the way down to the street level to, "I told you so, you can't trust the Irish. They'll do anything to get rid of us British. Blah, blah, blah . . ." That manifests itself in an incomplete, still in gestation peace process where those vulnerabilities that are all still relatively raw and easily accessible [become activated]. Absolutely, that's a big issue. (Interview with author, June 2020)

Others similarly indicated that an "economic centrist" approach to the Brexit debate (as termed by the same respondent) has been used by both sides to justify their respective constitutional agendas, translating into an activation of the deep-seeded mistrust "on the street level" between PUL and CNR communities. Sinn Fein's pro-Remain position leading up to the Brexit referendum reflected a volte-face from its previous long-standing Euroscepticism,[4] motivated by the interests of maintaining Northern Ireland's power-sharing institutions, preserving the island's economic benefits from membership in the single EU market (Murphy 2020), and maintaining support from its newer, growing, more "moderate" constituencies uncommitted to traditional Irish Nationalism. Its shift to a "pro-EU" party has led anti-Agreement dissident republicans and other critically leftist Nationalist groups to charge Sinn Fein with wanting to erode the sovereignty of any potential "new Ireland" to Brussels (see Trumbore and Owsiak 2019). Nonetheless, following the surprising victory of the "Leave" vote, fear of the problematic consequences that would likely result from the "hard Brexit" pushed by the main Unionist parties during negotiations over the terms of withdrawal has, for some, validated

Sinn Fein's call for an "all-Ireland" to preserve the trade and citizenship benefits of EU membership and sustain the peace process. A poll by Garry et al. (2018) found that Brexit increased the percentage of Catholics who would consider voting for a united Ireland. In addition—and quite surprisingly— several respondents indicated that an economic rationale for a united Ireland spearheaded by Nationalists amid the rise of disruptions to trade with other UK countries is garnering some consideration among moderate Unionist circles and the Unionist business class in particular. As one respondent explains:

> There's no doubt that Brexit is seen as an opportunity to now discuss the benefits of the unification of Ireland for social and economic reasons rather than purely just political reasons. Republicans are looking at how they can garnish support from the greater Unionist community, particularly the business community around that agenda. This isn't a United Ireland to get rid of the Brits. This is . . . [an] Ireland to stay in Europe . . . for business, security, and growth. (Interview with author, June 2020)

Indeed, DUP response to Theresa May's initial EU Withdrawal proposal resulted in "signs of fissuring in middle-class unionism." One prominent member of the Unionist middle class commented that "The DUP have convinced many 'soft' unionists like myself to seriously consider whether we would be better in a United Ireland." Another admitted to be "entertaining the idea of a new Ireland. . . . Everything is on the table" (Mallie 2018). For some Unionists, there is a sense that Nationalists are benefiting politically from the Brexit process by leveraging discussions in such a way as to make the idea of a united Ireland a "practical" social and economic issue more so than a purely ethnonational one. Nonetheless, rather than blaming Nationalists, many Unionist respondents explain how the DUP's Brexit strategy leaves no room for negotiation and has backed the party "into a corner," ultimately undermining its position in NI and UK politics moving forward. According to one interviewee, "The DUP . . . just painted themselves into a corner, found it very difficult to get out of and didn't have an adequate solution." To him, the lack of adequate solution was not masked by DUP rhetoric about "a slippery slope: 'if we're part of an economic united Ireland, how long before there is a border poll and we're part of an actual united Ireland?' That's the phraseology they used" (interview with author, June 2020).

More generally, since the NI Protocol decision was finalized, deep reflection about the direction of Unionism, by Unionists, is evident. The calculating nature of DUP politics to maximize its position as the most "pro-British" NI party frustrates many, who perceive the party as showing little concern about implications of Brexit on the terms of community relations theretofore upheld by the Agreement. As one Unionist respondent describes, messaging around Brexit exaggerated differences in opinion between PUL and CNR communities, contributing to divisions that could potentially have otherwise been moderated through employment of alternative discourses.[5] She criticizes Unionist politicians for suggesting that "if you were Protestant, you were, 'Oh, let's leave the European Union.' If you were Catholic, 'Let's stay.' That's nonsense. Forty-eight percent of Protestant women voted to stay in the EU. That misinformation of playing on people's fears here was very much so." The same respondent elaborates on how some of the residents she works with in her community-based organization "are starting to see the difficulty" with the DUP narrative on the implications of Northern Ireland's unique position within the UK and Ireland as a result of the Withdrawal Agreement. Some recognize, in her words, that "it opens up possibilities that you [NI] could be a hub for bringing in businesses from Europe, that [inaudible] not going to leave for England or not go to Scotland because of the connection between themselves and the Republic of Ireland. I think we're in a win-win situation" (interview with author, May 2020). A different respondent makes a similar point, indicating that the women she works with resisted the "sectarianization" of Brexit politics from early on:

> I think the one thing about Brexit was that we find from our women, they were saying, "Please do not turn it into a political football and please do not sectarianize it," because the assumption was that if you were a Protestant, you didn't want to be in Europe and if you were a Catholic, you did. In reality, a lot of women realized the impact of what it was going to be like for them, whether that was because their passport was not going to be valid. But obviously the big issue for the voluntary sector here was the . . . funding that came from Europe. While we get a package of some sort, it'll not match what we're losing. Even though the Westminster government is saying that it would, we know it won't. [The loss of] European Social Funds, things like that, that'll be an issue. (Interview with author, June 2020)

Todd (2017, 4) identifies how shifts in collective identity can occur "when exogenous shocks, and in particular power shifts, give windows of opportunity and incentives for change, which are framed and grasped by actors whose resources have themselves incrementally changed" or are expected to change. Respondents indicated that young people, and other sub-constituencies within broader Unionism (i.e., leaders of voluntary peacebuilding organizations) were more concerned about practical matters of Brexit that will impact their future opportunities than they were about "the border issue." As a PUL leader in the grassroots sector explains,

> There's a lot of anger by young people here, because Northern Ireland did decide to stay and a lot of them, who would have been looking to education overseas or

projects like Erasmus and stuff, where there's a lot of young people benefiting from that—if that's all gone, there's nothing being put in its place. . . . Anytime that we asked any politicians here who were pro Brexit [why they supported the Leave position], they really couldn't answer the questions. I could give them 100 reasons why we shouldn't leave. They had a lot of difficulty giving me some why we should: "Oh, all this money's"—no, it's not. (Interview with author, May 2020)

Another PUL respondent suggests that the DUP attempted to leverage calls by Sinn Fein for a border poll in the wake of the referendum to promote Unionist fear, after showing no apparent concern for the potential consequences of Brexit on the peacebuilding community during its Leave campaign. Rather than blaming Nationalists for escalating unification narratives, many Unionist respondents emphasized more so the role of Unionist parties for unwittingly assisting the Nationalist case for greater north-south connection post-Brexit by framing the issue in a way that was overreliant on emotive ethnonational attachments. Moreover, criticism of the major Unionist parties (but especially DUP) was most apparent when respondents conveyed worry about the consequences of Brexit on the future of their respective organizations. The following statement is a case in point:

The latest thing now is the border poll. That, again, that's the whip of fear to make people frightened of having a united Ireland or—The EU made that so much easier, that you could be a European citizen and nobody bothered [pushing for a united Ireland]. Already they put the tariffs up for stuff coming into Northern Ireland . . . after lying quite well. DUP said no such thing would happen. Interesting to see what happens down the line, but for us it's a massive loss, I have to say. In honesty we lose all that, we lose all those contacts. We lose all those other programs like Erasmus and different things. We will lose a lot of our core money. (Interview with author, May 2020)

The dire social and economic outlook for the future, including the sustainability of numerous EU-funded community-based peacebuilding programs, and rapid decline in DUP power following the dissolution of the Confidence and Supply Agreement, led many in the broader Unionist community to become increasingly critical of the Unionist status-quo. Within this space, where hegemonic constructs of ethnonational belonging become demystified and transgressed, the potential for widespread reconfigurations of ingroup identity increases. Todd argues that, in times of change, it is productive to focus on the subtle changes in the content of a collective identity rather than focus on identity categories. "In practice, the changes which make major impact are not, or not solely, the giving up or adoption of a [Unionist] . . . or a European, identity, but becoming a different sort of [Unionist] . . . or

European" (Todd 2005, 433). The "instability of some meaning configura-
tions . . . and dissonance between seemingly authoritative official meanings
and on-the-ground popular meanings" (Todd 2005, 434), moreover, are most
likely during periods of multi-institutional flux and uncertainty. It is implied
by some Unionist respondents that their attachment to a "European" identity
became more salient after the referendum. Internal Unionist rows over Brexit
signified a felt loss of the benefits constituting European identity, while fur-
thering their distance from the "official meanings" reflected in DUP politics,
namely that Brexit is about strengthening Northern Ireland's position in the
Union and defending against a slippery slope toward Irish unification. Even
after evidence accrued to suggest that some within Unionism are open to the
Protocol, the DUP refused to compromise its position on the "official meaning" of the issue to the Unionist community (Kula 2021). Yet, Brexit largely
symbolizes for some in broader Unionism an immanent social and economic
crisis, unwanted separation from the EU, British indifference to the NI peace
process, and DUP irresponsibility. Apparently, for many, the DUP's perceived
dishonesty about likely consequences of Brexit for their families and communities corresponds to a growing debate within Unionism as whether and
how to move forward politically and socially in the post-withdrawal period.

The perceived self-serving nature of British politicians illuminates to some
in the broader Unionist community the lack of recognition they receive from
Westminster, as well as the former's indifference to the principles of the
Agreement and stability of the NI peace process. One respondent explains
how the Tories "never worked out how complicated it [Brexit] would be,
how impactful it would be on the island of Ireland, how possibly negatively
transformative it would have been on the Good Friday Agreement. None
of this was worked out, frankly, because they didn't care" (interview with
author, May 2021). Indeed, there is evidence to corroborate this assertion.
Cowell-Meyers and Gallaher's (2020, 219) analysis of the Hansard record
on four key debates on the EU Withdrawal Act of 2018 in the House of
Commons (the first proposed Withdrawal Agreement) found "that the British
Parliament has departed markedly from its established pattern of bilateral-
ism, bipartisanship and deference to government in dealing with Northern
Ireland."[6] The British government has appeared to abandon its role as a key
"external ethnoguarantor" of Northern Ireland's peace process—a role which,
in partnership with the Irish government and "higher mediators" (the US and
the EU) had once been pivotal in transforming the conflict and enhancing
"the scale and nature of the economic assistance" to local peacebuilding projects (Byrne 2011, 11; see also Byrne 2007). As put by one respondent, "Boris
Johnson shafted the DUP . . . Dominic Cummings said Northern Ireland could
fall under the sea for all he cared. They were promised there wouldn't be a
border in the Irish Sea, and there is one." This new version of an old familiar

threat (i.e., British betrayal) is leading, in his view, to "a wakening up happening for Unionism" (interview with author, May 2021). One Loyalist identified "a feeling of insecurity" within Loyalism as a result of Brexit, but attributed such feeling to the DUP's "no surrender" stance during the 2019 withdrawal negotiations:

> if you look at what was going on with Brexit, the DUP had a really strong stance and they went in with Theresa May. They could have backed the good thing there, [and] there would've been no border down the Irish sea. The backstop was opened as a security measure, but they rejected that and they were foolish. Then Boris Johnson was able to [inaudible] them to suit his own needs and own agenda. He [unintelligible 00:18:34] them and then they ended up looking very foolish and silly. (Interview with author, June 2020)

Overall, while a renewed sense of threat via British betrayal has come to pervade the Unionist collective consciousness as a result of Brexit, this, according to many interviewees, did not empower insular Unionist party politics to the same extent that it had in the past. Rather, at least for sections of the Unionist community, it seems to have compounded a burgeoning distrust of the DUP and a recognition of the limits of the "no surrender" politics which brought it success in previous moments of constitutional uncertainty.

DEMOCRATIC VISIONS, AND A RISE OF THE "MIDDLE GROUND"?

Respondent discourses signify a configuration of a nuanced, reflexive Unionist political position that prioritizes the consent principle, democratic accountability, and the potential material consequences of Brexit across ethnoreligious lines over traditional ideological loyalties. For many, though, debates surrounding Brexit did not so much lead to the creation of "new" Unionist political visions as much as it facilitated a more open articulation of alternative conceptions of identity which had already taken root. The narratives of most respondents reflected a shared understanding of NI democracy, linked to neither historical ethnonational position, when explaining their frustration with DUP politics and the UK government handling of Brexit. Implicit in the particular construct of democracy employed in respondents' discourses is recognition that the interests of neither ethnopolitical bloc warrant greater attention than those of the other. As put by one Unionist interviewee,

> the problem with Brexit here was that the majority of people in Northern Ireland voted to stay. But because the DUP were the leading party, and because they went into that arrangement with [unintelligible 00:38:49]. . . . And the people

here, both Catholic and Protestant, would go, "Well you don't have a mandate
from us because we didn't vote for this." (Interview with author, May 2020)

Interestingly, this statement echoes a point made by Sinn Fein and members
of the broader Nationalist community, that "the DUP have wrongly assumed
it has authority to speak on behalf of all in Northern Ireland, despite the
fact the majority voted to stay in the EU" (Mallie 2018). Several Unionist
respondents make the same point, acknowledging that the majority position
on Brexit in NI—even if determined largely by the Catholic vote—should be
recognized during withdrawal negotiations, consistent with the principle of
consent but also reflective of a more universal democratic position rooted in
normative support for majority rule.

Some respondents also indicate how, among some networks of
cross-community peacebuilding practitioners, the Orange and Green fault line
separating positions on Brexit seemed to gradually blur as its implications on
their shared organizational interests began to illuminate. As one respondent
describes, "I think for a wee while it was quite divisive. . . . It became orange
and green for a while." Yet, as the implications of Brexit began to materialize,
"people started looking and going, 'as a community, we've done very well
out of European peace funding, for roads and things . . . and for things like
research by the universities," and their views "started to change" (interview
with author, June 2020). As Todd (2017, 4) explains, substantive change in
identity increases "when change in power relations make it clear to the public
that the identity status quo is no longer an option," facilitated by the emergence of new "cultural repertoires." For many, the DUP's mishandling of its
power in the Brexit process was a significant moment highlighting the need
for a more "forward-thinking" brand of Unionist politics.

Some reflected more commitment to a "European" identity than Unionist
or Loyalist identity when discussing the politics of Brexit in NI. Accordingly,
data corroborate an observation by Sinn Fein lawmaker John O'Dowd, who
says "more and more people are asking themselves the question, what is my
identity outside the European Union, what has Brexit done to my identity"
(Thomas and Ferguson 2020)? The "mandate from us" mentioned by an
above-cited respondent, refers to *both* Protestants and Catholics—a people
undefined primarily by ethnonational identity. Although more Catholics than
Protestants voted Remain, many Protestant respondents implied that the clear
position of the Northern Irish "people" on Brexit was Remain and that this
should have been taken more seriously by British and Unionist politicians.
At the same time, a few Nationalist respondents recognize the heterogeneity
of the PUL community and the open-mindedness of some elements within
it to rejecting hardline Ulster Loyalist politics and embracing a more con-
ciliatory approach to the Brexit crisis in NI. Also implying a belief that NI

democracy is being undermined by the Brexit process, a Nationalist explains how "the vast majority of people within NI wanted to remain within Europe. Albeit, the UK voted Leave but the Unionists and Loyalists, I think grasped what that meant for their local people. It wasn't just Catholics, Republicans, and Nationalists who voted to remain in Europe" (interview with author, June 2020).

There are other implications of Brexit on questions of identity, however. One respondent notes how the Brexit debate has led to a swelling-up of discussion among the "middle ground communities"—the growing number of residents who identify neither as British nor Irish—about their place in Northern Ireland's polity. Approximately one-third of NI residents identify neither with Irish Nationalism nor British Unionism, but rather designate their national identity as "Northern Irish" (Lowry 2019; see also Coymak 2015). Other indications of the rise of more nuanced political identities in the North were documented earlier in the peace process (see Ferguson and Gordon 2007). According to some respondents, Brexit has triggered a closer examination of just how the interests and identities of the "center ground" are, or are not, represented in the NI polity. As one participant in the study explains, "What's interesting is that middle ground . . . those people who don't identify as Irish or British, were then looking all around them [after the Brexit vote] and looking at the landscape and saying, 'Where do we fit here? Where do we want to go with this?' There is this bubbling up of the middle ground" (interview with author, June 2020). This "bubbling up of the middle ground" is reflected in the 2019 General Election results. Research by Hayward (2020b, 55) suggests that the "centre ground" turned out to the polls "in a way not seen for over a decade." Apparently, many voters who supported Alliance were "motivated by their pro-remain stance and by frustration at DUP-Sinn Fein ability to hold the region in limbo . . ." The Alliance Party and SDLP gained seats in the Executive as "previous DUP and Sinn Fein voters change[d] their minds" (Hayward 2020b, 55).

Respondents also suggest that Brexit has created an opportunity for leaders in the community sector to develop workshops which allow Nationalists and Unionists to discuss the underlying intercommunal tensions that it has brought back to the surface. In this way, Brexit is opening up new opportunities for intra-ethnic *and* cross-community dialogue about identity. One respondent describes how he harnessed the tensions surrounding Brexit to facilitate such cross-community discussions:

I give people an opportunity to talk about things like Brexit, and national identity, and why partition the people, and why a hundred years later we're still talking about partition, and we're still talking about borders, and why those are important. I think Brexit for me just opened up that debate. A lot of people who don't like conflict, or are conflict averse will come down and say, "God, do we need to talk about this?" Yes, we do. (Interview with author, June 2020)

As Todd (2017, 12) notes, "compromise" is not necessary for a constitutional moment to emerge; rather, an "openness to discussion," and a willingness to temporarily set aside ethnic loyalties might suffice. According to respondents, Brexit has propelled cross-community discussions, facilitated by local NGOs that critically examine longstanding historical misperceptions about the foundations of each ethnonational community. Moreover, cross-community discussions about Brexit indicate that the constitutional question was not the primary focus of many Leave voters during the referendum. As one cross-community activist explains, there were some similarities in reasons for voting "Leave" among NI residents and their counterparts in England and Wales, most notably, the threat perceived from increasing immigration. Brexit, for him, triggered the capacity to attract more public conversations about important issues beyond the constitutional question, including the growing presence of "newcomer communities":

One of the marginalized communities are the newcomer communities that are coming to Northern Ireland. Brexit also opened up that debate. . . . I suppose explicitly people were saying, "We don't want to be in the European Union anymore. We want to leave the EU simply because we don't have control over our own sovereignty here." Scratch below the surface and it was about immigration, and it was about newcomers coming to Northern Ireland and supposedly taking our jobs. That's not the case. . . . We need to deal with that element of racism and migration as well. That's a live issue at the moment. Brexit brought that up and made that much more explicit. In some respects, that was a good thing. (Interview with author, June 2020)

For this respondent, among others, the post-Brexit moment is seen as an opportunity to critically examine misperceptions of threat from various "Others." (In a sad irony, many of the groups leading this type of work are threatened by the economic consequences of Brexit, including the possible loss of EU Peace Fund grants.)

Although Brexit has presented opportunities for community leaders to facilitate important dialogue and challenge insular constructions of identity, these positive developments should not distract from other, less generative dynamics underway vis-à-vis the impact of Brexit on socio-political relations in NI. Focus on Unionist party politics in general, and DUP actions in particular, reveal that the reactionary nature of the "Ulster Loyalist" brand of Unionism remains powerful.

SIGNS OF A NEW "UNIONIST" POLITICS, OR BACK TO THE FUTURE?

The lack of a coherent Unionist strategy on dealing with the consequences of Brexit on the peace process has become increasingly clear to many grassroots leaders and journalists in NI. Some Unionist respondents indicated a reluctant belief (or at least hope) that the DUP's disappointing election results in 2019 would kickstart reflection among the party leadership on their relationship with Unionist constituencies and the broader NI population. One community leader implicated the DUP "fear factor" as an ongoing problem in Unionist politics, but also identified a shift in the party's discourse which began to manifest at the time of our conversation:

> Of course, the DUP will use that fear factor within Unionist communities, particularly when they need to mobilize the vote but there won't be any voting [in the near future] . . . because we have had one quite recently. . . . You can see a change in some circumstances at the minute. For example, we had the agricultural minister—along came hardcore DUP politicians saying that, "You know what . . . there's a closer link in economic terms to the Republic." (interview with author, May 2020)

Another respondent, who leads a community-based peacebuilding organization, provided the same example of potential movement in the DUP position (though she also indicates the intransigence that party officials had previously demonstrated):

> I think they tried to turn it into an Orange and Green vote which was wrong, but it's interesting that one of the DUP ministers come out just during the week and said about the Brexit scenario, that maybe Northern Ireland's got the best of both worlds at the moment in that they've got one foot in Europe and one foot in the United Kingdom, which is going to benefit them. But people like myself and others were saying way back, three years ago, [that] that was going to be the case, but they wouldn't have it. (Interview with author, June 2020)

These respondents refer to an instance in May 2020, when then DUP Agricultural Minister Edwin Poots—a longtime hardline Unionist politician—told the BBC that NI "would have the advantage of actually having access to the Single Market and to the UK market, and make NI an attractive place for inward investment" (Campbell 2020). Such narratives led some to believe, if only temporarily, in an emerging moderation within the DUP. As one Nationalist respondent notes, "DUP seem to have used this opportunity to retreat slightly from their previous position. . . . This was one of the more interesting parts of the whole Brexit experience" (interview with author, June 2020).

At the same time, many take care to envisage that the "pragmatism" reflected in DUP politics at that time was mostly a result of "the gains that Alliance had made in the past election and the reduction of the [DUP] numbers to 90 from 100," rather than a genuine transition in party leaders' thinking. As this government official elaborates, "The threat is still there. There's no doubt that the party whip is strong and the party line is strong. You'll even see that in the councils" (interview with author, June 2020). Following this interview, and the initial rollout of the NI Protocol, the caution this respondent demonstrated when describing prospects of DUP reform was validated. Poots was named party leader following the forced resignation of Arlene Foster who, in the words of one PUL respondent, was perceived to not be "doing a good enough job" representing Unionists' opposition to the Protocol. Hope that DUP was constructing a more moderate, "pragmatic" politics around Brexit seemed to fade in 2021, when the party appeared to fall into "war with itself" (Carroll 2021c). Following Poots's nomination of Paul Givan for the First Minister position in the NI Executive, widespread criticism from within his party for not consulting them before making the nomination, and for agreeing to a British government-brokered deal to revive the Executive, led to his ousting after less than a month as party leader. The deal proposed "commitment on a long-promised Irish language act," which "is anathema to many in the DUP" (Carroll 2021c). Poots was replaced by party whip Jeffrey Donaldson, who indicated that his top priority would be "to campaign against the Northern Ireland protocol" (Carroll 2021d). DUP critics contend that "the only explanation" for the party's leadership's hard opposition on the protocol is the belief that "it can get the British government to renege on the Good Friday Agreement" (McColl 2021).

Cillian McGrattan indicates that many Unionists feel that the principle of consent is violated by the Protocol, as it fails to acknowledge the majority Unionist position on the issue. In his view, "There's no doubt that the imposition of the Sea Border" violates the principle of consent. "It also leaves unionism without any solid ground on which to stand to exert leverage," in contrast to Nationalists, who "enjoy the vociferous encouragement of Dublin, the Biden White House and the EU" (quoted in Bradfield 2021). Unionist and Loyalist anger over the Protocol appeared to deepen in 2021, when the implementation of new regulations caused disruptions to trade, corresponding to a turn back to conventional DUP resistance politics (McClements 2021). One respondent reflects on these events when noting an "increase in Loyalist activity" including "street protests . . . being organized through towns, hamlets, villages throughout the North of Ireland here in relation to opposition to the Protocol." (These Loyalist protests, however, are much smaller than those that occurred in opposition to Sunningdale in 1974 and the Anglo-Irish Agreement in the 1980s, likely reflecting the significant extent to which the contemporary Protestant middle classes have withdrawn from ethnonational politics.) According to the same respondent, "I pick up from Loyalists that there is an increasing hardening of attitudes, particularly with the young people" (interview with author, June 2021).[7] Segments of Unionism and Loyalism committed to a hardline rejection of the Protocol may not represent the majority Unionist position on the issue, but do exert substantial political influence—as indicated, for example, when Arlene Foster "and two of her party's MPs . . . held talks with the LCC" in early 2021, "prompting rebukes from critics who said they were legitimising paramilitaries." The LCC is the Loyalist Communities Council, an organization that represents the main Loyalist paramilitary groups (UVF, Red Hand Commando, and UDA), and is staunchly opposed to the Protocol. These meetings happened just prior to the "worst rioting in Northern Ireland in years" that occurred in West Belfast in April 2021, attributed to Loyalist frustrations over the Protocol and perceptions of anti-Loyalist "two-tier policing" (BBC 2021).[8] Shortly thereafter, DUP Agriculture Minister Gordon Lyons "halted work on permanent post-Brexit border control posts in Northern Ireland" (Carroll 2021b). A month later, the LCC "sent a letter to British Prime Minister Boris Johnson and Ireland's Taoiseach, Micheal Martin . . . withdrawing support for the Good Friday Agreement in protest at Northern Ireland's Irish Sea Border with the rest of the UK" (Carroll 2021b). During the same time period (May 2021) a young LCC representative said he "wouldn't rule violence off the table" in response to the NI Protocol (Manley 2021; see also, Brennan 2021). For some in Loyalism, there is apparently a desire to see Brexit "collapse" the power sharing system. As one community activist elaborates,

> it's palpable the amount of fear and anxiety that's generated in there [within Loyalism]. I think the dilemma they have is that young Loyalists, even the older Loyalists, will quite happily see the institutions in Stormont collapse. See, they get nothing out of it. They have no vested interest in it. They feel that the Good Friday Agreement has probably not delivered on what they thought. In fact, it seems to be going the opposite way. They'll be quite happy for the political institutions here to collapse and quite happy for the DUP, Ulster Loyalists [inaudible] to walk away from those power-sharing agreements with Republicans and Nationalists. (Interview with author, May 2021)

The historically rooted instincts of Ulster Loyalism remain powerful. In February 2022, the DUP once again collapsed the Executive in protest over the Protocol, and warned that it would not return to participate in power-sharing institutions if the subsequent May 2022 elections result in Sinn Fein becoming the largest party in the Assembly (O'Carroll 2022).

For some community leaders in working-class Loyalist communities, however, there is neither a more inclusive construction of Unionist identity, nor a turn toward insular Loyalist populism, but rather a deepening sense of apathy. While some previously apathetic voters have turned to Alliance Party, roughly two-thirds are middle-class residents (Tonge 2020, 463). This is not to say that middle-class voters are necessarily more politically enlightened than their working-class counterparts. As McAuley (1997, 170) recognizes, there has always been a willingness, "by at least some sections of the Protestant working class, to reassess their own position, and to challenge the authority of the established Unionist political leadership." Yet as discussed in chapter 3, the working-class Loyalist party, the PUP, has been marginal in governance, stigmatized for its association with paramilitarism within mainstream "law and order Unionism" (see also, Bruce 2007, 122–130). And while the progressive segment of Loyalism continues to be critical of Unionist political elites' attempts at manipulation, they generally still hold ethnonational ideological commitment to conventional brands of Ulster Loyalism. For those disaffected by DUP threat politics in working-class PUL communities, there is a struggle to identify a feasible alternative. As one Loyalist respondent explains, "If you think about it, we never voted for people who could do things for us; we vote in Northern Ireland to keep the other side out." This person conveyed a frustration with the stasis of governance within a Sinn Fein-DUP run Assembly, but also acknowledged that, after turning away from DUP, she is unsure about what alternative party she could support: "With the DUP falling apart, the Ulster Unionist Party don't have the capacity even to take that [position as the leading Unionist party] on. It's so fractured now that I'm not even sure where I could go myself" (interview with author, May 2021). One former Loyalist paramilitary prisoner explains that the structure of segregation in urban areas of NI contributes to apathy within segments of Loyalism, referring to his own disengagement as a case in point:

They all vote in their silos. . . . It's linked to the history of fear. Irrespective of what you think about people's politics for both communities, if there is such a thing, people will not go out and vote for a Nationalist or a Republican if they live in an area that's—the Shankill is a typical example. The Shankill will never have a [Unionist] MP because they border with West Belfast and their electoral ward is categorized as West Belfast. The other side of the Shankill is in North Belfast where now we're seeing it predominantly on the race for Nationalism and a new MP with John Finucane [replacing long-time DUP MP Nigel Dodds]. Understandably, they'll not vote at all then go out and vote for someone that doesn't uphold their principles of Unionism and Loyalism. That feeds into one of my own answers to your questions earlier where my own engagement in voting terms with politics has been very little in the last two decades because I don't see anyone representing my form of [progressive Loyalist] politics in the area where I live. (Interview with author, June 2020)

Other respondents from working-class PUL communities convey a similar apathetic attitude toward local elections, underscored by exasperation with the sectarian politics of the DUP in particular and a lack of viable alternatives which represent their Unionist and Loyalist beliefs. Indeed, urban working-class Protestant wards have had the "highest" incidence of "non-voting" in some post-Agreement elections (Brewer 2013, 1; see also Delargy 2017).

It seems as though the apathy that once contributed to DUP success in the polls (Tonge 2008, 66) is no longer beneficial to the party amid the increasing Catholic presence in contested districts. Considering that the Agreement holds that the constitutional status of the North is subject to change and may be incorporated into the Republic of Ireland if a majority of the population of the island votes accordingly, the prospect of a united Ireland is a starkly realistic prospect for Unionists—especially since the rise in tensions over Brexit. As one respondent notes, the 2019 DUP loss in North Belfast "says volumes" about a growing Nationalist presence paralleled by Protestant voter apathy. Such apathy, moreover, is linked in part to negative perceptions of the consociational system itself. One Loyalist describes a perception of how a burgeoning disaffection with sectarian politics of fear, coupled with a lack of delivery on material interests for his North Belfast community, led some to avoid the polls altogether (though it is yet to be determined statistically if this had a decisive impact on the election results). As he explains,

Come here election time, you'll get, "If you don't vote for us, you'll get them." People went to vote for Nigel Dodds. And then some people say, "I'm not voting no more. I vote for him all the time, and he does nothing." If we end up with Sinn Féin, he doesn't take a seat in Westminster, [so] we're not going to lose out on anything because we don't get nothing with Nigel Dodds anyway. Where's Nigel Dodds now? . . . Now he's a Lord. A Lord for doing what? Absolutely nothing. Turning up to parades, contentious parades, shouting his mouth off about Ulster, shouting out against [inaudible]. That's all he was, a troublemaker. That's what they all are, both sides. (Interview with author, June 2020)

Overall, exasperation with threat politics has led some to a position of apathy rather than hope for a transformative brand of Unionism or Loyalism. The attitudes of this milieu of mostly Loyalist respondents generally do not signal signs of a potential "constitutional moment" in the same way as those from middle-class Unionist backgrounds. Certainly, a "new Ireland" is not something Loyalists would easily acquiesce to, and there is little mention among PUL respondents I spoke with of anything reflecting a burgeoning European identity. Loyalists generally have greater connection to the legacy of the Troubles, having participated in political violence or being close to others who have, and thus have trouble stomaching the prospect that what was fought and sacrificed for (i.e., the Union) could be compromised.[9] In addition, material interests at stake in regard to Brexit and the NI Protocol for other sections of Unionism (such as the business class) which underscore some degree of open-mindedness about Northern Ireland's constitutional identity, are of less concern in working-class Loyalist strongholds, wherein "peace dividends" are few and far between.

CONCLUSION

This chapter intended to identify emerging discourses in NI about Brexit which reflect the potential for a "constitutional moment" in Unionist collective identity. While findings corroborate previous observations of Brexit's divisive impact on intercommunal relations, they also, somewhat paradoxically, point to an inflection point in Unionism. Respondents' narratives reveal complex interpretations of the implications of Brexit and corresponding Unionist politics that do not simply reify an "us" versus "them" intercommunal dynamic, or re-emergence of the "border of the mind." Rather, such interpretations also illuminate a reaffirmation of the consent principle and more general commitment to democratic accountability as core to NI political society. The transitional Unionist political imaginations reflected by respondents above coincide with the continuation of a reactionary and fear-induced ethnopolitics among some segments of the PUL community, and a disaffection from NI politics altogether, among others. Brexit appears to have produced a paradox within Unionism: subtle indications of a "constitutional moment" have emerged, reflecting a potential for flux in socio-political identity facilitated by principles of "Ulster British" Unionism. At the same time, however, a reactionary Ulster Loyalism, underscored by a politics of fear and defeatism, has intensified, particularly within working-class Loyalist strongholds, paralleled by a deepening sense of apathy among others within the same communities. For some, "Brexit heightened suspicion in each community that the other side is once again going all out for political victory" (Teague 2019, 708). However, Sinn Fein's manipulation of uncertainties resulting from Brexit to promote the unification agenda has been shrugged off by others as something to be expected. More important to many Unionist's I spoke with was the role of the British government and main Unionist parties in creating a regional political dynamic which could strengthen Sinn Fein's position.

Many Unionist respondents did not interpret the situation as the DUP did, as merely another incident signaling the potential slippery slope toward unification. Instead, many blamed the DUP, not Nationalists, for creating this situation, and interpreted Brexit as a threat to their European identity. Newspaper reports also suggest that some "soft Unionists" from the business class are even willing to discuss the option of a united Ireland!

Connolly and Doyle (2019, 233) argue that the "way in which the provisions of the Good Friday Agreement and majority opinion in Northern Ireland were ignored, in order to pursue a concept of Brexit based on a narrow form of English nationalism, supported by a section of Ulster unionism, has started a debate on the future of the island which has gained momentum." Results here provide additional qualitative evidence to that point, and indicate emerging signs of Brexit as a constitutional moment in which new conversations and alliances are beginning to form, if not organizationally, then at least discursively. In this respect, findings corroborate Hayward's (2020b, 49) assertion that "Brexit has complicated, if not transcended, the traditional unionist/nationalist binary that defines political positions" in NI. Results reflect the strength of the consent principle as well as other inclusive democratic norms in underpinning the socio-political discourses about Brexit and its impacts on NI. The reaffirmation of the consent principle as core to a democratic NI, over above traditional notions of Ulster Loyalist identity or other exclusive ethnopolitical constructs reflects a moment where some Unionists are reconciling multiple identities (Unionist, European, etc.) and opting for the continuance of mutuality despite a show of domination by pro-unification Nationalists. Interests also play a role in shaping reconstructions of a joint Unionist-European identity, however. For instance, potential threats posed by Brexit to the business classes and community-based leaders reliant on EU funding have led to a critical reassessment of what "Unionism" should represent, and an increased salience of the importance of the European dimension of their identity as citizens of NI. Others suggest that a preoccupation with the party politics of Brexit has delayed movement on a variety of important forms of legislation needed to address deeply rooted social problems. As one government official explains, "the fact that there's been so much government time spent on it [Brexit], people are saying, what about all the other stuff? What about disability strategy? Mental health strategy? What about housing? Huge housing need within the Catholic working-class community that's not being met" (interview with author, May 2020). Socio-political fallout over Brexit distracts from efforts geared toward promoting various equality initiatives, undermining progress on social and economic issues.

Moreover, some degree of reconfiguration of Unionist identity does not necessarily suggest that official Unionist politics will follow suit. Respondents identify moments where DUP representatives signaled openness to accepting closer trade links with Ireland. However, as tensions over the Protocol deepened, so too has the DUP's hardline position on the issue, in appeal to its traditional base. The DUP withdrawal from power-sharing institutions in early 2022 reflects a doubling-down on its hardline Ulster Loyalist strategy; and its public discourse about the threat of Sinn Fein becoming the largest party in the North, which would relegate the DUP to a Deputy First Minister, rather than First Minister position, appears to be yet another attempt to enhance its prospects in the polls through promoting fear of burgeoning Nationalist power. The potential of tensions over the Protocol boiling over into political violence, and the influence of paramilitaries, continue to undermine the growth of a more inclusive Unionist politics as well. Yet, to many (as discussed in the subsequent chapter) the fragility of Northern Ireland's peace process, revealed in rows over Brexit, is deeply and structurally rooted in the consociational system of governance, which incentivizes the continuation of ethnonational and ethnoreligious binaries.

NOTES

1. The authors explain their point in more detail: "For unionists, if things are to stay the same (the Union continues and majority consent is affirmed), things will have to change (executive authority shared with nationalists and republicans as well as an all-Ireland dimension). For nationalists, if things are to change (a possible transition to Irish unity), then things will have to stay the same (unity can only be achieved on the basis of Unionist consent which means continuity of Northern Ireland's place within the Union). The essential point to note is that the principle of consent in this paradox involves mutuality" (Gormley-Heenan and Aughey 2017, 9).

2. The idea of the "sovereign people" also contains an explicitly ethnic component—"It is self-consciously ethnic in that its spiritual substance is a religious one" (i.e., evangelical Protestantism) (Aughey 1997, 22; see also Bruce 1986; Morrow 1997; McAllister 2005).

3. For example, the Sunningdale Agreement, proposed in 1973 by the British to allow the Irish government a consultative role in NI affairs, was fiercely resisted by Loyalist street protests and a labor strike which shut down industry, leading to the Agreement's collapse in 1974 (Bruce 2007, 102–108). The Anglo-Irish Agreement a decade later was rejected by leaders of the DUP and UUP who feared that its provision to increase cooperation between Britain and Ireland would amount to the beginning of a slippery slope toward Irish unification (Tonge 2002, 56–59). During and after the Troubles (1968–1998), it was often those opportunistic politicians, intent on benefiting themselves and their parties through sectarian conflict, who led in promoting a one-dimensional image of a paranoid Protestant Unionist "people" unified against Irish Nationalism, "Papism," and British betrayal.

4. In the early 2000s, Sinn Fein had "campaigned against various EU treaty reforms," including the Nice and Lisbon treaties (Murphy 2020).

5. A vast majority of Nationalists (88 percent) and Catholics (85 percent) voted Remain in the EU referendum, compared with 37 percent of those identifying as British and 40 percent as Protestants (see Dunin-Wasowicz 2018). However, fragmentation within Unionism vis-a-vis the referendum vote count is made more apparent when comparing votes by political party. For example, 89 percent of Traditional Unionist Voice (TUV) supporters voted Leave, compared to 70 percent of DUP voters and 54 percent of UUP voters (Garry and Coakley 2016).

6. The neglect of NI in the discourses of British politicians seem to reflect a lack of concern about the province among the broader UK population. Polls show that, even as the NI problem became central in debates over a potential British withdrawal deal with the EU, it has had little impact on the attitudes of the British public outside the six counties. According to a poll by British conservative Michael Ashcroft, "two-thirds of pro-Brexit voters would rather leave the Customs Union than avoid a hard border in Northern Ireland, and . . . six out of ten people surveyed 'would not mind either way' if Northern Ireland voted to leave the UK" (Buttersworth, 2019).

7. Earlier survey research shows that young Protestants are more pessimistic about the peace process than older Protestants and Catholics of all ages (see Smithey 2011, 15; Byrne 2011, 11).

8. Although official reports do not confirm the involvement of paramilitaries in the rioting, one DDR activist I interviewed during this period suggested that they must have had some organizational role. As he described: "When you look at the deaths that occurred within the Royal Family . . . those riots and stuff ended immediately. Suddenly [inaudible] themselves off the street. . . . Somebody [with power in the community] said to them, 'that's enough. No more of that.'"

9. See, chapter 3.

Chapter 6

"Peace Fatigue," Power Sharing, and Political Impediments to Community-based Peacebuilding

There has been a substantial increase in scholarly emphasis on the transformative role of "bottom-up" or "civil society" approaches to post-conflict transformation in recent years. Certainly, local community-based peacebuilding and transitional justice projects have unique strengths, such as, providing "clues as to what would or would not resonate at a national level, what kinds of 'reconciliation' have already occurred and what remains to be done" (Arriaza & Roht-Arriaza 2008, 170). Ethnographic research suggests that innovative solutions to local-level conflict by grassroots actors have informed the policy and practice of state institutions as well, including the police (Jarman 2006a). Knox's (2010, 26) study of community-based intergroup relation building in a West Belfast interface area suggests that historically segregated working-class communities "are capable of managing their own preferred destiny towards a more cohesive, integrated and shared society," and of "tackling the worst excesses of a deeply segregated society in a post-conflict era" (see also, Eriksson 2009; Smithey 2011). Mac Ginty (2014, 548) proposes that "everyday peace"—the facilitation of local-level intergroup co-existence through the bottom-up, "everyday diplomacy" of community-based stakeholders—is "an important building block of peace formation, especially as formal approaches to peacebuilding and statebuilding are often deficient."

Such arguments run counter to those of prominent pro-consociational scholars of NI, who argue that Protestant and Catholic communities are generally not interested in meaningful social integration, making the consociational political settlement the most practical approach to democratic governance (McGarry 2001). Under the consociational model of power sharing, methods such as grand coalition, mutual vetoes, and proportionality of authority are utilized to guarantee a minority group equal representation to the historically dominant group in the legislative process (Lijphart 1968). In NI, the power-sharing system erected under the Good Friday Agreement gives equal political representation to Unionists and Nationalists, as "matters that come before the legislature that are deemed to be 'key' can be endorsed only on a cross-community basis," requiring joint support from the largest Unionist and Nationalist parties (i.e., DUP and Sinn Fein since 2003) (Coulter and Murray 2008, 3). The "proportional electoral system" is also proposed by consociationalists to facilitate "moderation of party positions" on questions of state identity and promote greater competition among parties representing the same ethnopolitical bloc with distinct positions on social and economic issues (Tilley, Garry, and Matthews 2019, 1; see also, McGarry and O'Leary 2004; O'Leary 2001).

At the same time, consociational power-sharing arrangements have been criticized for "solidify[ing] intracommunal networks, rather than being concerned to promote intercommunal association" (Taylor 2001, 47; see also Dixon 2002; Selway and Templeman 2012). Findings from Tilley, Garry, and Matthews (2019, 15) suggest that while "moderation on the main ethno-national policy dimension [in NI] is clear,"[1] the emergence of increased co-ethnic party differences on social and economic issues is less evident.[2] Within the framework of the Agreement, in fact, ethnonational division is implicitly and perpetually framed as "the *only* major schism that needs to be addressed" in NI (Little 2004, 29), mitigating the willingness or ability of parties to meaningfully address other societal cleavages. "Ethnic outbidding" is a likely outcome in a consociational power-sharing system, more generally, as co-ethnic parties compete for recognition as the most committed to ingroup interests and as key guardians against outgroup threats (Horowitz 2000).

The debate between those advocating "top-down" consociational approaches to peacebuilding, and proponents of more "bottom-up" dimensions of conflict transformation tends to underplay the inextricable connections between evolving socio-political dynamics in civil society, including community-based peacebuilding, on the one hand, and the political practices of "the state," on the other. As Mann (1984, 194) observes, "there is no technique [in exercising ideological power] which belongs necessarily to the state, or conversely to civil society." Rather, "there is some kind of [dialectical] oscillation between the role of the two in social development." In practice, peacebuilding models are hybrid, constructed and maintained jointly and in complex ways by external agents, domestic political elites, and local actors (Mac Ginty 2010). Yet, the power to shape hybrid models of peace are certainly not shared equally among these groups. Their conflicting interests may correspond with divergent and contradictory agencies; and the disproportionate power of state and international organizations may have disruptive, cascading effects on the transformative potential of indigenous, "bottom-up" peacebuilding initiatives.

I argue here that Northern Ireland's consociational structure of governance, containing unique structural and ideological ambiguities, obviate a generative oscillation between the "development" goals pursued by the state and those of civil society groups committed to interethnic integration. Indeed, the "constructive ambiguity" in the identity of the post-accord state was inscribed through the very language of the Agreement (Nagle 2018). In the words of Brendan Murtagh, the "ambiguous language of the peace agreement," intended to satisfy the mutually exclusive ideological goals of Ulster Loyalism and Irish Nationalism, "was necessary so that all could sign on" (interview by Bollens 2018, 146). The Agreement states that NI will remain part of the UK, but also "sets out to accommodate nationalists' aspiration that they might in the future become citizens of a united Ireland" if a majority on both sides of the Irish border vote accordingly (Coulter and Murray 2008, 2). The "creative ambiguity" of the Agreement's language in this respect "creates significant embedded contradictions" and makes the implementation of peacebuilding initiatives susceptible "to political appropriation and manipulation by sectarian interests" (Bollens 2018, 209).

This chapter reports interview findings on how political manipulation of sectarian fears within the consociational framework shapes and undermines community-based peacebuilding work. More specifically, many respondents attribute the limitations of community-based peacebuilding to the (dys) functioning of the Assembly and the political strategies of the dominant Unionist and Nationalist parties. What many term the "Green and Orange politics" of NI has an ideological and organizational trickle-down effect, restricting the scope of social transformation envisioned and pursued at the grassroots level. At the same time, the politics of threat and resentment discussed in previous chapters are identified as creating periodic mini-crises which have degenerative impacts on the progress made by some community-based organizations in building positive interethnic relations on local levels. These interacting dynamics, coupled with other restraints on the work of community-based organizations—such as decreased funding from international donors, the inequitable distribution of funding, and consequences of inadequate progress by the state in addressing segregation, paramilitarism, and legacies of the Troubles—is contributing to what one respondent terms "peace fatigue" among practitioners, as well as a decline in their investment in cross-community projects. In these respects, the "Green and Orange politics" of NI continue to prevent meaningful institutional reforms which could enhance interethnic interdependency, while reifying ethnopolitical identities in ways which counteract the work of community-based peacebuilders— especially those who work in areas of concentrated disadvantage.

POLITICS, PEACE FUNDING, AND
THE COMMUNITY SECTOR

Respondents identify several problems with the bureaucratic processes involved in allocating funding to community-based peacebuilding and restorative projects in NI, noting that the increased role of state bodies in determining how funds are distributed is undermining grassroots actors' creativity and restricting the scope of the social changes they envision. The detrimental impacts of the decline in funding from international bodies and the state, in the view of many respondents, is compounded by a more general lack of state ideological investment in social integration.

More than 5,000 grassroots organizations have obtained over four billion pounds in funding from the International Fund for Ireland (IFI) and the European Peace and Reconciliation Fund (EU Peace Fund) since 1998 (see Fissuh et al. 2012). Over 21,000 applications for funding were approved by the EU Peace Fund by 1995; and 6,200 projects were supported by the IFI between 1986 and 2010 (Morrow, Faulkner-Bryne, and Pettis 2018, 18). The Northern Ireland Community Relations Council (CRC) provided grants worth upward of £3 million to support 279 projects committed to building intercommunity relations in 2012–2013 alone (Kelly and Braniff 2016). This significant investment has created what a few respondents call the "peace consultancy industry." With the creation of more community-based peacebuilding and restorative justice organizations through such investment also comes a greater economic dependency of communities on the short-term or medium-term grants received from local NGOs. While it may be unrealistic to expect these levels of aid to go on indefinitely, the decrease of funds is likely to result in a withdrawal of key actors in peacekeeping and peacebuilding initiatives. Yet reduction in overall funding is not the only reason for alarm. "[H]ow resources are targeted and the administrative requirements of some funders" are also of concern (Morrow, Faulkner-Bryne, and Pettis 2018, 7). Marking a shift from the first EU Peace Programs (Peace I, II, and III) in 2014, the model of Peace IV (2014–2020) funding "moved towards an enhanced role for public sector bodies," including the NI Executive "in the distribution of funds as well as the delivery of services" (ibid., 21–22). In addition to similar concerns of community-based peacebuilding practitioners noted by Morrow and colleagues—such as concern about funding streams connected to the NI Executive—respondents in the present study perceive a disdain of some politicians toward the voluntary sector, and voice their disappointment with the overly "invasive or prescriptive" nature of the funding process connected to the state. As one senior activist and scholar explains, funding is often now formed and shaped by the existing administration, including some large philanthropic funds that are in partnership with various arms of government. I mean, that's welcome at some levels. But compared to 20, 30, 40 years ago, you don't have the same cohort of, shall I say, unconditional funding, or funders that fund blue sky innovation to the same extent that we had then. So it's interesting that at a time of less violence, less threat, you have a more invasive, or a more prescriptive form of funding. (Interview with author, Co Antrim, May 2014)

The bureaucratic control of funders is perceived to be thwarting the creativity of recipients, creating an imbalance that is detrimental to community organizations' capacity to promote integration and reconciliation.[3]

There are class inequities in such "prescriptive" forms of funding, moreover. Byrne (2011, 76) found that many community-based organizations with innovative ideas and strong capacity to effect change on the ground were not able to secure funding due to difficulty with the application process, lack of assistance with it, and lack of resources (see also, Byrne et al. 2007; Buchanan 2008; Matic, Byrne, and Fissuh 2007). Some respondents in the present study make additional observations regarding the class inequities in peace fund distributions, perceiving those who decide what projects to fund as exercising classism (i.e., skepticism about working-class practitioners' ability to manage resources) in their decisions to restrict access of community-based organizations from working-class wards to peace monies. Respondents also charge state bureaucracies with allocating funding to organizations that are politically "safe," rather than those which deconstruct and challenge the Unionist-Nationalist binary and the dominant parties' corresponding policy positions. Organizations operated by middle-class professionals are perceived to obtain a greater share of financial support, resulting in the neglect of organizations that work intimately with those in marginalized communities most at risk of being victims and perpetrators of intergroup aggression. As a PUL respondent who works in ex-prisoner re-entry explains,

We've had the peace money since 1995. The name suggests that it's about peacebuilding because it's peace money. My argument would be that most of that has went to the middle classes with people who would have talked to each other anyway and has bypassed the very people that it should have been targeted at. They [middle-class professionals] come up with a rationale that these [working-class] people weren't capable of handling the money or using the money and that they should actually be the ones who should administer it and deliver it. (Interview with author, May 2021)

Another PUL respondent makes a similar point on how those working most directly with individuals and groups who pose the more serious risks to the peace process are not adequately supported by the peace funding bureaucracy:

> If you think about your local communities, where gangs are, unless you know the gangs and the gang members, you ain't getting in there to work with them. What has happened here is a lot of that money's just been spent with nice people talking to nice people and going away on a European trip when they should have been in with the very people who caused the problem to solve the problem. It doesn't happen. Even today a lot of the funding [follows this model]. (Interview with author, June 2020)

Others suggest that state funding decisions reflect a prioritization of the interests of middle-class and upper-class residents more generally. One Loyalist community leader reflects on his personal experience as a case in point:

> Money is pumped into the arts, the likes of big theaters and places like that. Not very many people from disadvantaged areas can actually pay to go to a theater, but the theaters are the ones that get a lot of the public funding, including the funding to keep them going. . . . [The young people I work with are] coming from families here that struggle day in, day out. . . . We can't afford to go to these places that are heavily funded by the government. . . . The new premises that we're looking at [to advance the educational work we do], we've been offered it by the Housing Executive, but we need to refurbish it. There's no money coming our way to refurbish this, but yet there's a lot of money going into these big art theater companies that only the well-to-do can afford. (Interview with author, June 2020)

Others similarly express concern that a less than adequate proportion of state funds are allocated to stakeholders in the peace process who would need it most, and in ways which would have the greatest overall impact. One respondent, for example, explains how working with stakeholders in areas of concentrated deprivation and ongoing paramilitary influence seems to be perceived as "too hard" for the state to bother; instead, projects are implemented where participants "work with the nice people." Intimated in her discussion is the view that state officials and politicians are fresh out of ideas on how to build good relations, or simply aren't interested. As she explains,

> the other day someone reminded me about the new Chief Constable, the one that was meant to lose his job but narrowly kept it. When he first arrived in Northern Ireland, he suggested that the social services take the children off all the paramilitaries. That was his answer to dealing with the problem [laugh] until someone pointed out to him that that just would—why would you do that? You need to have a reason to remove a child from their parents. Nobody has any real

ideas of how to change this. The community are having to fight for the very, very basics. There's so few people employed in the sector. There's very, very little infrastructure, resources, anything to bring communities together. They can go ahead and be with people from other traditions. We'll have to do it with them first, but there's no investment, none anymore. That used to come with peace money and the Good Relations [program]. There's no funds; certainly, not in this area [of North Belfast]. There's nothing for them. . . . Every year we have T:BUC—[Together:] Building a United Community—from the Executive Office. Every year there are camps. They're always [working with] the nice kids who don't cause any problems—the kids who would naturally be with other people [from different ethnic and national backgrounds] anyway—because the other ones are too hard [to work with]. "It's too hard to recruit them; too hard to have them there. . . . It's too hard, dealing with a legacy, too hard. Do you know what? We'll just not bother." (Interview with author, June 2020)

The experiences and perceptions of some respondents suggest that the allocation of peace monies reflects an agenda to support superficial images of cooperation, in line with the interests of dominant political parties, and to the exclusion of the particular interests of marginalized groups who suffer most from the ongoing ramifications of the conflict.

Consociational Problems

Organizations that espouse more imaginative visions of peace, through which structural sources of conflict such as poverty, class and gender inequities, and segregation would be addressed, are rarely endorsed by peace-funding bureaucracies according to several respondents. For example, a head of an organization that educates and empowers women from marginalized communities in Belfast comments on funders' relative overall neglect of women's organizations, and the uncertainty emerging in a post-Brexit environment in which political leadership shows little concern about an impending decline in international support for community-based peacebuilding, more generally. In 2020, she describes how her organization had, three years prior,

looked at how much women per head were being allocated in Europe, how much children were being allocated per head, and how much paramilitaries were being allocated per head. Women came out at £0.34 per head. Children came out at 1.34 per head. Paramilitaries were something like 360 per head. . . . The peace monies coming into Northern Ireland, did build a lot of structure and Europe did try very hard to keep that. If we lose it all, I'm just not sure how or what [we will do to carry on], because there's no plans. There's no plans being discussed here about what's going to come in its place or who's going to do it, or where the money's coming from. That means that women, again are going to be pushed further back, more marginalized than they ever were, because . . .

the needs of women are different than what they can be for males. . . . We have a young women's project here; a lot of them have children. You can't plan a nine to five placement if somebody has a child, or two or three. . . . So if you take all that away and just provide bog-standard training that these women can't access, then how are they ever going to improve? They're not. (Interview with author, May 2020)

Interviewees also perceive the withering interest of the NI state in community-based peacebuilding as a symptom of a broader limitation of the power-sharing process, namely, its lack of capacity to produce a shared space—psychosocially and physically—for the intercommunal dialogue necessary to forge a common ground necessary as a first step toward a more transformative mode of conflict transformation. Rather, a more noticeable consequence of NI politics, according to a senior leader in the interfaith community sector, is the consolidation of a

communal, pessimistic common-sense. . . . A lot of organizations are working for a different type of society, but many [work] within a mental model of not wishing for too much change, so that they won't get disappointed. But that huge imaginative peace, a peace beyond where we are now, beyond the simplified identities, I don't think that's a peace that most political parties or many civil society groups hope for, regretfully. . . . It is a bit about . . . want[ing] a wee bit more [social change] but not too much more that really challenges us fundamentally, to really rethink our core identities. . . . I think in the political community, you see how easily jointly agreed ideas can be derailed or, when fear and threat grow high, people withdraw from being more visionary. (Interview with author, Co Antrim, May 2014)

Several respondents contend that the problem of community-based peacebuilders' political alienation and withdrawal from "more visionary" work that challenges dominant ethnopolitical boundaries is inextricably linked with a power-sharing structure that incentivizes identity politics and even empowers the dominant parties to threaten withdrawing from government when their interests are challenged. This respondent directly implicates the politics of fear and threat in the withdrawal of community leaders from more "risky" but innovative approaches to cross-community peace work. Many others I interviewed similarly intimate how the structure of the power-sharing arrangement is stifling the transformation of identities, underscoring that "communal, pessimistic common sense." A respondent elaborates on this recurring theme in the data, when recognizing that

the Good Friday Agreement didn't talk about a form of oppositional politics. So I suppose it was the best we could get in those days. But . . . we won't have strong government until there's opposition permitted and sustained. And I suppose, you actually see the way identity politics is shaping at the moment, that the present parties are there in perpetuity. And that's unhealthy, in democratic terms. . . . One of the strengths of democracy is that every three, four, five years, citizens have the right to throw people out. . . . We can't really envision throwing the present parties out. . . . You've got a consociational agreement based on identity politics. If those identity politics become fragile or fragmented, the threat of identity politicians is that then the Agreement might fail. And previously, given the conditions to policing, to anti-discriminatory practices, to agreed public services and so on, the consent to those may well be withdrawn. (Interview with author, South Belfast, May 2014)

As indicated in chapter 4, for example, Sinn Fein threatened to withdraw its support for the PSNI following the arrest of Gerry Adams in 2014. The DUP has threatened on numerous occasions to withdraw from government, due to rows over policing and "culture war" issues in the Assembly (i.e., the prospect of an Irish Language Act, the 2012 Belfast City Council flag ruling, etc.). The collapse of the Executive in 2017, and again in 2022, is a stark reminder that such threats carry serious weight.[4] On a symbolic level, the identity politics exhibited in the operation of the Assembly (Noble 2013; Nolan 2014), underscoring the very logic of the consociational system, function to re-center ethnopolitical identity within public discourse to the exclusion of other identities, thereby obstructing the formation of shared, supra-ethnic meanings and interests. Such a dynamic is facilitated by the absence of "oppositional politics," moreover, and the corresponding lack of accountability held to the dominant Unionist and Nationalist parties. A PUL respondent who works on ex-combatant reintegration describes how

The peace was hard fought for and won. There's a document with signatures on it saying we have peace. We need to look past that. Everything in Northern Ireland goes back to the Troubles. Everything. We need to build stronger resilient communities who don't take this forward, but that doesn't seem to be something that the government are interested in. Unfortunately for us . . . we have no opposition. In any society, if you don't have an opposition to your government, they just do what they want. Ours is even worse than that because what we have are two people who are equal, equal [in] power. One's called a First Minister and the other a Deputy [First Minister]. . . . If one suggests something, especially if it's really good, the other one just naturally goes, "No." That's the way our government functions. It is obscene, absolutely obscene. . . . We need to end it and we need to say to them . . . "You've got us to the stage, now move on." We need political representation, not "I'm voting for you because you're going to keep him out." Our health service is on its knees; education is—don't even start with that. You've got infrastructure, transport, all of these things are just falling [unintelligible 00:45:32] and they're [politicians] arguing over how many people were at [Bobby Storey's] funeral [in violation of COVID-19 restrictions on public gatherings]. (Interview with author, May 2021)

A former UVF prisoner active in community-based restorative justice similarly describes how the "Orange and Green" nature of NI politics is obstructing progress in addressing the basic needs of the society and residents' everyday concerns, while increasing public costs:

> If you look at the much bigger political spectrum, across Stormont, you really just have Green and Orange politics. And our communities were probably better off when it [the Assembly] first started than it is now. There are a lot of people on the ground suffering from [inaudible]. They need things that every day people need. But it's still based on Orange and Green politics, not on the actual need. So if they get one, we get one. And if we want one, they want one. . . . And if you look at the money it costs to run a divided society in Northern Ireland, its atrocious. And all that money could have been pumped into hospitals or schools or local communities. (Interview with author, West Belfast, June 2014)

Indeed, as Deloitte and Touche's (2007, 6) report indicates, ethnoreligious segregation across institutions results in a "duplication or even multiplication of service delivery," costing NI upward of £1.5 billion more than "comparable regions" annually.

As noted by Nagle (2009a, 179), the position of both Irish Nationalist and British Unionist parties has been that economic growth will be "the remedy for a 'divided society'" while showing little interest in addressing sectarianism, segregation, and working-class alienation as a condition commensurate to the production of more positive economic outcomes. In fact, the NI Executive, in its *Building a Better Future: Draft Programme for Government 2008–2011*, explicitly states that "growing the economy is . . . top priority" (OFMDFM 2007, 2) while neglecting to advocate explicitly for "the development of integrated/shared communities where people wish to learn, live, work and play together; [and] to encourage communication, tolerance and trust in areas where communities are living apart"—goals explicitly stated in the previous *Programme for Government* (Nagle 2009a, 179; see also Community Relations Unit 2003).

As noted above, respondents emphasize how, since the onset of devolution in 2007, an "Orange and Green" framework of governance has become increasingly embedded in the polity, exacerbating economic inefficiencies resulting from ethnoreligious segregation and division. Accordingly, many also convey increasing frustration with what Barry (2017) terms the "shared out" nature of Northern Ireland's consociational system. Barry (2021, 3) describes Northern Ireland's government as "a One party Janus faced system, where each ethnic champion publicly appeals to its sectarian base for electoral power by blaming the 'Other' for all the Assembly's faults while privately collaborating with the very same 'Other' to ensure they remain the dominant power in the political process." This "One party Janus faced system" not only reveals itself in negotiations over resources for Catholic versus Protestant communities between Nationalist and Unionist parties, respectively, but, in the view of some respondents, is even illuminated through the same parties' provocations of street disorder. The distrust in the political process is reflected by some respondents, for example, in their stipulation that elected politicians from the more "hardline" wings of Nationalism and Unionism supposedly work collaboratively to escalate collective mentalities of threat from the Other. A PUL youth advocate believes, for example, that DUP and Sinn Fein prefer to have periodic disorder at interface areas to galvanize their respective political bases. His account intimates that the consociational system incentivizes an "us versus them" political framework mutually beneficial to the leading Unionist and Nationalist parties. In his view,

> The government—Sinn Féin, the DUP—have always had this wee pact going on. It goes quiet in one area and they need something to keep it [sectarian tensions] going. Funny enough, a riot appears, and then there's some money brought into that community to go to the community leaders who are all involved in the paramilitaries. Not all of them, but many of them. Then they ring the police out to keep it going and cause friction. . . . I don't have anything to back that up, but a lot of conversations that I've had with people, they would agree with me and say, "Yes, obviously that's pretty right." They're obviously not going to bring a document out saying that's what happened. Politically, it's a lot of what goes on. (Interview with author, June 2020)

Thus, according to this respondent, among others, perceptions of political manipulation on the ground corroborate speculation that both parties, Sinn Fein and DUP, "need the other to 'scare' their own voters and prospective voters into supporting them" (Barry 2021, 5), particularly within working-class ethnopolitical strongholds. Many implicate this dynamic, and the more general lack of political leadership to forge a path toward reconciliation and integration as key factors in their alienation from NI politics. There is a palpable sense of exasperation with, and withdrawal from the NI polity in many respondents' statements. For example, a Protestant from a border county suggests that "Community-based activists are fed up waiting" for state-led progress in reconciliation and integration. "But by the same token, they don't want to invest in politics. . . . They're so pissed off with politics. . . . I'm happily carrying on with my community-based work . . . [NI politics] is only a waste of time. Not going there. We'll do this in spite of the politicians" (interview with author, June 2020). To the extent that community-based leaders hold innovative political visions, their withdrawal from NI politics will likely only compound the problems of state-led peacebuilding.

Although it is possible that a "wee pact" has been made between DUP and Sinn Fein in some instances, this is not to say that the real ideological differences between them do not have stark consequences on the potential of government to function at even the most basic levels. Before the Assembly shut down for three years (2017–2020) due to the resignation of Martin McGuinness from the office of Deputy First Minster, rows over Brexit and an Irish Language Act, and allegations of then DUP leader Arlene Foster's role in the Renewable Heat Incentive scandal, Unionist and Nationalist parties constantly disagreed on legislation concerning various "bread and butter" issues (Coulter and Shirlow 2019; Gray et al. 2018). The mutual veto accorded to Sinn Fein and the DUP led to a "series of logjams" as the other parties expressed concern over being marginalized in the Assembly (Nolan 2014, 142). Disagreement over how to implement "welfare reform" provisions imposed by Westminster, before Sinn Fein finally surrendered to the whims of the British government, cost NI £5 million per month through most of 2013. The Assembly has not addressed education reform, "and the project for a Peace Building and Conflict Resolution Centre has been jettisoned" (Nolan 2014, 142; see also, McGlynn, Tonge and McAuley 2014; Carroll 2021). At the same time, "official recognition of and funding for Orange cultural themes and 'Ulster-Scots' . . . [reached] unprecedented levels" in the post-devolution period, seemingly reflecting Unionist parties' disinterest in reducing intercommunal tensions over "culture war" issues (Nolan 2014, 12). In 2012, the Office of the First Minister and Deputy First Minister of NI announced a plan to remove the peace walls by 2023. However, progress has been slow, blamed on the "lack of political progress, in the absence of a Northern Ireland Executive" for three years (Gray et al. 2018, 129). Progress on key issues in the Assembly were again stalled when the DUP chose to collapse the power-sharing institutions in protest over the NI Protocol in February 2022. DUP leadership suggested at this time that it would not participate in governance if Sinn Fein becomes the largest party in the Assembly after the May 2022 elections (O'Carroll 2022). DUP rhetoric about the dire prospect of Sinn Fein's Michelle O'Neill becoming First Minister (as opposed to Deputy First Minister)—coupled with its increased attention to Sinn Fein's calls for an all-Ireland "border poll" post Brexit (McCurry 2022)—is yet another example of the DUP's employment of threat politics to galvanize support in the polls. Even UUP leadership condemned DUP for undermining the democratic structures of power sharing, hoping to capitalize on the frustration at DUP tactics pervading undecided and more "moderate" Protestant/Unionist constituencies (O'Carroll 2022). Considering the paralysis of governance in the Assembly, it is not surprising how much "people are [still] disillusioned with the lack of movement at the political level that is needed to sustain the good work at the grassroots level" (Byrne 2011, 170). Indeed, interviewees elaborate on how such a phenomenon is largely a consequence of the sectarianized nature of political negotiation within Northern Ireland's consociational structure, the disregard of the voices of community leaders, and the intercommunity distrust resulting from the combination of mixed messaging about policy positions and ethnopolitical posturing in the Assembly. As a councillor and activist articulates it,

> I think part of the problem is that the political structure, at times, is so busy fighting with itself, that it has a negative impact and ripple effect on communities because they're not sure who or what to believe at the end of the day. I do think it keeps that sectarianism alive, which we're trying to stamp out [in our community-based work]. . . . I also think that government talks the talk, but it doesn't walk the walk. . . . It talks about the importance of engaging the community and voluntary sector and more in government, and then it doesn't do that. It brings out some kind of legislation or change in policy that actually doesn't get what's needed within a community because it's not listening to the voices of people in it. . . . I do think that sometimes politicians are stymied because it's not about supporting each other because it's the right thing to do, but it's about taking it back down to that sectarianism, "Well, if they get it, we have to get it," rather than identifying where the need actually is. (Interview with author, May 2020)

As indicated above, there is plenty of evidence to validate community leaders' disaffection from politics. Unfortunately, some have also withdrawn from cross-community work as a result of the divisive political atmosphere.

"Trickle-down" Implications on Community-based Peacebuilding

Several respondents perceive socio-political relations to have deteriorated to such an extent that they "see no point" in working on cross-community projects, to quote one participant in the study. Skepticism about the prospect of intercommunal integration, and a concomitant disinterest in cross-community dialogue are implied by respondents as inextricably linked to their disenchantment with consociational politics in NI. This is concerning, considering that dialogue between deeply divided ethnopolitical communities is integral to the development of "linguistic tractability and communicative transformation" (Byrne 2011, 176)—two core imperatives of peacebuilding (Ramsbotham 2010). A senior leader in restorative justice work in Belfast, for example, reveals that

I don't see the point of promoting cross community now, because I don't see that it's going to achieve anything. But I believe as a Protestant population we need to be careful of how we say things, because we don't want to be inciting our young people to go down another road. And our politicians need to be more proactive and show a leadership role. (Interview with author, West Belfast, June 2014)

Peacekeeping and peacebuilding work has been negatively impacted by the political environment in other ways as well. Former Loyalist paramilitary prisoners, for example, indicate that their perception of being stigmatized and exploited by Unionist political leadership undermines their willingness to continue "standing down" peace spoilers from within their community during contentious events (parades, protests, etc.). A former UVF paramilitary prisoner explains how his "disillusionment" with politics as a result of the exploitation of Loyalists by the main Unionist parties underscores his withdrawal from such peacekeeping activities. In his view,

When it comes to [Loyalist] ex-prisoners and ex-combatants, there's a lot of disillusionment. . . . Even DUP shuns them out. When it suits them they help them out, and when it doesn't suit you, you shun them. . . . [Former Loyalist paramilitary prisoners] over the years have faced down their own people trying to stop trouble at parades and everything else. But I wouldn't do it no more myself. . . . Why should I? (Interview with author, West Belfast, June 2014)

Many other former paramilitary prisoners continue to engage in vital peacekeeping work at interfaces, parades, and protests; however, some of the same individuals have disengaged in cross-community peace*building*. Other respondents with paramilitary backgrounds indicate that interest in facilitating meaningful cross-community dialogue and forming closer interethnic relationships has declined even as vital peace*keeping* work, such as preventing escalations of interface violence, continues. A PUL respondent who works on paramilitary disengagement explains how, due in part to political divisions in Stormont, there is a

current hardening of attitudes within Loyalism. The uncertainty, and the insecurity that [the Brexit Protocol] has created, I suppose, the conditions where there is a lower level of cross-community engagement . . . [Unintelligible 00:21:49] people won't see any value or worth in it. Those channels that exist between Loyalism and Republicanism still exist. They're still open . . . and still doing work on certain specific issues. In general, the cross-fertilization of ideas and support for each other and stuff has ended. Those don't occur anymore. They're nearly like—they only carry out interactions . . . like crisis prevention. . . . I don't see that there's any particular appetite for engaging in cross-community activity at this stage. (Interview with author, May 2021)

A Nationalist councillor with a history of grassroots intercommunity relation-building work similarly perceives a decline in local voluntary initiatives promoting cross-community integration among working-class Loyalist and Republican community leaders, and notes that the post-flag protest period has been marred by downward relations. In his perspective,

> the impact of the flag issue is still with us. It's just manifested itself in different ways. . . . I explained to you [how I worked with a Loyalist on a shared housing scheme] . . . as a[n example of] progress [back in 2014]; [since then] everything went, well, not backwards—it nearly went backwards. But certainly, we weren't able to build on all those good initiatives. . . . We should have been in a position to really capitalize on that. If anything, relationships have got worse, and we're in the process of building them back up again, which is quite sad, I have to say. (Interview with author, May 2021)

In the same interview, this respondent further acknowledged that rising tensions, largely rooted in rows between Unionist and Nationalist parties, undermine past achievements in the community sector and force grassroots leaders to focus on basic peacekeeping functions (i.e., violence prevention), rather than further entrenching cross-community relationships. He indicated that

> community tensions in North Belfast . . . [are] probably the worst that it's been in three to four years. . . . We've been on the ground, doing a lot of meetings, some of them public, some of them not so public, to try and get past—to get some grip of what's going on. Those tensions are still manifesting themselves nightly in some of the streets around North Belfast. . . . A lot of stuff is reacting to what's going on in the bigger picture, whether that's a stalled political process that has a vacuum that you're proactively trying to make sure doesn't slip into something really volatile on the streets. . . . I do lose hope sometimes, but I always get it back again. You have to. (Interview with author, May 2021)

Certainly, such grassroots work on preventing violent conflict escalation is notable and indicates ongoing cooperation between various actors across the ethnoreligious divide. Yet the need to continually revert back to de-escalation work is also an indication of how the "stalled political process" undermines the more generative work of third sector, bottom-up cross-community relation building. Other respondents also implicate the "stalled political process" in Stormont in the fluctuating tensions which periodically spill over into street disorder, requiring grassroots leaders to regularly engage in crisis management rather than working to construct shared meanings, interests, and institutions. Another Nationalist respondent makes a similar point:

There are some issues on the horizon where tensions are certainly simmering and potentially will grow. There's still, unfortunately, that ability for people to step back into their previous comfort zones, through fear or whatever. . . . I don't necessarily mean that the contact or relationship totally breaks down, but . . . they step back and the focus becomes entirely the next parade or an issue— flags, or whatever that issue is. (Interview with author, June 2020)

This cycle of periodic conflict re-escalation and de-escalation only compounds the problem of "peace fatigue," moreover. In the words of a respondent from a rural Unionist community,

We've been engaging with the same sets of stakeholders for nearly 30 years, if you think about it, in the buildup to the peace process itself and then the working out of the peace process; and now Brexit. . . . That's a long time for actors involved in it to be at it. . . . There's peace fatigue at a lot of levels. Very hard to come up with innovative solutions when you're genuinely fatigued, which is why we go around the same old problems every three or four years. Also because of that, we aren't really getting a recharge. (Interview with author, June 2020)

It is unlikely that all leaders in community peacebuilding organizations would necessarily subscribe to the view that cross-community relation building is on a downward trajectory. Some continue to work rigorously on building trust across the ethnoreligious divide and facilitating mutual understanding and respect, and a rich network of community organizations persists. Nonetheless, others have disengaged, or become occupied with more "urgent" responsibilities (de-escalating interface tensions, for example). Other participants in the study similarly indicate how periodic, politically-fueled mini-crises create cycles of conflict re-escalation which exacerbate the "peace fatigue" experienced by leaders of community-based organizations. Some such mini-crises occur on annual bases, exemplified by the regular increase in tensions over ethnopolitical parades that emerge in early summer and often become central themes of contentious debate between Unionist and Nationalist parties. A young community leader from an organization that brings at-risk Protestant and Catholic youth together explains how the young people he works with in his program are forced to discuss "tough political issues" with those from the other community, and learn that they can continue to "get on" even after disagreeing. As he explains, Protestant "people 21 years old I work with [who] didn't talk to a Catholic until they joined this group" spend much time engaging in positive interactions with Catholics, at their own initiative, "after a few weeks" in his program (interview with author, North Belfast, May 2014). The importance of building positive relationships between young people from polarized communities has been documented in research and underscores the benefit of the work done by these types of community-based projects. For example, studies have shown that those who have even one friend from an outgroup have "lower levels of both blatant and subtle prejudice, greater support for pro-out-group policies and more generalized positive attitudes to the entire out-group" than those who do not (Hughes et al. 2007, 38). The same respondent sees improvements in trust and interaction between most of the at-risk youth from Protestant and Catholic communities he works with throughout the spring; however, he also witnesses a re-fragmenting of such groups along ethnoreligious lines "as the parade season draws close." With the tenser period of the summer months comes a reconsolidation of ethnoreligious identity; in his words, "it seems like all the progress we made during the year is lost during the summer. Then we have to start all over" (interview with author, North Belfast, May 2014).

Such experiences of those involved in cross-community programs in poor and working-class wards risk underscoring a burgeoning sense of apathy, moreover. While many see benefits to these programs, they also perceive them to be counteracted by systemic problems of ethnopolitical division, including residential segregation, ethnocultural rituals, and youth violence (see also, Creary and Byrne 2014). There is little confidence among respondents that these voluntary programs translate into lasting cross-community relationships outside the safe spaces they provide. The high levels of ethnoreligious segregation in poor and working-class areas, in particular, seriously undermine the potential of innovative cross-community projects to build lasting intergroup trust and interdependency (see also Harland 2011, 422). Several respondents suggest that young people who have had contact with peers from the outgroup through integrated education or cross-community programs experience a heightened risk of being identified, harassed, and even attacked on the street. One respondent, who works with young people in an interfaith organization, suggests that "from young people's perspective particularly, the issue was that we brought groups of young people together, and then when they were back in their own communities, [and] they were out with their friends, these young people were easily identifiable, because they had known them from inter-community groups they had done" (interview with author, South Belfast, June 2014). Consequently, participation in cross-community programs, and even integrated educational programs, for many, becomes routine, with expectations for lasting change limited.

PEACE FATIGUE, PARAMILITARISM, AND INTERGENERATIONAL CONSEQUENCES OF THE TROUBLES

Interviewees contend that the "peace fatigue" experienced by long-standing leaders of community-based peacebuilding organizations is exacerbated by elected leaders' inadequate capacity or willingness to address key issues in the peace process, specifically, segregation, paramilitarism, and intergenerational consequences of the Troubles within families (domestic violence, addiction, trauma, etc.). The failure of the state to address these issues has cascading effects on working-class residents especially.

The influence of paramilitary elements in segregated wards of Belfast pose restraints on the cross-community work of grassroots organizations, in some cases by directly interfering in the organizations' work. A former elected official and current advocate for women and youth confirms that there is "a lot of cross-community stuff going on," but is hesitant about the extent to which it contributes to increased integration more broadly due to ongoing "paramilitary control." She goes on to describe an incident where her organization "looked at areas where there are patches of land between communities, where we could use that as some kind of play resource and try to bring . . . young children together. Then, the local paramilitary stepped in and said, 'Oh no, we're not having this.' It doesn't meet their aims at the end of the day" (interview with author, Belfast city center, May 2014). Paramilitarism's detrimental impacts on various aspects of social life is identified by respondents as a consequence of inadequate state investment in the structural transformation of working-class communities, as well as declining government interest in promoting third-sector peacebuilding initiatives. The potential for grassroots peacebuilding projects to facilitate a "rebalancing [of] local power away from victimizers and their supporters" (Arriaza & Roht-Arriaza 2008, 170) is undermined by the failure of the state to fully confront paramilitarism. A high-ranking official in government commissions argues that,

> reconciliation and peace has dropped off the [government] agenda entirely. I think the lack of funding for the [unintelligible 00:25:29] community sector has meant that a lot of those bodies that were really influential are not there anymore or are running on a shoestring. I don't think there's a government focus on peacebuilding anymore. Even paramilitarism—there were promises made on how to address paramilitarism, but that's gone on to the back burner. (Interview with author, May 2020)

This respondent corroborates a trend identified earlier by Morrow, Faulkner-Byrne, and Pettis (2018, 6), who report a decline in funding for more than half of the community-based peacebuilding organizations in their research. Forty percent of the organizations they surveyed indicated that reductions in funding "had negatively impacted their beneficiaries/target groups." The disappearance of positively influential organizations in the community sector risks putting off "the engagement of new generations, alongside the danger of considerable loss of learning" (ibid., 7). The impact of declining support for peacebuilding initiatives, both from international donors and the state, is especially detrimental to intercommunity capacity building in working-class areas of NI, which are disproportionately affected by paramilitarism and economically reliant on third-sector grants.

The insecurity experienced by communities in marginalized wards is only exacerbated by the social and economic impacts of austerity, Brexit, and the COVID-19 pandemic, moreover. As a government official explains,

I think people who are living in . . . marginalized communities are seeing very little benefit from peace. I think that then they're being hit disproportionately with COVID, with the shutting down of businesses, with education; they're feeling it. There's a double whammy happening to them. They don't believe they're politically represented. They still have paramilitarism in their communities. And because money has been withdrawn from those communities, a lot of the voluntary sector organizations are having to shut. They're not going to open again. That grassroots capacity is going. There isn't any initiative in my view of central government to drive that. . . . The ideal actors who were pushing that this has to be done, they've gone. Then people like the International Fund for Ireland and Atlantic Philanthropies—so people who did big box funding—they're all going. They're all on the way out. (Interview with author, May 2020)

At the same time, respondents argue that declining financial support for community-based organizations employing former paramilitaries, who mostly come from working-class and marginalized poor communities, is likely to increase such individuals' reliance on paramilitary networks for resources and social support. At the least, declining financial support for this milieu of community leaders will undercut their capacity to mediate intercommunity conflicts and defuse internecine paramilitary disputes. (Of course, as indicated in chapter 3, strong financial support for organizations connected to former paramilitary prisoners poses its own unique set of problems.) One Nationalist respondent who works to address the problem of violent paramilitary vigilantism explains that his colleagues continue basic peacekeeping work, but are doing less over time as a result of declining financial support from the state and international donors:

That's still happening at certain levels. People are still making phone calls. People are still meeting. The problem that a lot of people are flagging up is, this is not on my shoestring. Because the money's being cut to the voluntary sector, these people will lose their jobs, and with those jobs then will come all the connections that were made, and all the training processes and people will end up in paramilitarism. We're still having paramilitary shootings. In the last couple of weeks, there have been several [inaudible]. . . . This is still happening. . . . People are still living in fear. (Interview with author, June 2021)

A PUL respondent described a similar scenario, suggesting that a decline in international funding of community-based projects targeting paramilitary re-entry, and consequential reduction in grassroots capacity to contain intercommunal tensions, is compounded by declining political support, particularly from the "middle-class parties—SDLP, Alliance Party, and UUP." She indicates that her organization lost

funding in March [2021]. We're trying to hold it together. Unless people are paid to do the job, the job isn't going to get done, especially not a job like that where people really are taking risks to make things happen. . . . Until the money appears, it's like everything—just isn't happening. My fear is that the longer that goes on, the further away they get from actually engaging. . . . The project was needed more than ever. Now, it's not there. . . . To be perfectly honest with you, there's no appetite politically to do that anymore here unless it's very, very high profile; certainly not at the level on the ground here where I'm working. . . . There's that camp who sees the benefits, but unfortunately, the bigger camp—and certainly within the Protestant community—they would say, "Why are you giving these [former and active paramilitary] people money? They just need to go away." It's extremely difficult to work in that environment when they're saying, "The war is over. It was 20 years ago. Why are we still dealing with this?" . . . It's quite difficult to actually get people to support you and fund these projects when political parties are actually putting this stuff out. (Interview with author, June 2021)

Loyalist violence against the PSNI had already escalated in Belfast about a month before our interview, attributed by some to "political figures in Unionism [who] are winding young people up" over anger about the Protocol as well as accusations of "two-tier policing" by the PSNI (BBC 2021). With constitutional issues once again at the center of NI politics, and a simultaneous withdrawal of international and state support—economically and politically—for sustaining ex-combatant community-based peacebuilding initiatives, the likelihood of sectarian and political violence increases. Respondents also suggest that declining support for community-based organizations may only add to paramilitarism's attractiveness to young men who lack alternative visions for themselves. According to a respondent from a North Belfast PUL community,

When you're trying to say to a younger person, "Why don't you do this?" They go, "What? Then end up like you? End up like [inaudible]? He's no job. Your projects lose their funding all the time. Nobody supports them. Why would I want to do that?" I have no answer; they're absolutely right. . . . Young people now have a choice. We're back to the old Irish thing again; it's called immigration. That's the choice now. For a lot of people, even going to Britain isn't a choice for them anymore because they're not welcome there either. . . . If you're young—it's mostly males—if you're a young man and no prospect of a job or anything, you join a paramilitary. (Interview with author, May 2021)

Such attitudes, if widespread, risk undermining the intergenerational transmission of knowledge and social infrastructure necessary to carry on key peacebuilding and reconciliation work, while facilitating the reproduction of ethnocultures of masculinity detrimental to more transformative modes of peace.

Moreover, the same communities struggling most with paramilitarism and concomitant ethnocultures of hypermasculinity are also those containing young people who disproportionately experience a range of family problems which may exacerbate feelings of alienation and resentment, including domestic violence, depression, and addiction. For many, these problems are inextricably linked to the legacy of political and sectarian violence. Suicide rates in NI were at one time the lowest in the UK, but have doubled over the last 30 years and are now higher than the rates in England and Wales. Not surprisingly, people in NI who have experienced conflict-related trauma are more likely to consider suicide than those who have not, and these individuals reside disproportionately in poor and working-class neighborhoods (Nolan 2014, 111; see also Tomlinson 2012). A youth advocate reflects on her own personal observations to emphasize the serious extent of the problem of teen suicide attempts and its connection with the legacy of conflict:

They haven't grown up in an era where there was violence, but they're still feeling the ripple effect of the conflict. When you go to a school up the road here, a primary school, where an 8-year-old is trying to hang themselves, and an 8-year-old finds a piece of glass outside the school and cut himself 38 times, and another 9-year-old finds his brother for the fourth time trying to take his life, then you've got to say, there's something happening somewhere, from the community they're from, because of the pressure that they're under. And that is because you will have communities of the somebodies of yesterday who are the nobodies of today, and we know for a fact that the instances of domestic violence, all of that, control and power and everything within communities, is still there. (Interview with author, South Belfast, June 2014)

Pressures on young people of living in post-Troubles working-class communities are doubtless exacerbated by problems resulting from living with family who suffer from the psychological and legal consequences of violence and incarceration. About one-third of those categorized as economically inactive are people claiming long-term sickness benefits, and many of these individuals suffer from trauma related to the Troubles and addiction to prescription medications. An estimated 25 percent of Northern Ireland residents registered as "disabled" suffer from mental illness (Tomlinson 2016, 117), and about 15 percent of the population of the country deals "with some form of psychological trauma arising out of the Troubles" (Coulter 2018, 4; see also Fenton 2018, 144). Overall, "Northern Ireland has the second highest recipient rate of sickness/disability benefit recipients amongst the advanced economies" (Gray et al. 2018, 151). Disproportionately, those suffering from conflict-related trauma come from the most socio-economically deprived communities in the country (Fay, Morrissey, and Smyth 1999, 150; Devlin, McKay, and Russell 2018, 11). Importantly, several respondents implicate state inaction as partly responsible for the intergenerational transmission of these problems. It is implied by some that the "CNR versus PUL" framework of governance sustains the prioritization of ethnopolitical matters in public discourse and the legislative process, correspondingly diverting needed attention to widespread social problems affecting both ethnonational "communities"—especially poor and working-class residents who suffer disproportionately from the legacies of the Troubles. As a senior leader in the cross-community relation building sector puts it,

> You just sit and think, when is this [politics] going to be about the community? When is it going to be about what's right, what will help us get through this? The amount of death by suicide here in Northern Ireland is horrendous. I think people are starting to get fed up, ever since that battle against Catholic versus Protestant, for especially the two main parties [DUP and Sinn Fein, has come to define the political process]. . . . We're into third-generation families on medication and some of the ones I work with, their mothers were on Diazepam and different other drugs, and the daughter is and now grandchildren are coming up through that because it's not being addressed. Mental health [problems] after us having a war, or a whatever you want to call it here, none of that has really been addressed—what families went through living in certain areas [during the Troubles]. . . . With people, army soldiers, ex-combatants, and all under high pressure, and we haven't really addressed any of that either. (Interview with author, June 2020)

CONCLUSION

For many in NI, politics remains mostly about restricting the power of the Other, producing a dynamic in which ethnopolitical identity is perpetually re-activated and reproduced. In this vein, the political disaffection of those who find little appeal in the ethnic binary structure of the NI polity is largely a product of the consociational system, in which there is little room for dialogue or debate that fundamentally challenges the "two narrowly defined 'communities.'" In effect, the ethnopolitical foundations of political negotiation are "rendered 'static and unchanging' by the constant need" for dominant Unionist and Nationalist parties "to share power" (Little 2004, 29; quoted in Legg 2018, 62). Within this process, symbolic power—in this case, the "power of naming" those political identities requiring "agreement" (though they agree on little by the way of policy)—becomes the exclusive domain of actors adhering to "authentic" Orange and Green identities consistent with the dominant Unionist and Nationalist party frameworks. Community-based peacebuilders often find themselves struggling to neutralize intercommunal tensions they view as a result (at least in part) of efforts by ethnopolitical provocateurs from the dominant parties (i.e., DUP and Sinn Fein) to maintain the intercommunal divisions from which they mutually benefit. In various ways, these parties violate Section 75 of the Northern Ireland Act (1998), which requires compliance with two statutory duties: (1) the duty to "equality of opportunity," or the need for public authorities to "promote equality of opportunity between the nine equality categories" (including religious belief and political opinion); and (2) the duty to promote "good relations between persons of different religious belief, political opinion and racial group" (Equality Commission 2010, 7).

Political manipulation of housing insecurity, primarily by Unionist political elites (as discussed in chapter 1), and the structure of residential segregation that at once sustains, and is sustained by, sectarian fear and resentment, reinforces ingroup identification and ethnoreligious separation in ways which empower sectarian politics. These dynamics, coupled with deepening austerity measures—including state cuts to third-sector organizations—reflects how "devolution has promoted a mix between ethnosectarian resource competition and a constantly expanding neoliberal model of governance" (Murtagh and Shirlow 2013, 46). Underscored further by periodic escalations of intercommunal tensions arising from the manipulation of ethnocultural rituals and symbols, and compounded by the ongoing influence of paramiltarism, this dynamic undercuts local-level advancements by community-based organizations in building meaningful relationships between PUL and CNR stakeholders. Many respondents indicate a gradual disillusionment from NI politics as a result of this process, implying that such a politics stymies grassroots efforts in promoting shared institutions and strengthening identities which transcend ethnonational and ethnoreligious binaries—goals viewed by many as central to any successful post-conflict reconstruction model (Oberschall 2007). In this respect, the power-sharing system undermines a "development for peace" approach "that builds capacity, social inclusion, and equity within a community-based decision making system" to produce greater intergroup interdependency (Byrne 2011, 6; see also Jeong 2005, 124).

Knox (2010, 26) highlights "the need for local politicians to embrace a broader social justice agenda to reinforce the expressed wishes of communities to share rather than consolidate separation." More than a decade on, findings suggest that this need remains unmet, disputing the argument that the power-sharing system promotes "current strategies of creating a 'shared space' [which] can be critically viewed as a successful form of liberal multiculturalism" (Nagle 2009b, 132). The assertion that "Consociationalism and social transformation are . . . jointly supportive" in NI (Knox 2010, 26) may also be an overly optimistic exaggeration. Rather, according to many community-based leaders and government officials I interviewed, it is the paralysis resulting from political practices of exclusion, embedded within the consociational structure, that is mitigating their capacity to enhance "everyday diplomacy" while dampening their hope for greater social inclusion and integration. While it may be theoretically *possible* for consociational systems to accommodate bottom-up modes of social transformation and reconciliation, most respondents in this study perceive this structure of governance in NI as an impediment to the expansion of innovative peacebuilding work at the grassroots level. Those who frame peacebuilding in ways which transcend narrow definitions of ethnonational and ethnoreligious identity perceive themselves to be intentionally excluded from structures of peace funding connected to the state. There are particular class and gendered dimensions to this process as well, as it is largely women and community leaders from working-class communities who feel especially marginalized from centers of power within Northern Ireland's peacebuilding industry. In this respect, modes of exclusion/inclusion in the peace sector contribute to the dominant mode of social regulation discussed in the introduction: the (partial) integration of Protestant and Catholic middle-class communities, and separation and marginalization of working-class Loyalist and Republican communities. More broadly, the burden of dealing perpetually with the same problems of intercommunity distrust and hostility, underscored by the ethnopolitics of "the state," contributes to "peace fatigue" among leaders in Northern Ireland's community-based peace sector, who have become increasingly alienated from the polity even as they serve primary roles in holding it together. Although grassroots leaders continue to work to keep the peace and improve social outcomes within their respective communities, many perceive a "shared future" to be unlikely short of a transformation of the political structure. A "pessimistic common sense" at the grassroots level—or, the belief that intercommunal relations are incapable of genuine transformation within the consociational system—and the concomitant minimalization of the scope of change pursued by practitioners, has emerged in the post-accord period as a significant obstacle to conflict transformation. The decline of funding from international donors with relatively few prescriptive requirements on cross-community peacebuilding initiatives only further undermines the creation of projects intended to challenge and transform binary ethnopolitical identities.

NOTES

1. Although Nationalist and Unionist parties have committed to sharing power, tentatively, ongoing "moderation" in this respect is far from certain in the post-Brexit era. See chapter 5.

2. Although this trend was increasingly evident in Nationalism when comparing SDLP and Sinn Fein policy positions, it is most apparent when comparing policy positions of the UUP and DUP (see Tilley, Garry, and Matthews 2019).

3. Byrne et al. (2009) make a similar point regarding the restrictive dimensions of international economic aid to local third-sector NGOs in NI.

4. Interestingly, though, a few respondents believe that some government offices functioned more smoothly during the Assembly shutdown, when bureaucrats oversaw everyday operations of governance.

Conclusion

The preceding chapters examine how particular intersections of class, gender, place, and age shape distinct socio-political subjectivities and agencies in contexts of (low-intensity) ethnopolitical conflict and socio-economic inequality. As detailed in the introduction, measures of labor market participation, educational attainment, and poverty trends in NI are telling vis-à-vis shifts in the country's class structure since the Troubles. Catholics still "outscore Protestants on almost every measure of social deprivation," but the overall gap in economic advancement between Catholics and Protestants has narrowed greatly (Nolan 2014, 13). The ascendancy of a Catholic middle class has corresponded with an increase in inequality *within* the Catholic population. This dynamic, coupled with the erosion of the labor-market advantages once had in blue-collar PUL communities and the educational challenges faced by working-class boys especially, has resulted in intra-communal socio-economic inequalities that look increasingly similar in the broader PUL and CNR blocs.

The consolidation of these forms of inequality in NI has not occurred in a vacuum, but has emerged from a dynamic set forth during Direct Rule, when the British government sought to reconfigure the dominant mode of social regulation by investing substantially in middle-class public employment (for both Catholics and Protestants) while neglecting socio-economic problems in working-class CNR and PUL communities (McGovern and Shirlow 1997). Coulter (1997) examined how a withdrawal of a large segment of the Unionist middle class from politics during Direct Rule undermined the trajectory of peacemaking and development of a more generative Unionist politics. More than 20 years after the Agreement, there are now movements toward a (partial) middle-class withdrawal from contentious ethnopolitical issues in *both* Unionist and Nationalist communities, however, stifling the scope of conflict transformation.

Cultural mechanisms of social regulation which institutionalize codes of silence on issues of ethnonational and ethnoreligious identity have been integral to "integration" within predominantly middle-class sites of interaction (professional workplaces, third-level educational institutions, etc.), operating simultaneous to the ongoing marginalization of poor and working-class Loyalist and Republican communities. Young people from predominantly upper and middle-class communities, whose identities are largely constituted (at least publicly) through repression of ethnopolitical discourses and symbolic affiliations, tend to have more frequent contact with those from different backgrounds. Increased cross-community interactions and relationships are also undergirded by the opening of urban cosmopolitan spaces which are more accessible to relatively privileged segments of the population. Findings from chapter 1 reveal that—in certain contexts, at least—disengagement from ethnopolitical disputes signifies a desirable, upwardly mobile class status, where disassociation from interconnected "working-class" or "lower class" issues of sectarianism, conflict, and poverty reifies class boundaries. "Shared spaces" function in contradistinction from the interaction rituals in relatively deprived, segregated neighborhoods where more open attempts at physical and symbolic displays of ethnopolitical domination (via flags, parades, murals, etc.) continue to sectarianize the structure of space and the corresponding mental maps and self-perceptions of residents. A more general working-class masculinist culture among young men, long "outdated" in a post-industrial era in which traditional, decent-paying blue-collar jobs for men have mostly disappeared—and in an era of "peace" in which aggressive behavior in "defense" of communities is less accepted than it once was—leads some to status pursuits via cultures of paramilitarism. In Belfast and Derry, young, mostly working-class Loyalist and Republican men in the more segregated areas of the North continue striving for status as protectors of their communities. Others turn to "anti-social activity" and self-destructive behaviors. Some young people neglect both the official institutions of authority, as well as "extra-legal" or informal networks of neighborhood social control exercised by paramilitaries and are disenchanted with Northern Ireland's conflict culture. But most seem to have in common a shared community experience of alienation, rooted in legacies of conflict and trauma, compounded by poverty, and manifest as hypermasculinist (ethnic) identity. In the midst of overlapping social problems experienced in areas of concentrated disadvantage—including depression, suicidality, addiction, trauma, and family violence—attachment to ethnopolitical identities, underscored by powerful myths of ethnic origin and ingroup moral superiority, can channel frustrations, and the social energies they produce, into collective activities that bring (to some) a sense of meaning and connection while undermining intercommunal relation building. While some young men feel isolated both from the dominant society *and* from local cultures of paramilitarism, others feel cheated by history, deprived of their chance to "be somebody" through active participation in the conflict and resentful toward a peace process which they perceive has left them and their families behind. In effect, they associate corresponding feelings of loss pejoratively with the peace process—a phenomenon particularly evident in Loyalist communities, where a broader, shared feeling of status decline at the community level is connected psychosocially to belief that the state is increasingly facilitating a "Nationalist agenda."

Social immobility and stark levels of socio-economic inequality between working-class and middle-class Unionist *and* Nationalist communities have contributed to generalized feelings of discontent which can be manipulated by ethnopolitical and neo-paramilitary opportunists, who intend to derive legitimacy through constructions of threat to which they can subsequently respond tactically as "strong" community "protectors." Such processes in turn help to reproduce ethnocultures of masculinity which marginalize women from recognized community leadership positions and reify national and religious binaries. Some former Loyalist male paramilitary prisoners now serving as community leaders have called out Unionist political elites' neglect of problems facing working-class neighborhoods disproportionately and demonstrate a keen awareness of processes of ex-prisoner exploitation. Many of the same individuals have contributed to important grassroots peacekeeping initiatives as well. Yet, such efforts are paralleled by an ongoing embrace of hardline ethnopolitical mentalities and illicit practices of community control by some of the same men, inflicting additional strains on local communities and undermining the production of more inclusive identities. In such a social atmosphere, the integral community roles filled by women, and the unique perspectives they hold which could guide more transformative peacebuilding projects are compromised to appease the male community control facilitated by neo-paramilitarism.

Thus, the growth in "spaces of innovation"—that is, spaces in which cultural production can fulfill "its own logic as a field," and thereby "suspend or reverse the dominant principle of hierarchization" (Bourdieu 1983, 38–39)—does not mean that "old" social rules and parameters governing the integrity of "pure" ethnopolitical space, in both physical and symbolic terms, have simply gone away. Rather, in the post-accord era, they have apparently become more concentrated in segregated, working-class neighborhoods experiencing combined problems of socio-economic anxiety, legacies of violence, and paramilitarism. In more "mixed," middle-class communities, ethnonational identification continues, but in generally subtler ways. While some families in underserved communities have shown openness to dialogue and good faith toward prospects of integration, they also must live in segregated and isolated spaces inscribed by ethnopolitical ritual and symbology which powerfully shape the development of identity. Within such environments, the threat of sectarian attack, rituals of ethnonational territorial ownership, and legacies of segregation and violence counteract residents' movement toward peacebuilding. The impacts of different everyday experiences of upper-class and middle-class residents versus those living in areas of concentrated disadvantage have additional social and political implications, however.

Lijphart (1968, 138) stipulates that, in divided transitional societies, "popular apathy and disinterest in politics and its apparent dullness have a positive value" in disengaging and demobilizing militant ethnopolitical movements and rechanneling popular focus into "non-political" spheres. According to this perspective, a disengaged populace may help to sustain a fragile power-sharing system centered on elite negotiations by reducing scrutiny on ethnonational parties for cooperating with the Other. The apathy which purportedly helps sustain Northern Ireland's consociational system, however, has important class dimensions which may ultimately function to facilitate the more divisive ethnopolitics its proponents wish to defuse. The alleged withdrawal of segments of the middle classes from local ethnopolitical issues, coupled with stark levels of religious segregation in underserved areas disproportionately, produces distinct psychosocial channels through which support is sought by the dominant ethnonational parties—Sinn Fein (and especially) the DUP. To perpetuate their mutual hegemony in the power-sharing government and maintain commitment from their traditionally working-class bases, while increasing their appeal to more privileged sectors of the Unionist or Nationalist communities whose socio-economic interests are increasingly shared, multifaceted and sometimes contradictory political strategies are pursued. The promotion of fear and resentment is particularly notable in disadvantaged PUL communities. At the same time, the main Unionist parties, DUP and UUP, prioritize policy positions most favorable to upper and middle class constituents, and "separate themselves" from issues pejoratively associated with poor and working-class communities when communicating with constituents in sites frequented predominantly by the upper strata. By "conspiring in silence to avoid contested issues," in the words of one prominent peacemaker, privileged segments of the population indirectly maintain the ideological or discursive space in which constructions of ethnopolitical fear and resentment, and the joint dynamics of segregation, poverty, and insecurity underscoring such emotions, can thrive (interview with author, Antrim, May 2014).

Following Atashi (2009, 51), Byrne (2011, 6) argues that "transformational strategies should provide tangible resources to communities marred by violence and deprivation to create structures to distribute them fairly to prevent divisions between the 'gots' and the 'left outs.'" However, the transformative justice and conflict transformation literature overwhelmingly frames the "gots" and the "left-outs" in terms of "horizontal inequality." Since most intra-state conflicts are fought along ethnic lines, this is understandable. Yet, as peace processes move forward over the course of years or even decades after a peace deal is signed—as in NI—other forms of inequality and structural violence, which to some extent transcend ethnic, religious, or national identities may become increasingly entrenched, signaling the merits of reforms in some respects and, somewhat paradoxically, creating new pressures on the sustainability of the peace process, in others.

For example, frameworks which suggest that reducing horizontal ethnic or national inequalities will weaken tribal loyalties have impacted policy making—an overall positive trend. Yet, there are apparent limitations to policies following this prescription in mitigating conflict in NI. For instance, the NI Executive report, *Together: Building a Better Society*, suggests that promoting economic growth will by itself improve community relations by closing the socio-economic deficit between Catholics and Protestants. Economic progress is framed in the report as a "moral, rational and political project in which material prosperity will overwrite tribal allegiances" (Murtagh 2011, 1120). Framing of the "gots" and "left outs" in solely ethnonational or ethnoreligious terms, however, risks distorting the reality that particular post-conflict social, economic, and political structures contributing to the reproduction of inequalities along lines of class, place, and gender have similar impacts on Catholic *and* Protestant working-class communities—even if they are experienced subjectively in ethnopolitical terms—and facilitate reproductions of grievance which help to reconstitute insular identities rooted in the legacy of the conflict. As Mac Ginty and Williams (2009, 6) explain, "the perception of unevenness" in resource allocation is more important than objective measures of unevenness, and is especially "salient in societies with identity-based divisions in which groups may interpret their share of resources through an ethnic, religious or racial lens." Often, perceived competition over newly available resources is sectarianized or ethnicized through ethnopolitical discourse (Paris 2004, 9). *Perception* of disadvantage is key, and how individuals or groups perceive their relative status in the society depends on interpretations of lived experience through discursive frames propounded by political and cultural leaders in public discourse. Although in NI the "horizontal inequalities" between Catholics and Protestants overall has narrowed substantially, large sections of poor and working-class communities in both ethnopolitical blocs remain socially marginalized. Collective feelings of insecurity or hopelessness may be translated through sectarianized discourses which frame class issues (among others) in the language of ethnonational loss or threat. Even in the case where there is acute awareness of the complicity of a group's own political leadership in shaping their marginalization and exploiting their votes, ethnic or national ingroup identities and discourses can be so powerful due to their historical trajectory to militate against an emergence of supra-ethnic political identities. Indeed, this is the hope of some political elites and "community leaders" in NI who thrive on sectarian asperity.

Hence, a key observation documented in the previous chapters is that shifts in modalities of social stratification and marginalization within and across the broader CNR and PUL "communities" have important implications on the capacity of political elites to appropriate sectarian fear and resentment. Middle-class disengagement from grassroots politics and the problems facing mainly working-class communities contribute to the continued realization of the former's vested economic and social interests in the status quo. Political leaders—but Unionists especially—have benefitted from a dual strategy of appealing to middle-class voters through upholding their privileges via policy frameworks, while at the same time appropriating ongoing feelings of fear, threat, or resentment disproportionately felt by poor and working-class constituents through contentious, ethnopolitical discourses. In a sense, class difference increasingly cuts across ethnoreligious lines and might, in certain instances, result in the decentering of the traditional binary identities in shaping social and institutional relations. However, such a condition is disproportionate to middle-class Catholic and Protestant communities, which have benefitted materially from the status quo, and opt to remain silent about contentious ethnopolitical issues in order to "get on." For many in these communities, "boundary deactivation"—a "shift toward new or multiple boundaries and towards decreased difference between within-boundary and cross-boundary interactions" (Tilly 2003, 21)—is an everyday experience. For less well-off communities, a shared sense of unfair economic conditions does not translate into a cross-community, working-class politics, even as some in this milieu—both Protestant and Catholic—acknowledge the similar life circumstances they share with poor and working-class residents in the "other community." Rather, a "single us–them boundary" more centrally shapes everyday social life, requiring differentiation "between within boundary and cross-boundary interaction" (Tilly 2003, 21) at greater frequency. This is largely due to the compounding effects of deepening poverty, ennui and social and economic marginalization on longstanding sectarian mentalities, and the incitements to conflict in the discourses of certain political elites and "community leaders." While internal criticism of the main Unionist and Nationalist parties by some community and (former) paramilitary leaders persists, it has not corresponded with the widespread development of a multicultural politics of class. For example, Loyalist criticism of mainstream Unionist leadership for neglecting important social and economic issues has done little to push the latter toward a more effective and tempered negotiating position vis-à-vis Sinn Fein. Loyalist criticism of elected Unionist leaders for neglecting issues of underdevelopment in their communities is paralleled by a persistent fear of the rise of Nationalism, sustaining a political culture in which voting across historical ethnonational lines is rare, empowering the very elected officials often seen as ineffectual on quality-of-life matters.

More generally, findings indicate how structural economic inequality and immobility in communities most directly impacted by conflict, historically and contemporaneously, facilitate aggressive leadership strategies which restrict the formation of cross-community coalitions and undermine opposition from "moderate" parties. Within conditions of economic and social immobility, provocations of "culture wars" (over flags, parades, etc.), the politicization of policing, and consistent pressures toward ingroup loyalty undercut progress made in intergroup cooperation via community-based peacebuilding projects. Although Brexit has resulted in discourses which indicate early signs of a "constitutional moment" in *sections* of middle-class Unionism, it has also empowered the "hardline" positions of Unionism by re-centering Ulster Loyalist culture in Unionist party politics and empowering Nationalist discourses promoting the unification of Ireland.

A quite different dynamic is underway in Nationalist politics, with respect to Sinn Fein's attempt to "get rid of its baggage" (i.e., its historical connection to IRA violence) and become a "catch-all party" that appeals to various segments of Northern Ireland's population, in the words of one Republican respondent (interview with author, East Belfast, June 2014). Indeed, the "association between contemporary Sinn Féin and its violent past means that it has to work especially hard to persuade voters of its increased policy moderation" (Tilley, Garry, and Matthews 2019, 15). The changing nature of a large segment of the Catholic middle class's relationship with the state since the Troubles—from one of distrust and resentment to tacit acquiescence to the status quo—has corresponded to a widening psychosocial and ideological gulf between them and working-class Republican communities who have experienced no meaningful "peace dividend" in over 20 years of official "peace." Maximizing support from across CRN communities thus requires a careful balancing act which is difficult to sustain. Sinn Fein's attempt to end the long political row over welfare reform, which threatened to collapse the Assembly in 2015 revealed emerging struggles facing the party with respect to its capacity to balance its legacy as a Republican socialist party with continuing its success in keeping the Assembly intact and appealing to a broad range of Nationalist voters, young people, immigrant populations, and others identifying with neither Unionist nor Nationalist traditions. For example, Sinn Fein resisted austerity until November 2015, when it mostly acquiesced to the UK government's agenda (Coulter 2018). Sinn Fein signed off on a political deal "designed to bring an end to gridlock within the power sharing administration," requiring the party to "modify . . . its objections to austerity" and relinquish local control over issues concerning disability benefits and the roll out of Universal Credit to Westminster (O'Hara 2016).

The message conveyed by a socialist party unaffiliated with Nationalism or Unionism—The People Before Profit Alliance (PBP)—that Sinn Fein's action on welfare reform amounted to an abandoning of its working-class base, seemed to resonate with Nationalist voters in some districts experiencing concentrated deprivation. Two PBP candidates, Gerry Carroll and Eamonn McCann, took seats away from Sinn Fein and the SDLP in West Belfast and Derry, respectively. Yet, overall Sinn Fein has maintained its position as the dominant Nationalist party in NI despite internal fractures over the direction of its peace strategy within the more militant Republican wards. This is due, in part, to pressure felt within the broader Nationalist community to ally in opposition to Unionism by supporting the "mainstream" party thought to be the more ardent defenders of their interests (Evans and Tonge 2009; Mitchell, Evans, and O'Leary 2009; Tilley, Garry, and Matthews 2019). Moreover, disputes over the implementation of Brexit has seemingly once again empowered Sinn Fein's constitutional politics, galvanizing its core base while subjugating class politics (Economist 2020; Coulter 2018). The goal of a united Ireland retains ideological importance principally within relatively deprived Republican communities experiencing a disproportionate impact from the legacy of the Troubles. At the same time, the loss of support from middle-class Catholic voters to Alliance Party in the 2019 elections—probably a result of Sinn Fein's return to pro-unification rhetoric and its role in the Assembly's three-year shutdown (Hayward 2020b)—is indicative of the difficult challenge the party faces in balancing support from diverse segments of the CRN community.

The withdrawal of segments of the middle classes from ethnopolitics may likely compound the difficulty of the dominant parties to maintain intraethnic class alliances. In such a scenario, reliance on divisive ethnopolitics may become especially strategic vis-à-vis less privileged districts, but may also further alienate those sections of the middle classes who have constructed simultaneous supra-ethnic identities that accommodate their largely "mixed" everyday social environments and shared material interests. For Sinn Fein, a key goal is to tap into the cultural solidarity that still exists, to some extent, across working-class and middle-class Nationalist communities and maintain its image as the party for "social justice" and "equality" among non-Unionist constituencies without alienating middle-class Nationalist voters, whose material interests increasingly align with those of middle-class Unionism. Put differently, Sinn Fein faces the challenge of moderating its messaging and policy framework enough to appeal to middle-class Nationalists and non-affiliated voters, while in the process not alienating its traditional working-class urban base, whose "tribalism," linked inextricably with Irish Republican unification ideology, largely constitutes the party's "hardline" appeal even as it may moderate on socio-economic policy—or at least shy away from more aggressively pursuing traditional Irish socialist prerogatives. Contradictions between Sinn Fein's rising success as the anti-austerity party of opposition in the South, and its more "cautious" politics in the North, may bring additional challenges to maintaining this diverse coalition of supporters.

A quite different dynamic occurs in broader Unionism. Unlike Sinn Fein, with many of their elected officials being former IRA associates coming from, and often still residing within, relatively deprived working-class communities, most Unionist politicians come from middle-class areas less affected by legacies of conflict than areas occupied by Loyalists. While opposition to Nationalism unites Unionists across classes, the various disconnects between middle-class Unionism and working-class Loyalism limits the ethnosocial channels Unionist political elites can tap into in galvanizing support from a fragmented constituency. This is a significant dynamic impacting the more noticeably contentious Unionist political tactics, and is not coincidental to their disproportionate role in manipulating culturally sensitive ethnopolitical symbols. On the contrary—and notwithstanding the ongoing influence of small though committed anti-accord dissident Republican groups—Sinn Fein leaders and associated former Republican paramilitary prisoners are relatively more capable of steering the behaviors of the more militant, urban, working-class CNR communities in ways which are commensurate with the party's more diversified political strategy. Respondents acknowledge Sinn Fein's more inclusive politics as more effective than the evangelical Protestant dogma of the DUP, and the insular nature of Unionist party politics more generally. One Loyalist respondent, for example, describes how Sinn Fein has been effective in employing equality narratives to broaden their electoral appeal. In his view, compared to DUP,

> Even the UUP is more progressive. The DUP is full of, "We've got this Christian ethos," that they want the shops to close on a Sunday. Kids' parks used to be chained up. You know the swings? They used to chain them all together on a Sunday, so kids couldn't use the park on a Sunday. That was one of the things that they had [in their policy agenda]. Even the LGBT community—they don't like that . . . Sinn Féin has been very smart, and they're opening up to the LGBT community. They're opening up to immigrants because that's more folks and more folks and more folks. They're inviting immigrants into their areas and communities. . . . In the Protestant communities, ethnic minorities get their windows broke and get pulled out and they're losing out on all those folks. (Interview with author, June 2020).

Corroborating this respondent's observation, McHugh and Cromie (2015) note that "a racist hate crime was reported every three hours on a typical day in Northern Ireland" in 2014, disproportionately in PUL neighborhoods where many immigrant families can find vacant homes.

TOWARD AN ALTERNATIVE
SUPRA-NATIONAL POLITICS?

To discount the positive developments in peacebuilding and governance would present a misleading picture of the state of post-accord NI. As Paul Teague argues, power sharing in NI, despite its problems, underpinned significant advances "towards creating a new democratic equal status between Catholics and Protestants, which held out the promise of spilling back and disrupting established attitudes inside both unionism and nationalism" (Teague 2019, 699). As documented in chapter 5, Unionist respondents' embrace of hybrid identities transcending conventional Unionism suggests that a culture of mutuality remains strong regardless of simmering ethnonational tensions over Brexit. At the same time, many respondents believe that the consociational structure has run its course, and that inclusive reconfigurations of identity occur *in spite* of the agendas of the dominant parties. Respondents refer to the tendency of the Assembly election cycle to reproduce polarized identities and undermine peacebuilding initiatives which challenge mutually-exclusive notions of "community." Findings presented in chapter 6 lend support to critiques of Northern Ireland's power-sharing system, which emphasize how the dominant paradigm of state-led peacebuilding follows "a political order predicated on agreement, [wherein] there is little room for dialogue or debate," and the "two narrowly defined 'communities' . . . [are] rendered 'static and unchanging' by their very need to share power" (Legg 2018, 62; see also Little 2004, 28).

For long-term conflict transformation to be successful, changing attitudes of historically polarized groups toward one another and "removing incompatibilities between the groups" are imperative (Byrne 2011, 8). To facilitate greater intergroup compatibility and interdependency, Lederach (2005, 79) argues for the simultaneous construction of "vertical capacity" and "horizontal capacity" in post-conflict societies. Vertical capacity involves "relational spaces" that connect individuals and groups from the top and bottom of societal and institutional hierarchies, whereas "horizontal capacity" refers to the building of sustainable relationships at the community level across ethnic or religious lines, providing a foundation for gradual increases in interdependency and, thus, integration (see also Levin and Rabrenovic 2004). In some institutional contexts, the middle classes have increased their "horizontal capacity," but predominantly in politically "neutral" ways which do not fundamentally challenge ethnopolitical structures. Grassroots leaders from poor and working-class communities, including ex-combatants, have built horizontal capacity with former outgroup enemies with whom they collaborate in peacebuilding work. However, community leaders from the more segregated and disadvantaged residential areas are confronted with a range of problems that hinder their capacity to facilitate a broader, long-term connection between the Protestant and Catholic residents they serve, including paramilitarism, economic stasis, and mental health problems, addiction and family disruption rooted in the Troubles. Respondents also intimate that the lack of political leadership promoting cross-community initiatives, and revolving disruptions to local peacebuilding projects resulting from politically-fueled mini-crises, lead many to withdraw from horizontal capacity building. Socio-political mini-crises largely fomented by rows between Nationalist and Unionist political elites, and provocations of ethnopolitical entrepreneurs, empower those social forces which militate against the fertilization of constructive cross-community relations, and lead community-based leaders to withdraw from capacity-building work to focus on more "urgent" peacekeeping functions.

Furthermore, many community leaders describe how the "Orange versus Green" nature of Northern Ireland's consociational politics has crept into peace funding decision-making processes, undermining both vertical and horizontal integration. The declining state support for cross-community peacebuilding initiatives, coupled with the aforementioned problems of politically fueled escalations of sectarian tensions and neglect of the policy concerns of poor and working-class constituents, results in decreased faith in the power-sharing system. Vertical integration is undermined as some working-class community stakeholders feel excluded and consequently disengage from formal politics—a dynamic most evident within PUL communities, wherein a "leadership gap" ultimately empowers shadow political elements (i.e., paramilitaries). Horizontal integration is simultaneously undermined by the lack of investment in community peacebuilding projects, both financially and symbolically, translating to less sustainable "everyday diplomacy" beyond the most basic levels (such as preventing interface violence or rioting). Within such an environment, accusations that the "other community" receives more from the peace, or is favored by state institutions, may gain influence since resource deprivation within a community is felt in isolation, and linguistic tractability is mitigated.

Although the present study focuses on just one research site, it is likely that the theoretical implications are relevant for other post-conflict societies as well. The ever deepening entrenchment of neoliberal globalization has produced great wealth for some while exacerbating the marginalization of much of the world's poor (Davis 2007). The increase in a "precariat" class of insecure and redundant workers risks exacerbating the "status frustrations" (Standing 2014, 971) of those who also struggle disproportionately with legacies of violence in post-conflict societies. The consequent growth of class inequalities within other post-colonial societies with histories of ethnic or national conflict thus holds the potential to fuel simmering mentalities of threat and loss which risk taking sectarian, racist, or otherwise dangerous forms—especially when promoted by political entrepreneurs in communities where ethnocultures of masculinity remain entrenched. As Brubaker and Laitin (1998) suggest, theoretical generalizations are best supported through a systematic comparison of qualitative, in-depth case studies of particular (post) conflict societies. Through such comparisons, wherein unique geographical and cultural phenomena are accounted for, the explanatory capacity of the combined evidence of social processes which cut across diverse societies will be enhanced. Additional studies should critically assess whether the theoretical implications of findings documented here are evident in other divided societies in transition, and examine whether more global theoretical conclusions regarding the combined impacts of increased intragroup class divisions, shifts in distributions of power across ethnonational groups, and provocations of political elites can be drawn.

Finally, despite the obstacles to social integration and political transformation documented here, it is appropriate to conclude on a positive note. Although some community leaders are withdrawing from cross-community work, others continue to press on despite the obstacles. And there is much "single community" work being undertaken by local NGOs, such as restorative justice, community renewal, and youth and women's empowerment initiatives, which positively impact local communities in ways which may potentially sow the seeds for future growth in cross-community relations. Even for those respondents pessimistic about the degree of socio-political change that might emerge from ongoing community-based efforts, recognition of the complex nature of political, social, and economic problems facing their communities reflects the knowledge and wherewithal they hold to challenge the hierarchies and socio-political practices which restrict the scope of peacebuilding and conflict transformation. As findings documented in chapter 5 suggest, Unionists' rejection of divisive DUP and UUP politics corresponds to a reflexive stance, and an openness to more inclusive constructs of political identity. Moreover, the apathy and exasperation with the stasis of consociational governance in NI and the ethnopolitics of threat and grievance exercised by dominant parties provides a psychosocial space where new productions of identity aligning Nationalists, Unionists, and others could potentially emerge. In this respect, "an apathy charged with [Jacques] Ranciere's sense of 'dissensus,' a mode of disengagement that could engineer 'a debate' on the sectarian structure of the Northern Ireland state" (Legg 2018, 68, citing Ranciere 2003)—as well as the structures of inequality that help sustain it— has already emerged to some extent. Whether this "dissensus" will provide a foundation for an emergent politics which transcends historical ethnonational and sectarian binaries, however, remains uncertain.

References

Adams, G. 2014. "The Jean McConville Killing: I'm Completely Innocent. But What Were My Accusers' Motives?" *The Guardian*, May 7. https://www.theguardian.com/commentisfree/2014/may/07/jean-mcconville-killing-gerry-adams-innocent-accusers

Adorno, T. W. 1991. *The Culture Industry: Selected Essays on Mass Culture*, edited by J. M. Bernstein. London: Routledge.

Allan, K. 2006. *Contemporary Social and Sociological Theory: Visualizing Social Worlds.* Thousand Oaks, CA: Pine Forge Press.

Anastasiou, H. 2008. *The Peacebuilding Elements of the Belfast Agreement and the Transformation of the Northern Ireland Conflict*. Frankfurt am Main: Peter Lang.

Arendt, H. 1963. *On Revolution*. New York: Penguin.

Arextaga, B. 1997. *Shattering Silence: Women, Nationalism and Political Subjectivity in Northern Ireland.* Princeton, NJ: Princeton University Press.

Arriaza L. and N. Roht-Arriaza. 2008. "Social Reconstruction as a Local Process." *The International Journal of Transitional Justice* 2 (2): 152–172.

Ashe, F. 2008. "Gender and Ethno-nationalist Politics." In *Northern Ireland After the Troubles: A Society in Transition*, edited by C. Coulter and M. Murray, 156–174. Manchester & New York: Manchester University Press.

Ashe, F. 2009. "From Paramilitaries to Peacemakers: The Gender Dynamics of Community-based Restorative Justice in Northern Ireland." *The British Journal of Politics and International Relations* 11 (2): 298–314.

Ashe, F. 2012. "Gendering War and Peace: Militarized Masculinities in Northern Ireland." *Men and Masculinities* 15 (3): 230–248.

Ashe, F. 2019. *Gender, Nationalism and Conflict Transformation: New Themes and Old Problems in Northern Ireland Politics.* London & New York: Routledge.

Ashe, F. and K. Harland. 2014. "Troubling Masculinities: Changing Patterns of Violent Masculinities in a Society Emerging from Political Conflict." *Studies in Conflict and Terrorism* 37: 747–762.

Atashi, E. 2009. "Challenges to Conflict Transformation from the Streets." In *Conflict Transformation and Peacebuilding: Moving from Violence to Sustainable Peace*, edited by B. Dayton and L. Kriesberg, 45–60. London: Routledge.

Aughey, A. 1997. "The Character of Ulster Unionism." In *Who Are the "People"? Unionism, Protestantism and Loyalism in Northern Ireland*, edited by P. Shirlow and M. McGovern, 16–33. London and Chicago: Pluto.

Bairner, A. 1999. "Soccer, Masculinity, and Violence in Northern Ireland: Between Hooliganism and Terrorism." *Men and Masculinities* 1 (3): 284–301.

Barker, R. 2001. *Legitimating Identities: The Self-Presentations of Rulers and Subjects.* Cambridge & New York: Cambridge University Press.

Barnard, H. 2018. *Poverty in Northern Ireland 2018.* York: JRF.

Barnes., S. M. 2001. "The Contribution of Democracy in Rebuilding Postconflict Societies." *American Journal of International Law* 95 (1): 86–101.

Barry, J. 2017. "From Power Sharing to Power Being Shared Out." *Green European Journal,* July 6. https://www.greeneuropeanjournal.eu/from-power-sharing-to -power-being-shared-out/

Bayley, D. H. 2008. "Post-conflict Police Reform: Is Northern Ireland a Model?" *Policing* 2 (2): 233–240.

BBC News. 2013. "West Belfast 'Second Highest in UK for Child Poverty.'" BBC, February 20. https://www.bbc.com/news/uk-northern-ireland-21506734

BBC News. 2013a. "Historical Enquiries Team Treats State Cases With 'Less Rigour.'" BBC, July 3. https://www.bbc.com/news/uk-northern-ireland-23161353

BBC News. 2014. "Sinn Fein Accused of 'Blackmailing' PSNI over Gerry Adams." BBC, May 4. https://www.bbc.com/news/uk-northern-ireland-27272696

BBC News. 2021. "NI Assembly to be Recalled over Loyalist Violence." BBC, April 6. https://www.bbc.com/news/uk-northern-ireland-56649459

BBC News. 2021b. "Belfast: Rioting 'was Worst seen in Northern Ireland in Years," BBC, April 8. https://www.bbc.com/news/uk-northern-ireland-56664868

Beetham, D. 2013. *The Legitimation of Power (2nd Edition).* New York & London: Palgrave Macmillan.

Belfast Interface Project. 2017. *Interface Barriers, Peacelines and Defensive Architecture.* Belfast: BIP.

Belfast Telegraph. 2010a. "Officer is Hit on Head with Concrete Block as Rioters go on Rampage; Policewoman Lucky to be Alive After Brutal Attack. *Belfast Telegraph,* July 13.

Belfast Telegraph. 2010b. "Pipe Bombers Tried to Kill Mary Kelly and Undo Her Community Relations Work. Last Night a Show of Unity Showed They Failed." *Belfast Telegraph,* April 21.

Belfast Telegraph. 2012a. "'No Excuse' for Flag-vote Violence." *Belfast Telegraph,* December 4.

Belfast Telegraph. 2012b. "A Tale of Two City Halls Sparked the Monday Madness." *Belfast Telegraph,* December 5.

Belfast Telegraph. 2013. "Special Advisers Bill: Stormont Assembly Passes SPAD Bill." *Belfast Telegraph,* June 3. https://www.belfasttelegraph.co.uk/news/northern -ireland/special-advisers-bill-stormont-assembly-passes-spad-bill-29316948.html

Belfast Telegraph. 2013b. "Robinson Slams Anti-Police Violence." *Belfast Telegraph Online,* July 16. https://www.belfasttelegraph.co.uk/news/northern-ireland/ robinson-slams-anti-police-violence-29422028.html

Belfast Telegraph. 2014. "New Gerry Adams Mural is Painted in West Belfast as Sinn Fein President Remains Held over Jean McConville Murder." *Belfast Telegraph*, May 2. https://www.belfasttelegraph.co.uk/news/northern-ireland/new-gerry -adams-mural-is-painted-in-west-belfast-as-sinn-fein-president-remains-held-over -jean-mcconville-murder-30239341.html

Bell, C. 2018. *Political Power-sharing and Inclusion: Peace and Transition Processes* (PA-X Report, Power-Sharing Series). Global Justice Academy, University of Edinburgh.

Bell, C. and K. Zulueta-Fulscher. 2016. *Sequencing Peace Agreements and Constitutions in the Political Settlement Process.* 9PSRP Report in Cooperation with IDEA. Stolkholm: International IDEA.

Bell, J. 2018. "Sinn Fein Criticize Police for Derry Disorder Arrests." *Belfast Telegraph*, July 16. https://www.belfasttelegraph.co.uk/news/northern-ireland/sinn -fein-criticise-police-for-derry-disorder-arrests-tuvs-allister-hits-out-at-hyprocrisy -37123149.html

Belloni, R. 2010. "Civil Society in War-to-Democracy Transitions," in *From War to Democracy: Dilemmas of Peacebuilding*, edited by A. K. Jarstad and T. Sisk, 182–210. Cambridge: Cambridge University Press.

Berdal M., G. Collantes-Celador, and M. Z. Buzadzic. 2012. "Post-war Violence in Bosnia and Herzegovina," in *The Peace in Between*, edited by A. Surke and M. Berdal, 75–94. London & New York: Routledge.

Bew, P., P. Gibbon, and H. Patterson. 1979. *The State in Northern Ireland*. Manchester: Manchester University Press.

Bew, P. and H. Patterson. 1985. *The British State and the Ulster Crisis: From Wilson to Thatcher.* London: Verso.

Bew, P., P. Gibbon and H. Patterson. 2002. *Northern Ireland, 1921–2002: Political Forces and Social Classes.* Northampton, MA: Interlink Publishing Group.

Billig, M. 1995. *Banal Nationalism.* London: Sage.

Birrell, D. 1972. "Relative Deprivation as a Factor in Conflict in Northern Ireland." *The Sociological Review* 20 (3): 317–343.

Black, R. 2014. "UDA Feud Ratcheted Up as Rebel Loyalist is Shot: Three Arrested Including Rival Duo." *Belfast Telegraph*, August 22. https://www.belfasttelegraph. co.uk/news/northern-ireland/uda-feud-ratcheted-up-as-rebel-loyalist-is-shot-three -arrested-including-rival-duo-30527430.html

Bollens, S. A. 2018. *Trajectories of Conflict and Peace: Jerusalem and Belfast since 1994.* London & New York: Routledge.

Borooah, V. and C. Knox. 2015. *The Economics of Schooling in a Divided Society: The Case for Shared Education.* Houndmills, Basingstoke, Hampshire: Palgrave Macmillan.

Bourdieu, P. 1983. "The Field of Cultural Production, or: The Economic World Reversed," in P. Bourdieu, *The Field of Cultural Production: Essays on Art and Literature*, 29–73. London: Polity.

Bourdieu, P. 1984. *Distinction: A Social Critique of the Judgement of Taste.* Translated by R. Nice. Cambridge, MA: HarvardUniversity Press.

Bourdieu, P. 1991. *Language and Symbolic Power*, edited by J. B. Thompson and translated by G. Raymond & M. Adamson. Cambridge, MA: Harvard University Press.

Bradfield, P. 2021. "US Offers no Response as Unionists React with Anger to Joe Biden Stance on NI Protocol—Parties Agree that Irish Sea Border Breaches Consent Principle of Belfast Agreement." *News Letter,* March 19.

Bradshaw, J., G. De Lazzari and J. Andrade. 2018. *Performance in TIMSS 2015 of Disadvantaged Pupils in Northern Ireland.* Slough: NFER.

Braniff, M. and S. Whiting. 2017. "Deep Impact: The Fiction of a Smooth Brexit for Northern Ireland." *Juncture* 23 (4): 244–249.

Brass, P. R. 1997. *Theft of an Idol: Text and Context in the Representation of Collective Violence.* Princeton: Princeton University Press.

Brennan, S. 2021. "From Warrior Regimes to Illicit Sovereigns: Ulster Loyalist Paramilitaries and the Security Implications for Brexit." *Small Wars and Insurgencies.* DOI: 10.1080/09592318.2021.1895588

Brewer, J. 2013. "Culture, Class and Protestantism in Urban Belfast." *Discover Society*, November 5. https://discoversociety.org/2013/11/05/culture-class-and-protestantism-in-urban-belfast-2/

Brubaker, R. 1999. "The Manichean Myth: Rethinking the Distinction Between Civic and Ethnic Nationalism." In *Nation and National Identity: The European Experience in Perspective,* edited by H. Krissi, K. Armingeon, H. Siegrist and A. Wimmer, 55–72. Chur and Zurich: Verlag Ruegger.

Brubaker, R. 2002. "Ethnicity Without Groups." *European Journal of Sociology* 43 (2): 163–189.

Brubaker, R. and D. Laitin. 1998. "Ethnic and Nationalist Violence." *Annual Review of Sociology* 24: 423–452.

Brubaker, R. and F. Cooper. 2000. "Beyond 'Identity.'" *Theory and Society* 29 (1): 1–47.

Bruce, S. 1986. *God Save Ulster: The Religion and Politics of Paisleyism.* Oxford: Oxford University Press.

Bruce, S. 2007. *Paisley: The Religion and Politics of Northern Ireland.* Oxford: Oxford University Press.

Bryan, D. 2000. *Orange Parades: The Politics of Ritual, Tradition and Control.* London: Pluto.

Bryson, J. 2019. "Exclusive: Unionist Voice Reveals that at least 72 % of Northern Ireland's most Senior Judges come from a Catholic Background." *Unionist Voice*, June 3. http://unionistvoice.com/policingandjustice/exclusive-unionist-voice-reveals-that-at-least-72-of-northern-irelands-most-senior-judges-come-from-a-catholic-background/

Buchanan, S. 2008. "Transforming Conflict in Northern Ireland and the Border Counties: Some Lessons from the Peace Programmes on Valuing Participative Democracy." *Irish Political Studies* 23 (3): 387–409.

Bush, K. 2013. "The Politics of Post-conflict Space: The Mysterious Case of Missing Graffiti in 'Post-Troubles' Northern Ireland." *Contemporary Politics* 19 (2): 167–189.

Buttersworth, B. 2019. "The Majority of Britons Don't Care if Northern Ireland Leaves the UK, Poll Finds." *iNews*, April 3. https://inews.co.uk/news/uk/the-majority-of-britons-dont-care-if-northern-ireland-leaves-the-uk/

Byrne, J., C. Gormley-Heenan, and G. Robinson. 2012. *Attitudes to Peace Walls.* University of Ulster and Office of First Minister and Deputy First Minister.

Byrne, J. and N. Jarman. 2011. "Ten Years After Patten: Young People and Policing in Northern Ireland." *Youth and Society* 43 (2): 433–452.

Byrne, S. 2007. "Mired in Intractability: The Roles of External Ethno-guarantors and Primary Mediators in Cyprus and Northern Ireland." *Conflict Resolution Quarterly* 24 (2): 149–172.

Byrne, S. 2009. "The Politics of Peace and War in Northern Ireland." In *Regional and Ethnic Conflicts: Perspectives from the Front Lines*, edited by Carter, J., G. Irani, and V. Volkan, 212–226. New York: Prentice Hall.

Byrne, S. 2011. *Economic Assistance and Conflict Transformation: Peacebuilding in Northern Ireland.* London & New York: Routledge.

Byrne, S., E. Fissuh, and M. Matic. 2007. "The International Fund for Ireland: Economic Assistance and the Northern Ireland Peace Process." *Peace and Conflict Studies* 14 (2): 49–73.

Byrne, S. and L. Keashly. 2000. "Working with Ethno-political Conflict: A Multi-modal Approach." *International Peacekeeping* 7 (1): 87–120.

Byrne, S., O. Skarlato, E. Fissuh, and C. Irvin. 2009. "Building Trust and Goodwill in Northern Ireland: The Impact of Economic Aid on the Peace Process." *Irish Political Studies* 24 (3): 337–364.

Campbell, C., N. Aolain, and C. Harvey. 2003. "The Frontiers of Legal Analysis: Reframing Transition in Northern Ireland." *Modern Law Review* 66 (3): 317–345.

Campbell, J. 2019. "Northern Ireland Unemployment Rate Hits Historic Low." *BBC News*, 14 May. https://www.bbc.com/news/uk-northern-ireland-48266312

Campbell, J. 2020. "Does the DUP Now Want a 'Best of Both World' Brexit?" *BBC News*, May 30. https://www.bbc.com/news/uk-northern-ireland-52847831

Campbell, N. 2021. "Decisions Imminent: DUP say Things can't go on over NI Protocol and Sinn Fein's 'Equality Talk.'" *Belfast Telegraph*, August 26. https://www.belfasttelegraph.co.uk/news/brexit/decisions-imminent-dup-say-things-cant-go-on-over-ni-protocol-and-sinn-feins-equality-talk-40790089.html

Carroll, R. 2021. "Irish-language Row Threatens to Derail Northern Ireland Government." *The Guardian*, June 14. https://www.theguardian.com/politics/2021/jun/14/irish-language-row-threatens-to-derail-northern-ireland-government

Carroll, R. 2021b. "Brexit: Loyalist Paramilitary Groups Renounce Good Friday Agreement." *The Guardian*, March 4. https://www.theguardian.com/uk-news/2021/mar/04/brexit-northern-ireland-loyalist-armies-renounce-good-friday-agreement

Carroll, R. 2021c. "Edwin Poots Resigns as DUP Leader after 21 Days in Post." *The Guardian*, June 17. https://www.theguardian.com/uk-news/2021/jun/17/edwin-poots-resigns-as-dup-leader-after-21-days

Carroll, R. 2021d. "Jeffrey Donaldson to Lobby Against NI Protocol as New DUP Leader." *The Guardian*, June 22. https://www.theguardian.com/politics/2021/jun/22/jeffrey-donaldson-only-nominee-for-dup-leadership

Cassidy, K. J. 2008. "Organic Intellectuals and the New Loyalism: Re-Inventing Protestant Working-class Politics in Northern Ireland." *Irish Political Studies* 23 (3): 411–430.

Cebulla, A. and J. Smyth. 1995. "Industrial Collapse and Post-Fordist Overdetermination in Belfast." In *Development Ireland: Contemporary Issues*, edited by P. Shirlow, 81–93. London: Pluto.

Center for Opportunity and Equality. 2017. *Understanding the Socio-economic Divide in Europe.* January 26, Paris: OECD.

Clarke, L. 2014. "Jean McConville: The Murder Still Haunting Republicans After 42 Years." *Belfast Telegraph*, May 13.

Coakley, J. 2008. "Has the Northern Ireland Problem Been Solved? *Journal of Democracy* 19 (3): 98–112.

Cochrane, F. 2020. *Breaking Peace: Brexit and Northern Ireland.* Manchester: Manchester University Press.

Cockburn, C. 2004. *The Line: Women, Partition, and the Gender Order in Cyprus.* London & New York: Zed Books/Palgrave McMillan.

Collier, P. and A. Hoeffler. 2004. "Greed and Grievance in Civil War." *Oxford Economic Papers* 56 (4): 563–595.

Collins, J. 2014. "Adams Arrest May Not Go as Planned." *North Belfast News*, May 10, p. 12.

Collins, P. H. 2002. *Black Feminist Thought: Knowledge, Consciousness, and the Politics of Empowerment (2nd Edition).* London & New York: Routledge.

Collins, P. H. 2004. "Black Feminist Thought in the Matrix of Domination." In *Social Theory: The Multicultural and Classic Readings (Third Edition)*, edited by C. Lemert, 535–546. Boulder & Oxford: Westview.

Committee on the Administration of Justice (CAJ). 2016. *CAJ Annual Report 2016.* Belfast: CAJ.

Committee on the Administration of Justice (CAJ). 2019. *Submission to the Committee of Ministers from the Committee on the Administration of Justice (CAJ) in Relation to the Supervision of the Cases Concerning the Action of the Security Forces in Northern Ireland.* Belfast: CAJ.

Community Relations Unit. 2003. *A Shared Future.* Belfast: Community Relations Unit, OFMDFM.

Connolly, E. and J. Doyle. 2019. "Brexit and the Changing International and Domestic Perspectives of Sovereignty over Northern Ireland." *Irish Studies in International Perspective* 30: 217–233.

Coulter, C. 1997. "The Culture of Contentment: The Political Beliefs and Practices of the Unionist Middle Class." In *Who Are the "People"? Unionism, Protestantism and Loyalism in Northern Ireland*, edited by P. Shirlow and M. McGovern, 114–139. London & Chicago: Pluto.

Coulter, C. 2014. "Under Which Constitutional Arrangement Would You Still Prefer to be Unemployed? Neoliberalism, the Peace Process and the Politics of Class in Northern Ireland." *Studies in Conflict and Terrorism* 37: 763–776.

Coulter, C. 2018. "Northern Ireland's Elusive Peace Dividend: Neoliberalism, Austerity, and the Politics of Class." *Capital & Class* 43 (1): 123–138.

Coulter, C. and M. Murray. 2008. Introduction to *Northern Ireland After the Troubles: A Society in Transition*, edited by C. Coulter and M. Murray, 1–28. Manchester & New York: Manchester University Press.

Coulter, C. and P. Shirlow. 2019. "From the 'Long War' to the Long Peace." *Capital & Class* 43 (1): 3–21

Cowell-Meyers, K. and C. Gallaher. 2020. "Parsing the Backstop: Northern Ireland and the Good Friday Agreement in the Brexit Debates." *British Politics* 16 (3): 219–238.

Coymak, A. 2015. "The Dynamics of Citizenship, Multiple Identities and Intergroup Trust Amongst Young People in Northern Ireland." Ph.D. dissertation, Queen's University Belfast.

Coymak, A. and E. O'Dwyer. 2020. "Does Brexit Mean a Return to Sectarianism? Beyond the 'Border Issue,' the Future of Social Identities in Northern Ireland from a Political Psychological Perspective." *Development* 63 (1): 74–78.

Creary, P. and S. Byrne. 2014. "Youth Violence as Accidental Spoiling? Civil Society Perceptions of the Role of Sectarian Youth Violence and the Effect of the Peace Dividend in Northern Ireland." *Nationalism and Ethnic Politics* 20 (2): 1–23.

Cross, G. 2021. "Centenary Poll: British Identity on Decline in NI with More Young People Identifying as Northern Irish." *Belfast Telegraph*, May 3. https://www.belfasttelegraph.co.uk/news/northern-ireland/centenary-poll-british-identity-on-decline-in-ni-with-more-young-people-identifying-as-northern-irish-40379972.html

Dahanayake, J. 2020. "Queen's Sees 38 Per Cent Increase in First-generation University Students Since 2017." *The Queen's University Journal*, October 2. https://www.queensjournal.ca/story/2020-10-01/university/queens-sees-38-per-cent-increase-in-first-generation-university-students-since-2017/

Darby, J. 2001. *The Effects of Violence on Peace Processes.* Washington, DC: United States Institute of Peace Press.

Davis, M. 2007. *Planet of Slums*. London: Verso.

Delargy, J. 2017. "Vote? Young People in the North Don't See the Point." *The Irish Times*, October 9. https://www.irishtimes.com/news/politics/vote-young-people-in-the-north-don-t-see-the-point-1.3248904

Deloitte and Touche. 2007. *Research into the Financial Cost of the Northern Ireland Divide*. Belfast: Deloitte and Touche.

Department of Education (DE). 2012. *Research Briefing PIRLS 2011 and TIMSS 2011 Achievement of Year 6 Pupils in Northern Ireland*. Belfast: DE.

Department of Enterprise, Trade and Investment. 2015. "Statistics and Economic Research." http://www.detini.gov.uk/stats-labour-market-unemployment

Department of Justice (DOJ). 2018. *Northern Ireland Crime Survey*. Belfast, DOJ.

Devlin, A., K. McKay, and R. Russell. 2018. *Multiple Deprivation in Northern Ireland*. Belfast: Northern Ireland Assembly Research and Information Service.

Dickson, D. and O. Hargie. 2006. "Sectarianism in the Northern Ireland Workplace." *International Journal of Conflict Management* 17 (1): 45–65.

Dixon, P. 2002. *Northern Ireland: The Politics of War and Peace.* Basingstoke: Palgrave.

Douglas, N. 1997. "Political Structures, Social Interaction and Identity Change in Northern Ireland." In *In Search of Ireland*, edited by B. Graham, 151–173. London: Routledge.

Dowler, L. 1998. "'And They Think I'm a Nice Old Lady': Women and War in Belfast, Northern Ireland." *Gender, Place and Culture* 5: 159–176.

Drewett, Z. 2021. "Food Supplies at Risk as Brexit Border Issues Hit Northern Ireland." *Newsweek*, January 13. https://www.newsweek.com/food-supplies-risk-brexit-border-issues-hit-northern-ireland-1561137

Drissel, D. 2007. "Urban Schism, Social Strains: Exploring the Collective Identities of Youth in Contemporary Belfast." *The International Journal of Diversity in Organizations, Communities and Nations* 7 (4): 177–186.

Dunin-Wasowicz, R. 2018. "In Northern Ireland, There is Both Division and Consensus Between Different Ethno-national Groups on Brexit." London School of Economics and Political Science, February 21. https://blogs.lse.ac.uk/brexit/2018/02/21/in-northern-ireland-there-is-a-strong-division-in-how-different-ethno-national-groups-voted-in-the-referendum/

Duffy, R. 2021. "'A Bad Week for the PSNI': How an Arrest at a Belfast Massacre Memorial has put Pressure on Policing." *The Journal.ie*, February 8. https://jrnl.ie/5348726

Dwyer, C. D. 2012. "Expanding DDR: the Transformative Role of Former Prisoners in Community-based Reintegration in Northern Ireland." *The International Journal of Transitional Justice* 6: 274–295.

The Economist. 2020. "Brexit and Sinn Fein's Success Boost Talk of Irish Unification." February 15. https://www.economist.com/briefing/2020/02/13/brexit-and-sinn-feins-success-boost-talk-of-irish-unification

The Economist. 2021. "Northern Irish Catholics are Becoming Less Devout: But Cultural Attachment to their Faith is Undiminished." *Economist: Britain,* July 31. https://www.economist.com/britain/2021/07/29/northern-irish-catholics-are-becoming-less-devout

Edwards, A. and C. McGrattan. 2011. "Terroristic Narratives: On the (Re)invention of Peace in Northern Ireland." *Terrorism and Political Violence* 23: 357–376.

Edwards, A. and C. McGrattan. 2013. "What We Talk about When We Talk about Peace." *Terrorism and Political Violence* 25: 351–354.

Eisner, E. W. 1998. *The Enlightened Eye: Qualitative Inquiry and the Enhancement of Educational Practice.* Upper Saddle River, NJ: Merrill.

Elliott, M. 2007. "Religion and Identity in Northern Ireland." In *The Long Road to Peace in Northern Ireland*, edited by M. Elliot, 175–191. Liverpool: Liverpool University Press.

Ellison, G. 2007. "A Blueprint for Democratic Policing Anywhere in the World? Police Reform, Political Transition, and Conflict Resolution in Northern Ireland." *Police Quarterly* 10 (3): 243–269.

Ellison, G. and J. Smyth. 2000. *The Crowned Harp: Policing Northern Ireland.* London: Pluto.

Equality Commission Northern Ireland. 2010. *Section 76 of the Northern Ireland Act 1998: A Guide for Public Authorities.* Belfast: ECNI.

Equality Commission Northern Ireland. 2017. *Fair Employment Monitoring Report Number 27.* Annual Summary of Monitoring Returns, 2016. Belfast: ECNI.

Eriksson, A. 2009. "A Bottom-up Approach to Restorative Justice in Northern Ireland." *The International Journal of Transitional Justice* 3 (3): 301–320.

Evans, J. and J. Tonge. 2009. "Social Class and Party Choice in Northern Ireland's Ethnic Blocs." *West European Politics* 32 (5): 1012–1030.

Evans, J. and J. Tonge. 2013. "Catholic, Irish and Nationalist: Evaluating the Importance of Ethno-national and Ethno-religious Variables in Determining Nationalist Political Allegiance in Northern Ireland." *Nations and Nationalism* 19 (2): 357–375.

Farrell, N. 2015. "Castlederg Republican Parade: DUP Accuse Police of 'Wilful Blindness' as Court Case is Dismissed Against Organizer." *Belfast Telegraph*, February 18. https://www.belfasttelegraph.co.uk/incoming/castlederg-republican -parade-dup-accuse-police-of-wilful-blindness-as-court-case-is-dismissed-against -organiser-31003204.html

Fay, M. T., M. Morrissey, and M. Smyth. 1999. *Northern Ireland's Troubles: The Human Costs.* London: Pluto.

Fearon, J. and D. Laitin. 1996. "Explaining Interethnic Cooperation." *The American Political Science Review* 90 (4): 715–735.

Fearon, J. and D. Laitin. 2000. "Violence and the Social Construction of Ethnic Identity." *International Organization* 54 (4): 845–877.

Fenton, S. 2018. *The Good Friday Agreement.* London: Biteback Publishing.

Ferguson, N. and M. Gordon. 2007. "Intragroup Variability among Northern Irish Catholics and Protestants." *The Journal of Social Psychology* 147 (3): 317–319.

Ferree, M. M., W. Gamson, J. Gerhards, and D. Rucht. 2002. *Shaping Abortion Discourse: Democracy and the Public Sphere in Germany and the United States.* Cambridge, UK: Cambridge University Press.

Figueiredo, R. J. P. and B. Weingast. 1998. "The Rationality of Fear: Political Opportunism and Ethnic Conflict." In *Civil Wars, Insecurity, and Intervention*, edited by B. F. Walter and J. Snyder, 262–302. New York: Columbia University Press.

Finlay, A. 2001. "Defeatism and Northern Protestant 'Identity.'" *Global Review of Ethnopolitics* 1 (2): 3–20.

Finlayson, A. 1997. "Discourse and Contemporary Loyalist Identity." In *Who Are the "People"? Unionism, Protestantism and Loyalism in Northern Ireland*, edited by P. Shirlow and M. McGovern, 72–94. London and Chicago: Pluto.

Finlayson, A. 1999. "Loyalist Political Identity After the Peace." *Capital & Class* 23 (3): 47–75.

Fissuh, E., O. Skarlotta, S. Bryne, P. Karari, and A. Kawser. 2012. "Building Future Coexistence or Keeping People Apart? The Role of Economic Assistance in Northern Ireland." *International Journal of Conflict Management* 23 (3): 248–265.

Gagnon, V. P. Jr. 1995. "Ethnic Nationalism and International Conflict: The Case of Serbia." *International Security* 19 (3): 130–166.

Gamson, W. A. and A. Modigliani. 1989. "Media Discourse and Public Opinion on Nuclear Power: A Constructionist Approach." *American Journal of Sociology* 95 (1): 1–37.

Ganiel, G. 2009. "'Battling in Brussels': The DUP and the European Union." *Irish Political Studies* 24 (4): 575–588.

Garry, J. and J. Coakley. 2016. "Brexit: Understanding Why People Voted as They Did in the Choice of a Lifetime." *The Belfast Newsletter*, 15 October. http://www.newsletter.co.uk/news/brexit-understanding-why-people-voted-as-they-did-in-the-choice-of-a-lifetime-1-7630272

Garry, J. K., B. McNicholl, B. O'Leary, and J. Pow. 2018. *Northern Ireland and the UK's Exit from the EU: What do People Think?* London: UK in a Changing Europe.

Gibney, J. 2014. "Opinion: Clear that Arrest of Adams was a Sham." *The Irish News*, May 15.

Giddens, A. 1984. *The Constitution of Society*. Berkeley: University of California Press.

Gilmartin, L. 2015. "'Negotiating New Roles': Irish Republican Women and the Politics of Conflict Transformation." *International Journal of Feminist Politics* 17: 58–76.

Ginifer, J. 2003. "Reintegration of Ex-combatants." In *Sierra Leone: Building the Road to Recovery,* edited by S. Meek, T. Thusi, J. Ginifer, and P. Coke, 39–52. Pretoria, South Africa: Institute for Security Studies.

Goeke-Morey, M. C., L. K. Taylor, C. E. Merrilees, and E. M. Cummings. 2016. "Predictors of Strength of In-group Identity in Northern Ireland: Impact of Past Sectarian Conflict, Relative Deprivation, and Church Attendance." *Journal of Community Applied Social Psychology* 25 (4): 283–295.

Gormally, B. 2001. *Conversion from War to Peace: Reintegration of Ex-prisoners in Northern Ireland*. Basingstoke: Palgrave.

Gormley-Heenan, C. 2006. "Chameleonic Leadership: Towards a New Understanding of Political Leadership During the Northern Ireland Peace Process." *Leadership* 2 (1): 53–75.

Gormley-Heenan, C. and R. Mac Ginty. 2008. "Ethnic Outbidding and Party Modernization: Understanding the Democratic Unionist Party's Electoral Success in the Post-Agreement Environment." *Ethnopolitics* 7 (1): 43–61.

Gormley-Heenan, C. and A. Aughey. 2017. "Northern Ireland and Brexit: Three Effects on 'the Border in the Mind.'" *British Journal of Politics and International Relations.* Online first, DOI 10.1177/1369148117711060

Gotham, K. F. 2003. "Toward an Understanding of the Spatiality of Urban Poverty: the Urban Poor as Spatial Actors." *International Journal of Urban and Regional Research* 27 (3): 723–737.

Graham, B. and C. Nash. 2006. "A Shared Future: Territoriality, Pluralism and Public Policy in Northern Ireland." *Political Geography* 25 (3): 253–278.

Graham, B. and P. Shirlow. 1998. "An Elusive Agenda: The Development of a Middle-ground in Northern Ireland." *Area* 30 (3): 245–254.

Gray, A. M., J. Hamilton, G. Kelly, B. Lynn, M. Melaugh, and G. Robinson. 2018. *Northern Ireland Peace Monitoring Report Number Five.* Belfast: Community Relations Council.

Gready, P. and S. Robins. 2014. "From Transitional Justice to Transformative Justice: A New Agenda for Practice." *The International Journal of Transitional Justice* 12: 368–378.

Guelke, A. 2017. "Britain after Brexit: The Risk to Northern Ireland." *Journal of Democracy* 28 (1): 42–52.

Guhathakurta, M. 2008. "The Chittagong Hill Tracts (CHT) Accord and After: Gendered Dimensions of Peace." In *Gendered Peace: Women's Struggles for Post War Justice and Reconciliation*, edited by D. Pankhurst, 187–204. London: Routledge.

Gurr, T. R. 1970. *Why Men Rebel.* Princeton, NJ: Princeton University Press.

Gurr, T. R. 2000. *People versus States.* Washington, D.C: United States Institute of Peace Press.

Hall, S. 1988. *The Hard Road to Renewal: Thatcherism and the Crisis of the Left.* London: Verso.

Hamber, B. and G. Kelly. 2009. "Beyond Coexistence: Towards a Working Definition of Reconciliation." In *Reconciliation(s): Transitional Justice in Postconflict Societies*, edited by J. Quinn, 286–310. Montreal, Quebec: McGill-Queen's University Press.

Hamber, B. and R. Wilson. 2002. "Symbolic Closure through Memory, Reparation and Revenge in Post-conflict Societies." *Journal of Human Rights* 1 (1): 35–53.

Handrahan, L. 2004. "Conflict. Gender, Ethnicity and Post-conflict Reconstruction." *Security Dialogue* 35: 429–445.

Harland, K. 2000. *Men and Masculinity: An Ethnographic Study into the Construction of Masculine Identities in Inner City Belfast.* Ph.D. dissertation, University of Ulster, Northern Ireland.

Harland, K. 2011. "Violent Youth Culture in Northern Ireland: Young Men, Violence, and the Challenges of Peacebuilding." *Youth and Society* 43 (2): 414–432.

Harland, K., and S. McCready. 2007. "Work with Young Men." In *International Encyclopaedia Men & Masculinities*, edited by M. Flood, J. K. Gardiner, B. Pease, and K. Pringle, 665. London: Routledge.

Harland, K. and S. McCready. 2015. *Boys, Young Men and Violence: Masculinities, Education and Practice.* New York: Palgrave McMillan.

Hartzell, C. and M. Hoddie. 2003. "Institutionalizing Peace Power Sharing and Post-Civil War Conflict Management." *American Journal of Political Science* 47: 318–332.

Hayes, B. C., I. McAllister, and L. Dowds. 2005. "The Erosion of Consent: Protestant Disillusionment with the 1998 Northern Ireland Agreement." *Journal of Elections, Public Opinion and Parties* 15 (2): 147–167.

Hayner, P. B. 2002. *Unspeakable Truths.* New York: Routledge.

Hays, R. A. 2013. "Policing in Northern Ireland: Community Control, Community Policing, and the Search for Legitimacy." *Urban Affairs Review* 49 (4): 557–592.

Hayward, K. 2004. "Defusing the Conflict in Northern Ireland: Pathways of Influence for the European Union." Working paper series in EU Border Conflicts Studies, No. 2, January, 1–30. Belfast: Queen's University.

Hayward, K. 2009. *Irish Nationalism and European Integration: The Official Redefinition of the Island of Ireland.* Manchester: Manchester University Press.

Hayward, K. 2020a. "Why it is Impossible for Brexit Britain to 'Take Back Control' in Northern Ireland." *Territory, Politics, Governance* 8 (2): 273–278.

Hayward, K. 2020b. "The 2019 General Election in Northern Ireland: The Rise of the Centre Ground?" *The Political Quarterly* 91 (1): 49–55.

Hayward, K. and McManus, C. 2019. "Neither/Nor: The Rejection of Unionist and Nationalist Identities in Post-Agreement Northern Ireland." *Capital & Class* 43 (1): 139–155.

Hearn, J. 1997. "The Implications of Critical Studies on Men." *Nora* 3: 48–60.

Hearty, K. 2014. "The Great Awakening? The Belfast Flag Protests and Protestant/Unionist/Loyalist Counter-memory in Northern Ireland." *Irish Political Studies* 30 (2): 157–177.

Hearty, K. 2015. "Legislating Hierarchies of Victimhood and Perpetrators: The Civil Service (Special Advisers) Act (Northern Ireland) 2013 and the Meta-Conflict." *Social & Legal Studies* 25 (3): 333–353.

Hearty, K. 2018. "Discourses of Political Policing in Post-Patten Northern Ireland." *Critical Criminology* 26: 129–143.

Herbolzheimer, K. 2019. "Negotiating Inclusive Peace in Colombia," in *Navigating Inclusion in Peace Processes*, edited by A. Carl, 48–51. London: Conciliation Resources.

Herrault, H. and B. Murtagh. 2019. "Shared Space in Post-conflict Belfast." *Space and Polity* 23 (3): 251–264.

Hewstone, M. E., E. Cairns, A. Voci, K. Hamburger, and U. Niens. 2006. "Intergroup Contact, Forgiveness, and Experience of 'the Troubles' in Northern Ireland." *Journal of Social Issues* 62 (1): 99–120.

Hiller, H. and L. DiLuzio. 2004. "The Interviewee and the Research Interview: Analysing a Neglected Dimension in Research." *Canadian Review of Sociology* 41 (1): 1–26.

Hood, A. and T. Waters. 2017. *Living Standards, Poverty and Inequalities in the UK 2017–2018 and 2021–2022.* London: Institute for Fiscal Studies.

Horgan, J. 2008. "Deradicalization or Disengagement?" *Perspectives on Terrorism* 2 (4): 3–8.

Horgan, J. and J. Morrison. 2011. "Here to Stay? The Rising Threat of Violent Dissident Republicanism in Northern Ireland." *Terrorism and Political Violence* 23 (4): 642–669.

Horowitz, D. 2000. *Ethnic Groups in Conflict.* Berkeley & Los Angeles: University of California Press.

Hughes, J., A. Campbell, and R. Jenkins. 2011. "Contact, Trust and Social Capital in Northern Ireland: A Qualitative Study of Three Mixed Communities." *Ethnic and Racial Studies* 34: 967–985.

Hughes, J., A. Campbell, M. Hewstone, and E. Cairns. 2007. "Segregation in Northern Ireland." *Policy Studies* 28 (1): 33–53.

Hutton, B. 2021. "Bobby Storey Funeral: 'No Police Bias' in Decision Not to Prosecute Attendees." *The Irish Times*, May 17. https://www.irishtimes.com/news /crime-and-law/bobby-storey-funeral-no-police-bias-in-decision-not-to-prosecute -attendees-1.4567320.

Irish News. 2014. "Council Elections 2014—'Ireland's Place is in Europe'—While Sinn Fein may be Poised to Enjoy its Most Successful European Election Ever, Martina Anderson Tells Political Reporter John Manley that She is not Taking Her Seat for Granted." *The Irish News*, May 17.

Irish News. 2021. "DUP Infighting Continues as Internal Meeting Turns into 'Total Shambles.'" June 17. https://www.irishnews.com/news/northernirelandnews /2021/06/17/news/dup-infighting-continues-as-internal-meeting-turns-into-total -shambles--2358872/

Irish Times. 2010. "Dawn Purvis Resigns as PUP Leader." June 3, 2010. https://www. irishtimes.com/news/dawn-purvis-resigns-as-pup-leader-1.859071

Irish Times. 2013. "DUP: 'Rioters are Wrong but so is the Parades Commission.'" July 15. https://www.irishtimes.com/news/crime-and-law/dup-rioters-are-wrong -but-so-is-the-parades-commission-1.1464015

Irish Times. 2013b. "Woodvale Hurly-burly Calls Shared Future into Question." *The Irish Times*, August 8.

Jacoby, T. 2008. *Understanding Conflict and Violence: Theoretical and Interdisciplinary Approaches*. London: Routledge.

Jamieson, R., P. Shirlow and A. Grounds. 2010. *Ageing and Social Exclusion among Former Politically Motivated Prisoners in Northern Ireland*. Report for the Changing Ageing Partnership. Institute of Governance, School of Law, Queen's University Belfast.

Jarman, N. 1997. *Material Conflicts: Parades and Visual Displays in Northern Ireland*. Oxford & New York: Berg.

Jarman, N. 2004. "From War to Peace? Changing Patterns of Violence in Northern Ireland, 1990–2003." *Terrorism and Political Violence* 16 (3): 420–438.

Jarman, N. 2006a. "Policing, Policy and Practice." *Anthropology in Action* 13 (1–2): 11–21.

Jarman, N. 2006b. "Peacebuilding and Policing—The Role of Community Based Initiatives." *Shared Space* 3: 31–44.

Jeong, H. W. 2005. *Peacebuilding in Postconflict Societies: Strategy and Process*. Boulder, CO: Lynne Rienner.

Jerrim, J. and N. Shure. 2016. *Achievement of 15-Year-Olds in Northern Ireland: PISA 2015 National Report*. London: UCL.

Jordan, H. 2021. "Eir Rage: Ex-Red Hand Commando Ran Online Hate Campaign Against Kids' Irish Lessons." *Sunday World*, August 10. https://www.sundayworld. com/news/northern-ireland-news/ex-red-hand-commando-ran-online-hate -campaign-against-kids-irish-lessons-40736860.html

Kapferer, B. 1988. *Legends of People/Myths of State: Violence, Intolerance, and Political Culture in Sri Lanka and Australia.* Washington, D.C.: Smithsonian Institute Press.

Kearney, V. 2016. "Northern Ireland Terror Threat Level Raised in Great Britain." *BBC News,* May 11. http://www.bbc.com/news/uk-36267052

Kelly, B. 2012. "Neoliberal Belfast: Disaster Ahead?" *Irish Marxist Review* 1 (2): 44–59.

Kelly, G. and M. Braniff. 2016. "'A Dearth of Evidence' Tackling Division and Building Relationships in Northern Ireland." *International Peacekeeping* 23 (3): 442–467.

Kelso, P. 2021. "Brexit: Supermarkets Warn of 'Cliff-edge' for Northern Ireland Supplies." *Sky News,* January 13. https://news.sky.com/story/brexit-supermarkets -warn-of-cliff-edge-for-northern-ireland-supplies-12186740

Kingma, K. 2001. *Demobilisation and Reintegration of Ex-combatants in Post -war and Transition Countries.* Eschborn, Germany: Deutsche Gesellschat fur Technische Zusammenarbeit.

Klingebiel, S., L. Garke, C. Kreidler, S. Lobner, and H. Schutte. 1995. *Promoting the Reintegration of Former Female and Male Combatants in Eritrea.* Bonn, Germany: Deutsches Institut fur Entwicklungspolitik.

Knox, C. 2002. "'See No Evil, Hear No Evil': Insidious Paramilitary Violence in Northern Ireland." *Journal of Criminology* 42 (1): 164–185.

Knox, C. 2010. "Peace Building in Northern Ireland: A Role for Civil Society." *Social Policy and Society* 10 (1): 13–28.

Knox, C. 2016. "Northern Ireland: Where is the Peace Dividend?" *Policy & Politics* 44 (3): 485–503.

Korpi, W. 1974. "Conflict, Power and Relative Deprivation." *American Political Science Review* 68 (4): 1569–1578.

Kula, A. 2021. "Unionists Rebut SF Claim about Support for the Protocol." *News Letter,* June 24. https://www.newsletter.co.uk/news/politics/unionists-rebutt-sf -claim-about-support-for-the-protocol-3284454

Lamont, M. 1992. *Money, Morals and Manners.* Chicago & London: University of Chicago Press.

Lawther, C. and K. Hearty. 2021. "Through the Looking Glass: Memory, Myth and Policing the Past." *Policing and Society: An International Journal of Research and Policy.* Online first: https://doi.org/10.1080/10439463.2021.1994569

Lazenbatt, A., U. Lynch, and Eileen O'Neil. 2001. "Revealing the Hidden 'Troubles' in Northern Ireland: The Role of Participatory Rapid Appraisal." *Health Education Research* 16: 567–578.

Lederach, J. P. 1997. *Building Peace: Sustainable Reconciliation in Divided Societies.* Washington, D.C.: United States Institute of Peace Press.

Lederach, J. P. 2005. *The Moral Imagination: The Art and Soul of Building Peace.* Oxford: Oxford University Press.

Legg, G. 2018. *Northern Ireland and the Politics of Boredom.* Manchester: Manchester University Press.

Levin, J. and G. Rabrenovic. 2004. *Why We Hate.* Amherst, NY: Prometheus.

Lijphart, A. 1968. *The Politics of Accommodation: Pluralism and Democracy in the Netherlands.* Berkeley: University of California Press.

Lijphart, A. 1999. *Patterns of Democracy.* New Haven & London: Yale University Press.

Little, A. 2002. "Feminism and the Politics of Difference in Northern Ireland." *Journal of Political Ideologies* 7: 163–177.

Little, A. 2004. *Democracy and Northern Ireland: Beyond the Liberal Paradigm?* Basingstoke: Palgrave Macmillan.

Loader, I. 1997. "Policing and the Social: Questions of Symbolic Power." *British Journal of Sociology* 48 (1): 1–18.

Loader, I. and A. Mulcahy. 2003. *Policing and the Condition of England: Memory, Politics, and Culture.* New York & Oxford: Oxford University Press.

Lowry, B. 2019. "The Politics of Neither: How Northern Ireland is Shunning Unionism and Nationalism." *The Guardian*, June 25. https://www.theguardian.com/commentisfree/2019/jun/25/northern-ireland-unionism-nationalism-tribalism

Lysaght, K. 2002. "Dangerous Friends and Friendly Foes—Performances of Masculinity in the Divided City." *Irish Geography* 35: 51–62.

Mac Ginty, R. 2006. *No War, No Peace: The Rejuvenation of Stalled Peace Processes and Peace Accords.* London: Palgrave Macmillan.

Mac Ginty, R. 2010. "Hybrid Peace: The Interaction Between Top-Down and Bottom-up Peace." *Security Dialogue* 41 (4): 391–412.

Mac Ginty, R. 2014. "Everyday Peace: Bottom-up and Local Agency in Conflict-Affected Societies." *Security Dialogue* 45 (6): 548–564.

Mac Ginty, R. and A. Williams. 2009. *Conflict and Development.* London & New York: Routledge.

Mallie, E. 2018. "Some Unionists are Thinking the Unthinkable about Living in a United Ireland." *The Irish Times*, December 9. https://www.irishtimes.com/news/ireland/irish-news/some-unionists-are-thinking-the-unthinkable-about-living-in-a-united-ireland-1.3725241

Manley, J. 2021. "Widespread Concern at LCC Warning that Violence is 'Not Off the Table.'" *The Irish News,* May 20. https://www.irishnews.com/news/northernirelandnews/2021/05/20/news/widespread-concern-at-lcc-warning-that-violence-is-not-off-the-table--2328374/

Mann, M. 1984. "The Autonomous Power of the State: Its Origins, Mechanisms and Results." *European Journal of Sociology* 25 (2): 185–213.

Marijan, B. and D. Guzina. 2014. "Police Reform, Civil Society, and Everyday Legitimacy: A Lesson from Northern Ireland." *Journal of Regional Security* 9 (1): 51–66.

Masciulli, J., M. A. Molchanov, and W. A. Knight. 2009. "Political Leadership in Context." In *Ashgate Research Companion to Political Leadership,* edited by Masciulli, J., M. A. Molchanov, and W. A. Knight, 3–27. London & New York: Routledge.

Mason, J. 2002. *Qualitative Researching (2nd Edition).* Thousand Oaks, CA: Sage.

Matic, M., S. Byrne, and E. Fissuh. 2007. "Awareness and Process: The Role of the European Union Peace II Fund and the International Fund for Ireland in Building the Peace Dividend in Northern Ireland. *Journal of Conflict Studies* 27 (1): 105–125.

McAdam, D., S. Tarrow, and C. Tilly. 2001. *Dynamics of Contention: Cambridge Studies in Contentious Politics*. New York & London: Cambridge University Press.

McAdam, N. 2011. "Riot a 'Wake-up Call': Baggott; We Must Redouble Efforts to Make Country a Safe Place, says PSNI Chief." *Belfast Telegraph,* June 24, 2011.

McAlister, S., P. Scraton, and D. Haydon. 2014. "Childhood in Transition: Growing up in 'Post-conflict' Northern Ireland." *Children's Geographies* 12 (3): 297–311.

McAllister, R. J. 2005. "Religious Identity and the Future of Northern Ireland." *Policy Studies Journal* 28 (4): 843–857.

McAuley, J. 1994. *The Politics of Identity: A Loyalist Community in Belfast*. London: Avebury.

McAuley, J. 1997. "'Flying the One-Winged Bird': Ulster Unionism and the Peace Process." In *Who Are the "People"? Unionism, Protestantism and Loyalism in Northern Ireland,* edited by P. Shirlow and M. McGovern, 158–175. London and Chicago: Pluto.

McAuley, J. 2005. "Whither New Loyalism? Changing Loyalist Politics after the Belfast Agreement." *Irish Political Studies* 20 (3): 323–340.

McAuley, J. W. 2015. *Very British Rebels? The Culture and Politics of Ulster Loyalism*. London: Bloomsbury.

McAuley, J. and J. Tonge. 2007. "For God and the Crown: Contemporary Political and Social Attitudes amongst Orange Order Members in Northern Ireland." *Political Psychology* 28 (1): 33–52.

McAuley, J., J. Tonge and P. Shirlow. 2010. "Conflict, Transformation and Former Loyalist Paramilitary Prisoners in Northern Ireland." *Terrorism and Political Violence* 22 (1): 22–40.

McCall, C. 2003. "Shifting Thresholds, Contested Meanings: Governance, Cross-Border Co-operation, and the Ulster Unionist Identity." *European Studies* 19: 81–103.

McCall, C. 2011. "Culture and the Irish Border: Spaces for Conflict Transformation." *Cooperation and Conflict* 46: 201–221.

McCall, C. and I. O'Dowd. 2008. "Hanging Flower Baskets, Blowing in the Wind: Third-sector Groups, Cross-border Partnerships, and the EU Peace Programs in Ireland." *Nationalism and Ethnic Politics* 14 (1): 29–54.

McCambridge, J. 2021. "Principal 'Sickened' After Online Hate Campaign Forces Irish Language Nursery to Relocate." *Irish Examiner*, July 28. https://www.irishexaminer.com/news/arid-40347800.html

McClements, F. 2017. "Dissident Republicans Parade Through Derry's Bogside." *The Irish Times*, April 17. https://www.irishtimes.com/news/ireland/irish-news/dissident-republicans-parade-through-derry-s-bogside-1.3051984

McClements, F. 2018. "Fifty Years On From Civil Rights, NI Segregation 'Simply Not Tacked.'" *The Irish Times,* June 15. https://www.irishtimes.com/news/ireland/irish-news/fifty-years-on-from-civil-rights-ni-segregation-simply-not-tackled-1.3532237

McClements, F. 2019. "Arlene Foster Accuses PSNI of 'Heavy-handed' Policing of Flute Band." *The Irish Times*, August 13. https://www.irishtimes.com/news/politics/arlene-foster-accuses-psni-of-heavy-handed-policing-of-flute-band-1.3985476

McClements, F. 2019a. "Arlene Foster Against Return of 50:50 PSNI Recruitment." *The Irish Times*, December 16. https://www.irishtimes.com/news/ireland/irish-news/arlene-foster-against-return-of-50-50-psni-recruitment-1.4117250.

McClements, F. 2021. "The Northern Ireland Protocol: 'All Shades of Unionist are Really Angry.'" *The Irish Times*, February 20. https://www.irishtimes.com/news/ireland/irish-news/the-northern-ireland-protocol-all-shades-of-unionist-are-really-angry-1.4489813

McColl, P. 2021. "Is the DUP Trying to Bring Down Power-sharing in Northern Ireland?" *Open Democracy*, June 18. https://www.opendemocracy.net/en/opendemocracyuk/dup-trying-bring-down-power-sharing/

McCormack, F. E. 2017. "Fear, Silence, and Telling: Catholic Identity in Northern Ireland." *Anthropology and Humanism* 42 (1): 50–71.

McCurry, C. 2022. "DUP Leader Accuses Sinn Fein of Pushing 'Radical All-Ireland Agenda." *Bloomberg,* March 19. https://www.bloomberg.com/news/articles/2022-03-19/dup-leader-accuses-sinn-fein-of-pushing-radical-all-ireland-agenda

McDonald, H. 2009. "11-plus Returns in Northern Ireland." *The Guardian,* February 6. https://www.theguardian.com/politics/blog/2009/feb/06/northern-ireland-11-plus

McDonald, H. 2013. "Belfast: It's Not Just the Flag. They Want to Take Everything British Away." *The Guardian*, January 12. https://www.theguardian.com/uk/2013/jan/13/belfast-protest-flag-young-loyalists

McEvoy, K. and B. Gormally. 1997. "'Seeing' is Believing: Positivist Terrorology, Peacemaking Criminology, and the Northern Ireland Peace Process." *Critical Criminology* 8 (1): 9–30.

McEvoy, K. and P. Shirlow. 2009. "Re-imagining DDR: Ex-combatants, Leadership and Moral Agency in Conflict Transformation." *Theoretical Criminology* 13: 31–59.

McGarry, J. 2001. "Northern Ireland, Civic Nationalism and the Good Friday Agreement." In *Northern Ireland and the Divided World: Post-Agreement Northern Ireland in Comparative Perspective,* edited by J. McGarry, 109–136. Oxford: Oxford University Press.

McGarry, J. and B. O'Leary. 1995. *Explaining Northern Ireland: Broken Images.* London: Blackwell.

McGarry, J. and B. O'Leary. 2004. *The Northern Ireland Conflict: Consociational Engagements.* Oxford: Oxford University Press.

McGarry, J. and B. O'Leary. 2006. "Consociational Theory, Northern Ireland's Conflict, and its Agreement Part 1." *Government and Opposition* 41 (1): 43–63.

McGarry, R. 2015. "War, Crime and Military Victimhood." *Critical Criminology* 23 (3): 255–275.

McGlynn, C., J. Tonge, and J. McAuley. 2014. "The Party Politics of Post-devolution Identity in Northern Ireland." *British Journal of Politics and International Relations* 16: 273–290.

McGlynn, L., U. Niens, E. Cairns, and M. Hewstone. 2004. "Moving Out of Conflict: The Contribution of Integrated Schools in Northern Ireland to Identity, Attitudes, Forgiveness and Reconciliation." *Journal of Peace Education* 1 (2): 147–163.

McGovern, M. and P. Shirlow. 1997. "Counter-Insurgency, Deindustrialization and the Political Economy of Ulster Loyalism." In *Who Are the "People"? Unionism, Protestantism and Loyalism in Northern Ireland*, edited by P. Shirlow and M. McGovern, 176–198. London and Chicago: Pluto.

McGrattan, C. 2014. "Policing Politics: Framing the Past in Post-conflict Divided Societies." *Democratization* 21 (3): 389–410.

McHugh, M. 2014. "My Arrest Has Galvanized Party's Campaign, Says Adams." *Belfast Telegraph*, May 13.

McHugh, M. and C. Cromie. 2015. "A Race Hate Crime Happens Every Three Hours in Northern Ireland, Depressing New PSNI Figures Reveal." *Belfast Telegraph*, May 12. https://www.belfasttelegraph.co.uk/news/northern-ireland/a-race-hate-crime-happens-every-three-hours-in-northern-ireland-depressing-new-psni-figures-reveal-31215898.html

McKinney, S. 2010. "Bomb 'Mistimed' to Kill Police Officers." *The Irish News,* August 4.

McNay, L. 2012. "Suffering, Silence and Social Weightlessness: Honneth and Bourdieu on Embodiment and Power." In *Embodied Selves*, edited by S. Gonzalez-Arnal, G. Jagger, and K. Lennon, 230–248. London: Palgrave Macmillan.

McQuaid, R. and E. Hollywood. 2008. *Educational Migration and Non-return in Northern Ireland.* Belfast: Equality Commission for Northern Ireland.

Mead, G. H. 1959. *The Philosophy of the Present.* Amherst, NY: Prometheus.

Mesev, V., P. Shirlow, and J. Downs. 2009. "The Geography of Conflict and Death in Belfast, Northern Ireland." *Annals of the Association of American Geographers* 99 (5): 893–903.

Miles, M. B. and A. M. Huberman. 1984. *Qualitative Data Analysis.* London: Sage.

Miller, D. 2007. *Queen's Rebels: Ulster Loyalism in Historical Perspective.* Dublin: University College Dublin Press.

Mitchell, C. 2006. *Religion, Identity, and Politics in Northern Ireland: Boundaries of Belonging and Belief.* Burlington, VT: Ashgate.

Mitchell, C. 2008. "The Limits of Legitimacy: Former Loyalist Combatants and Peace-Building in Northern Ireland." *Irish Political Studies* 23 (1): 1–19.

Mitchell, C. and J. R. Tilley. 2004. "The Moral Minority: Evangelical Protestants in Northern Ireland and Their Political Behaviour." *Political Studies* 52: 585–602.

Mitchell, P., G. Evans, and B. O'Leary. 2009. "Extremist Outbidding in Ethnic Party Elections is not Inevitable: Tribune Parties in Northern Ireland." *Political Studies* 57 (2): 397–421.

Moore, G., N. Loizides, N. A. Sandal, and A. Lordos. 2013. "Winning Peace Frames: Intra-Ethnic Outbidding in Northern Ireland and Cyprus." *West European Politics* 37 (1): 159–181.

Morning Star. 2013. "Belfast Hit by Another Night of Rioting." *Morning Star*, January 8.

Morrow, D. 1997. "Suffering for Righteousness' Sake? Fundamental Protestantism and Ulster Politics." In *Who Are the "People"? Unionism, Protestantism and Loyalism in Northern Ireland*, edited by P. Shirlow and M. McGovern, 140–157. London & Chicago: Pluto.

Morrow, D., L. Faulkner-Bryne, and S. Pettis. 2018. *Funding Peace: A Report on the Funding of Peace and Reconciliation Work in Northern Ireland and Ireland 2007 –2017.* Belfast: Corrymeela.

Moser, A. 2007. "The Peace and Conflict Gender Analysis: UNIFEM's Research in the Solomon Islands." *Gender and Development* 15 (2): 231–239.

Mulcahy, A. 2013. *Policing Northern Ireland: Conflict, Legitimacy and Reform.* London: Routledge.

Muldoon, O., K. Trew, J. Todd, N. Rougier, and K. McLaughlin. 2007. "Religious and National Identity after the Belfast Good Friday Agreement." *Political Psychology* 28 (1): 89–103.

Mujamdar, S. 2013. *Prose of the World: Modernism and the Banality of Empire.* New York: Columbia University Press.

Mulvenna, G. 2015. "Labour Aristocracies, Triumphalism, and Melancholy: Misconceptions of the Protestant Working-class and Loyalist Community." In *The Contested Identities of Ulster Protestants*, edited by T. Burgess & G. Mulvenna, 159–176. Hampshire: Palgrave MacMillan.

Murphy, J. 2013. *Policing for Peace in Northern Ireland: Change, Conflict and Community Confidence.* London: Palgrave MacMillan.

Murphy, M. C. 2020. "What Sinn Fein's Election Success Means for Irish Relations with the EU and Brexit." *The Conversation*, February 13. https://theconversation. com/what-sinn-feins-election-success-means-for-irish-relations-with-the-eu-and -brexit-131507

Murphy, M. C. and J. Evershed. 2019. "Between the Devil and the DUP: The Democratic Unionist Party and the Politics of Brexit." *British Politics.* Doi: 10.1057/s41293-019-00126-3

Murtagh, B. 2011. "Desegregation and Place Restructuring in the New Belfast." *Urban Studies* 48 (6): 1119–1135.

Murtagh, B. and P. Shirlow. 2013. "Devolution and the Politics of Development in Northern Ireland." *Environment and Planning C Politics and Space* 30 (1): 46–61.

Musemwa, M. 1995. "The Ambiguities of Democracy: The Demobilization of the Zimbabwean Ex-combatants and the Ordeal of Rehabilitation 1980–1993." *Transformation* 26: 31–47.

Nagel, J. 1998. "Masculinity and Nationalism: Gender, Sexuality and the Making of Nations." *Ethnic and Racial Studies* 21: 242–269.

Nagle, J. 2009a. "Potemkin Village: Neo-liberalism and Peace-building in Northern Ireland?" *Ethnopolitics* 8 (2): 173–190.

Nagle, J. 2009b. "The Right to Belfast City Centre: From Ethnocracy to Liberal Multiculturalism?" *Political Geography* 28: 132–141.

Nagle, J. 2018. "Between Conflict and Peace: An Analysis of the Complex Consequences of the Good Friday Agreement." *Parliamentary Affairs* 71 (2): 395–416.

Nascimento, D. 2011. "The (In)visibilities of War and Peace." *International Journal of Peace Studies* 16 (2): 43–58.

News Letter. 2012. "Class is a Major Issue, Claims Protest Speaker." *News Letter*, December 20.

News Letter. 2013a. "SDLP Councillor Stands Firm After Gun Attack." *News Letter,* January 7.

News Letter. 2013b. "Young Believe Other Side are Enemies." *News Letter,* January 24.

New York Times. 2010. "Scandal Tests Catholics' Trust in Leadership." *New York Times: Europe*, March 28. https://www.nytimes.com/2010/03/29/world/europe/29catholics.html

Nilsson, A. 2005. *Reintegrating Ex-combatants in Post-conflict Societies.* Swedish International Development Cooperation Agency.

Noble, E. 2013. "A Field Study of Consociationalism in the Northern Ireland Assembly: A Moderating Influence or Threat to Democracy?" *The Macalester Review* 3 (1). http://digitalcommons.macalester.edu/macreview/vol3/iss1/3.

Nolan, P. 2013. *Northern Ireland Peace Monitoring Report No. 2.* Belfast: Community Relations Council.

Nolan, P. 2014. *Northern Ireland Peace Monitoring Report No. 3.* Belfast: Community Relations Council.

Nolan, P., D. Bryan, C. Dwyer, K. Hayward, K. Radford and P. Shirlow. 2014. *The Flag Dispute: Anatomy of a Protest.* Belfast, UK: Community Relations Council.

Norris, P. 2008. *Driving Democracy.* New York & Cambridge: Harvard University Press.

Northern Ireland Equality Commission. 2015. Investigation Report on DSD Compliance With Equality Scheme. http://www.equalityni.org/Footer-Links/News/Employers-Service-Providers/Investigation-report-on-DSD-compliance-with-equali

Northern Ireland Housing Executive (NIHE). 2016. *Community Cohesion Strategy 2015–2020.* Belfast: NIHE.

Northern Ireland Statistics and Research Agency. 2017. *Northern Ireland Annual Survey of Hours and Earnings.* Belfast: NISRA.

Novosel, T. 2013. *Northern Ireland's Lost Opportunity: The Frustrated Promise of Political Loyalism.* London: Pluto.

Oberschall, A. 2007. *Conflict and Peace Building in Divided Societies: Responses to Ethnic Violence.* London: Routledge.

O'Brien, M. 1981. *The Politics of Reproduction.* London: Routledge and Kegan Paul.

O'Carroll, L. 2022. "Stormont 'Could Disappear Forever,' says Ulster Unionist Leader." *The Guardian*, February 13. https://www.theguardian.com/politics/2022/feb/13/stormont-could-disappear-forever-says-ulster-unionist-leader-doug-beattie

O'Connor, F. 1994. *In Search of a State: Catholics in Northern Ireland.* Belfast: Blackstaff.

O'Doherty, C. 2011. "Widespread Violence, Riots Mark 12th." *Irish Voice*, July 13.

O'Dowd, N. 2014. "Boston College Tapes was a 'Get Adams' Project from the Beginning." *Irish Central*, May 3. https://www.irishcentral.com/news/boston -college-tapes-was-a-get-adams-project-from-the-beginning

OFMDFM. 2007. "Building a Better Future: Draft Programme for Government 2008–2011." Belfast: OFMDFM.

O'Hara, M. 2016. "Anti-austerity Party Challenges Sectarian Politics and Cuts in Northern Ireland." *The Guardian*, May 17. https://www.theguardian.com /society/2016/may/17/anti-austerity-party-challenges-sectarian-politics-and-cuts -innorthern-ireland

O'Hearn, D. 2000. "Peace Dividend, Foreign Investment, and Economic Regeneration: The Northern Irish Case." *Social Problems* 47 (2): 180–200.

O'Leary, B. 2001. "Comparative Political Science and the British-Irish Agreement." In *Northern Ireland and the Divided World*, edited by J. McGarry, 53–88. Oxford: Oxford University Press.

Olick, J. K. and D. Levy. 1997. "Collective Memory and Cultural Constraint: Holocaust Myth and Rationality in German Politics." *American Sociological Review* 62: 921–936.

O'Neill, J. 2020. "PSNI Recruitment: Sinn Fein Backs New Campaign." *BBC News*, February 4. https://www.bbc.com/news/uk-northern-ireland-51359592

O'Rawe, M. and L. Moore. 2001. "A New Beginning for Policing in Northern Ireland?" In *Human Rights, Equality and Democratic Renewal in Northern Ireland*, edited by C. Harvey, 184–214. Oxford and Portland: Hart.

O'Rourke, C. 2015. "Feminist Scholarship in Transitional Justice: A De-Politicising Impulse?" *Women's Studies International Forum* 51: 118–127.

Paris, R. 2004. *At War's End: Building Peace After Conflict.* Cambridge: Cambridge University Press.

Parver, C. and R. Wolf. 2008. "Civil Society's Involvement in Post-conflict Peacebuilding." *International Journal of Legal Information* 36 (1): 51–79.

Patterson, H. 2006. *Ireland since 1939: The Persistence of Conflict.* London: Penguin.

Peterson, S. V. 1999. "Political Identities: Nationalism as Heterosexism." *International Feminist Journal of Politics* 1: 34–65.

Pickering, P. M. 2006. "Generating Social Capital for Bridging Ethnic Divisions in the Balkans." *Ethnic and Racial Studies* 19 (1): 79–103.

Potter, A. 2008. "Women, Gender and Peacemaking in Civil Wars." In *Contemporary Peacemaking: Conflict, Peace Processes and Post-war Reconstruction (2nd Edition)*, edited by J. Darby and R. Mac Ginty, 105–119, Basingstoke: Palgrave.

Potter, M. 2014. *Review of Gender Issues in Northern Ireland.* Research and Information Service Research Paper, Northern Ireland Assembly, January 28.

Powell, A. 2018. *Labour Market Statistics: UK Regions and Countries.* Briefing Paper 7950, 1 August. London: HC Library.

Powell, B. M. 2014. "Policing Post-war Transitions: Insecurity, Legitimacy and Reform in Northern Ireland." *Dynamics of Asymmetric Conflict: Pathways toward Terrorism and Genocide* 7 (2–3): 165–182.

Quinn, C. 2018. "West Tops Child Poverty League." *BelfastMedia.com*, November 27. https://belfastmedia.com/west-tops-child-poverty-league-2

Racioppi, L. and K. O'Sullivan. 2001. "'This We Will Maintain': Gender, Ethno -Nationalism and the Politics of Unionism in Northern Ireland." *Nations and Nationalism* 7: 93–112.

Ramsbotham, O. 2010. *Transforming Violent Conflict: Radical Disagreement, Dialogue and Survival.* Cambridge: Polity.

Ranciere, J. 2003. "Comment and Responses." *Theory and Event,* 6 (4). http://doi.org /10.1353/tae.2003.0017

Reevell, P. 2020. "Few Cheer in Northern Ireland as Brexit Finally Happens." *ABC News,* February 1. https://abcnews.go.com/International/cheers-northern-ireland -brexit-finally/story?id=68685258

Reinisch, D. 2019. "Unfortunately, the Threat from Militant Republicans is Here to Stay." *Irish Examiner,* April 27. https://www.irishexaminer.com/breakingnews/ views/analysis/unfortunately-the-threat-from-militant-republicans-is-here-to-stay -920364.html

Renshon, J. 2006. *Why Leaders Choose War.* Westport: Praeger.

Richmond, O. 2005. *The Transformation of Peace.* London: Palgrave.

Ritchie, M. 2002. "Processes of Nation Building." Coiste.com 4 (3).

Rolston, B. 2006. "Dealing with the Past: Pro-state Paramilitaries, Truth & Transition in Northern Ireland." *Human Rights Quarterly* 28 (3): 652–675.

Rolston, B. 2007. "Demobilization and Reintegration of Ex-combatants: The Irish Case in International Perspective." *Social and Legal Studies* 16 (2): 259–280.

Ross, M. H. 2007. *Cultural Contestation in Ethnic Conflict.* Cambridge: Cambridge University Press.

Rotberg, R. 2000. "Truth Commissions and the Provision of Truth, Justice and Reconciliation." In *Truth V. Justice,* edited by R. Rotberg and D. Thompson, 2–21. Princeton, NJ: Princeton University Press.

Rothschild, J. 1981. *Ethnopolitics: A Conceptual Framework.* New York: Columbia University Press.

Rowan, B. 2012. "Protesters Won't be Told What to Do, You Have to Involve Them, Insists UDA Chief." *Belfast Telegraph,* December 12.

Rowthorn, R. 1981. "Ireland's Intractable Crisis." *Marxism Today,* December: 26–35.

Ruane, J. and J. Todd. 1996. *The Dynamics of Conflict in Northern Ireland: Power, Conflict, and Emancipation.* Cambridge: Cambridge University Press.

Ruppe, C. 2014. "Devoted to Being British: Young Unionists' Identities After the Good Friday Agreement." *The Annual of Language & Politics and Politics of Identity (ALPPI).* Prague: Charles University, Volume VIII.

Rutherford, A. 2013. "Communities United on a Night of Hatred; Praise for Solidarity Amid Riot, but Alleged Police Advice Causes Anger." *Belfast Telegraph,* July 30.

Rydgren, J. 2007. "The Power of the Past: A Contribution to a Cognitive Sociology of Ethnic Conflict." *Sociological Theory* 25 (3): 225–244.

Rydgren, J. and D. Sofi. 2011. "Interethnic Relations in Northern Iraq: Brokerage, Social Capital and the Potential for Reconciliation." *International Sociology* 26 (1): 25–49.

Rydgren, J., D. Sofi, and M. Hallsten. 2013. "Interethnic Friendship, Trust, and Tolerance." *American Journal of Sociology* 188 (6): 1650–1694.

Sales, R. 1997a. *Women Divided: Gender, Religion and the Politics in Northern Ireland*. London: Routledge.

Sales, R. 1997b. "Gender and Protestantism in Northern Ireland." In *Who Are the "People"? Unionism, Protestantism and Loyalism in Northern Ireland*, edited by P. Shirlow and M. McGovern, 140–157. London and Chicago: Pluto.

Sasson, T. 1995. *Crime Talk: How Citizens Construct a Social Problem*. New York: Aldine de Gruyter.

Seidman, S. 2008. *Contested Knowledge: Social Theory Today (Fourth Edition)*. Malden, MA: Blackwell.

Selway, J. and K. Templeman. 2012. "The Myth of Consociationalism? Conflict Reduction in Divided Societies." *Comparative Political Studies* 45 (12): 1542–1571.

Sheriff, R. 2000. "Exposing Silence as Cultural Censorship: A Brazilian Case." *American Anthropologist* 102 (1): 114–132.

Shirlow, P. 1995. "Contemporary Development Issues in Ireland." In *Development Ireland: Contemporary Issues*, edited by P. Shirlow. London: Pluto.

Shirlow, P. 1997. "Class, Materialism and the Fracturing of Traditional Alignments." In *In Search of Ireland*, edited by B. Graham, 87–107. London: Routledge.

Shirlow, P. 2003a. "'Who Fears to Speak': Fear, Mobility, and Ethno-sectarianism in the Two 'Ardoynes.'" *The Global Review of Ethnopolitics* 3 (1): 76–91.

Shirlow, P. 2003b. "Ethnosectarianism and the Reproduction of Fear in Belfast." *Capital & Class* 80: 77–94.

Shirlow, P. 2006. "Belfast: the 'Post-conflict' City." *Space and Polity* 10 (2): 99–107.

Shirlow, P. 2008. "Belfast: A Segregated City." In *Northern Ireland After the Troubles: A Society in Transition*, edited by C. Coulter and M. Murray, 73–87. Manchester & New York: Manchester University Press.

Shirlow, P. 2012. *The End of Ulster Loyalism?* Manchester: Manchester University Press.

Shirlow, P., B. Graham, F. O' hAdhmaill, and D. Purvis. 2005. *Politically Motivated Former Prisoner Groups: Community Activism and Conflict Transformation*. Belfast: University of Ulster.

Shirlow, P. and M. McGovern. 1997. Introduction to *Who Are the "People"? Unionism, Protestantism and Loyalism in Northern Ireland*, edited by P. Shirlow and M. McGovern, 1–15. London and Chicago: Pluto.

Shirlow, P. and M. McGovern. 1998. "Language, Discourse and Dialogue: Sinn Fein and the Irish Peace Process." *Political Geography* 17 (2): 171–186.

Shirlow, P, and B. Murtagh. 2006. *Belfast: Segregation, Violence, and the City*. London: Pluto.

Shirlow, P. and R. Pain. 2003. "The Geographies and Politics of Fear." *Capital & Class* 80: 15–26.

Shuttleworth, I., B. Foley, M. Gould, and T. Champion. 2020. "Residential Mobility in Divided Societies: How Individual Religion and Geographical Context Influenced Housing Moves in Northern Ireland 2001–2011." *Population, Space and Place* 27. https://doi.org/10.1002/psp.2387

Simpson, C. 2021. "Jean Smyth-Campbell Killing: Supreme Court Backs Earlier Ruling on PSNI Independence." *The Irish Times*, December 16. https://www.

irishnews.com/news/northernirelandnews/2021/12/16/news/jean-smyth-campbell-killing-supreme-court-backs-earlier-ruling-on-psni-independence-2536813/

Smithey, L. 2011. *Unionists, Loyalists, and Conflict Transformation in Northern Ireland.* Oxford: Oxford University Press.

Smyth, J. 2013. "Northern Ireland Plunges Back into Crisis as Loyalists Vent Fury." *Financial Times (London),* January 10.

Smyth, J. and A. Cebulla. 2008. "The Glacier Moves? Economic Change and Class Structure." In *Northern Ireland After the Troubles: A Society in Transition,* edited by Coulter, C. and M. Murray, 175–191. Manchester and New York: Manchester University Press.

Sonnenschein, N., Z. Bekerman, and G. Horenczyk. 2010. "Threat and the Majority Identity." *Group Dynamics: Theory, Research, and Practice* 14 (1): 47–65.

Standing, G. 2014. "Understanding the Precariat through Labour and Work." *Development and Change* 45 (5): 963–980.

Starmer, K. 2007. "Monitoring the Performance of the Police Service in Northern Ireland in Complying with the Human Rights Act 1998." *Policing* 1 (1): 94–101.

Steinhoff, P. and G. Zwerman. 2008. "Introduction to the Special Issue on Political Violence." *Qualitative Sociology* 31: 213–220.

Stevenson, C. 2010. "Beyond Divided Territories: How Changing Popular Understandings of Public Space in Northern Ireland can Facilitate New Identity Dynamics." Institute for British-Irish Studies, University College Dublin, Working Paper No. 102.

Stewart, F. (Ed). 2008. *Horizontal Inequalities and Conflict.* London: Palgrave Macmillan.

Strauss, A. and J. Corbin. 1990. *Basics of Qualitative Research.* London: Sage.

Sunshine, J. and T. R. Tyler. 2003. "The Role of Procedural Justice and Legitimacy in Shaping Support for Policing." *Law and Society Review* 37 (3): 513–548.

Svenson, I. and K. Brouneus. 2013. "Dialogue and Interethnic Trust." *Journal of Peace Research* 50 (5): 563–575.

Sweeney, J. 2014. "U-turn Over OTR Letters a Victory for Justice: DUP." *Belfast Telegraph,* September 3.

Tajfel, H. and J. C. Turner. 1986. "The Social Identity Theory of Intergroup Behavior." *Psychology of Intergroup Relations* 5: 7–24.

Tam, T., M. Hewstone, J. Kenworthy, and E. Cairns. 2009. "Intergroup Trust in Northern Ireland." *Personality and Social Psychology Bulletin* 35 (1): 45–59.

Taylor, R. 2001. "Northern Ireland: Consociation or Social Transformation?" In *Northern Ireland and the Divided World: Post-Agreement Northern Ireland in Comparative Perspective,* edited by J. McGarry, 37–52. Oxford: Oxford University Press.

Taylor, R. 2008. *Global Change, Civil Society and the Northern Ireland Peace Process: Implementing the Political Settlement.* Basingstoke: Palgrave Macmillan.

Teague, P. 2019. "Brexit, the Belfast Agreement and Northern Ireland: Imperiling a Fragile Political Bargain." *The Political Quarterly* 90 (4): 690–704.

Teddie, C. and A. Tashakkori. 2009. *Foundations of Mixed Methods Research.* Los Angeles, London, New Delhi, Singapore, Washington, D.C: Sage.

Telegraph. 2014. "Gerry Adams Arrested: Sinn Fein Trying to Blackmail Police, Says Peter Robinson." *Telegraph*, May 4. https://www.telegraph.co.uk/news/uknews/northernireland/10807446/Gerry-Adams-arrested-Sinn-Fein-are-trying-to-blackmail-police-says-Peter-Robinson.html

Thomas, N. and A. Ferguson. 2020. "Bewildered and Angry, Northern Ireland Unionists Fret Over Place in UK." *Reuters,* December 31. https://www.reuters.com/article/us-britain-eu-nireland-idUSKBN295149

Tilley, J., J. Garry, and N. Matthews. 2019. "The Evolution of Party Policy and Cleavage Voting under Power-Sharing in Northern Ireland." *Government and Opposition.* Online first: doi:10.1017/gov.2019.20

Tilly, C. 2003. *The Politics of Collective Violence*. Cambridge: Cambridge University Press.

Todd, J. 1986. "Two Traditions in Unionist Political Culture." *Irish Political Studies* 2 (1): 1–26.

Todd, J. 2005. "Social Transformations, Collective Categories, and Identity Change." *Theory and Society* 34 (4): 429–463.

Todd, J. 2017. "From Identity Politics to Identity Change: Exogenous Shocks, Constitutional Moments and the Impact of Brexit on the Island of Ireland." *Irish Studies in International Affairs* 28: 1–16.

Todd, J. 2018. "Everyday Narratives, Personalized Memories and the Remaking of National Boundaries." *Innovation: The European Journal of Social Science Research* 32 (3): 315–330.

Tomlinson, M. 2012. "War, Peace and Suicide: The Case of Northern Ireland." *International Sociology* 27 (4): 464–482.

Tomlinson, M. 2016. "Risking Peace in the 'War against the Poor'? Social Exclusion and the Legacies of the Northern Ireland Conflict." *Critical Social Policy* 36 (1): 104–123.

Tonge, J. 2002. *Northern Ireland: Conflict and Change*. London: Longman.

Tonge, J. 2008. "From Conflict to Communal Politics: The Politics of Peace." In *Northern Ireland after the Troubles: A Society in Transition*, edited by C. Coulter and M. Murray, 49–72. Manchester & New York: Manchester University Press.

Tonge, J. 2017. "Supplying Confidence or Trouble? The Deal between the Democratic Unionist Party and the Conservative Party." *The Political Quarterly* 88 (3): 412–416.

Tonge, J. 2020. "Beyond Unionism versus Nationalism: The Rise of the Alliance Party of Northern Ireland." *The Political Quarterly* 91 (2): 461–466.

Tonge, J., M. Braniff, T. Hennessey, J. McAuley, and S. Whiting. 2014. *The Democratic Unionist Party: From Protest to Power.* Oxford: Oxford University Press.

Topping, J. R. 2008a. "Diversifying from Within: Community Policing and the Governance of Security in Northern Ireland." *The British Journal of Criminology* 48: 778–797.

Topping, J. R. 2008b. "Community Policing in Northern Ireland: A Resistance Narrative." *Policing & Society* 18 (4): 377–396.

Topping, J. R. and J. Byrne. 2012. "Paramilitary Punishments in Belfast: Policing Beneath the Peace." *Behavioral Sciences of Terrorism and Political Aggression* 4 (1): 41–59.

Trumbore, P. F. and A. P. Owsiak. 2019. "Brexit, the Border, and Political Conflict Narratives in Northern Ireland." *Irish Studies in International Affairs* 30: 195–216.

Tucker, R. C. 1995. *Politics as Leadership, 2nd Edition.* Columbia, MO: University of Missouri Press.

Turner, C. 2015. "Transitional Constitutionalism and the Case of the Arab Spring." *International & Comparative Law Quarterly* 64: 267–291.

Tyler, T. R. 2006. *Why People Obey the Law.* Princeton and Oxford: Princeton University Press.

Van Dijk, T. A. 2006. "Discourse and Manipulation." *Discourse and Society* 17 (3): 359–383.

Walsh, J. 2013. "New Protests, Same 'Troubles' as Riots Roil Belfast." *Christian Science Monitor,* July 16. https://www.csmonitor.com/World/Europe/2013/0716/New-protests-same-troubles-as-riots-roil-Belfast

White, R. W. 1989. "From Peaceful Protest to Guerrilla War: Micromobilization of the Provisional Irish Republican Army." *American Journal of Sociology* 94 (6): 1277–1302.

Whitehead, T. 2014. "Northern Ireland Tensions at Boiling Point Over Adams' Arrest." *Telegraph,* May 3. https://www.telegraph.co.uk/news/uknews/northernireland/10805252/Northern-Ireland-tensions-at-boiling-point-over-Gerry-Adams-arrest.html

Whyte, J. 1990. *Interpreting Northern Ireland.* Oxford: Clarendon Press.

Wildavsky, A. 2006. *Cultural Analysis,* edited by B. Swedlow. New Brunswick: Transaction.

Wilkinson, S. I. 2002. *Votes and Violence.* Cambridge & New York: Cambridge University Press.

Wilson, L. 2017. *Decent Work in Northern Ireland: The Challenge of Insecure and Low Pay,* NERI Research in Brief, no. 48. Belfast: Nevin Economic Research Institute.

Women's Policy Group. 2016. "Women's Manifesto: Northern Ireland Assembly Elections 2016." www.ictuni.org/download/pdf/womens_manifesto_final.pdf

Young, C. 2013. "Parade Tensions—Unionists Criticized Over Statement on PSNI Report." *The Irish News,* August 9.

Young, D. 2021. "Nationalist Crisis of Confidence in Policing After Memorial Arrest Row—O'Neill." *Belfast Telegraph,* February 7. https://www.belfasttelegraph.co.uk/news/northern-ireland/nationalist-crisis-of-confidence-in-policing-after-memorial-arrest-row-oneill-40061969.html

Young, D. and R. Black. 2020. "Perception of Two-tier Policing over Bobby Storey Funeral 'Must be Addressed.'" *Belfast Telegraph,* December 11. https://www.belfasttelegraph.co.uk/news/northern-ireland/perception-of-two-tier-policing-over-bobby-storey-funeral-must-be-addressed-39852476.html

Yuval-Davis, B. 1997. *Gender and Nation.* Cambridge, MA: Polity Press.

Zalewski, M. 2005. "Gender Ghosts in McGarry and O'Leary and Representations of the Conflict in Northern Ireland." *Political Studies* 53 (1): 201–221.

Zartman, I. W. 2005. "Need, Greed, and Creed in Intrastate War." In *Rethinking the Economics of War: The Intersection of Need, Greed, and Creed,* edited by C. Arnson and I. W. Zartman, 256–284. Baltimore, MD: John Hopkins University Press.

Zuckerman, E. and M. Greenberg. 2004. "The Gender Dimensions of Post -conflict Reconstruction: An Analytical Framework for Policymakers." *Gender and Development* 12 (3): 70–82.

Zwerman, G. 1994. "Mothering on the Lam: Politics, Gender Fantasies and Maternal Thinking in Women Associated with Armed, Clandestine Organizations in the United States." *Feminist Review* 47 (Summer): 33–56.

Index

Adams, Gerry, 17, 54, 64; arrest of, 16, 129–32, 134, 139n7, 173
addiction, and legacy of the Troubles, 182, 185–86, 192, 201
The Agreement, 1, 108, 133, 166, 191; equality and social integration as result of, 2, 9, 24n7; and "peace dividends," 34; and DUP political strategy, 50–51, 84, 156; and republican perceptions of betrayal, 64, 88n13; attitudes of young people toward, 74; class politics since, 86; ex-combatant community-based peacebuilding since, 89; and release of paramilitary prisoners, 90, 118n2; Loyalist ex-prisoner alienation since, 109–10; Loyalist paramilitary contributions to, 111; lack of British government prioritization of, 118n3, 150; and the principle of consent, 141–42; implications of Brexit on, 147, 150, 157–59; "constructive ambiguity" of, 167; and identity politics, 172–73. *See also,* European Union (EU)
Alliance Party, 184; and the flag protest, 59, 66–68; increased support for, 44, 71, 153, 156, 158, 198
Anderson, Martina, 130

An Garda Siochana, 76
Anglo-Irish Agreement, 157, 162n3
anomie, 72
apathy, 181; of middle-class Catholics, 13, 42; of Loyalists, 158–60; and consociational politics, 194, 202
Arendt, Hannah, 144
Ashcroft, Michael, 163n6
the Assembly, 13, 70, 177, 197; shut down of, 14, 25n10, 173, 176, 189n4, 198; DUP and Sinn Fein dominance in, 44, 158, 167, 174–75; exclusion of Loyalists from, 82, 110–11; cooperation between Nationalists and Unionists in, 84; Republican ex-prisoners serving in, 94. *See also,* Northern Ireland Executive
Atlantic Philanthropies, 183
austerity, 112, 183, 187, 197; DUP support for, 50–51

Boston College, 130
Bourdieu, Pierre, 5, 28, 144
Brexit, 7–8, 13, 16–18, 20, 25n9, 162, 183, 200; and constitutional politics, 21, 141–42, 145–47, 159, 198; and divisions in Unionism, 85, 143, 148–52; and European identity, 152, 161; and the "middle ground," 153;

About the Author

Curtis C. Holland is assistant professor at the State University of New York at Old Westbury, where he teaches for the criminology and sociology programs. Professor Holland received his Ph.D. in sociology from Northeastern University (USA) in 2016 and has published articles on a range of issues relating to the sociology of ethnic conflict, violence, peacebuilding, and security.